The Only Girl

The Only Girl

My Life and Times on the

Masthead of *Rolling Stone*

Robin Green

Little, Brown and Company

New York Boston London

Little, Brown and Company
Hachette Book Group
1290 Avenue of the Americas, New York, NY 10104
littlebrown.com

First Edition: August 2018

Little, Brown and Company is a division of Hachette Book Group, Inc. The Little, Brown name and logo are trademarks of Hachette Book Group, Inc.

The publisher is not responsible for websites (or their content) that are not owned by the publisher.

The Hachette Speakers Bureau provides a wide range of authors for speaking events. To find out more, go to hachettespeakersbureau.com or call (866) 376-6591.

Photograph of Jerry Garcia copyright © Annie Liebovitz

ISBN 978-0-316-44002-8
LCCN 2018935533

10 9 8 7 6 5 4 3 2 1

LSC-C

Printed in the United States of America

Contents

For Mitch

Why is she driven to tell the tale? Usually it's to go back and recover some lost aspect of the past so it can be integrated into current identity.

—Mary Karr, *The Art of Memoir*

It's my party and I'll cry if I want to.

—Seymour Gottlieb, "It's My Party"

I have a good memory, but not an infallible one, as I learned when I checked facts and timelines with friends, family, and colleagues. The rest, though, this being a memoir, is subjective, reflecting my own peculiar point of view of everything that occurred. I haven't reordered or compressed events to suit the story, as some memoirists do, though I did reconstruct dialogue in places where I could remember the tenor of the scene but not exactly what was said. Some names are changed. Mostly, however, it is all as it was.

The Only Girl

Introduction

RSX
The *Rolling Stone* Ex-Employee
Fortieth Reunion

One day in late summer 2007, a weird blast from the past showed up in my e-mail, an e-vite to the fortieth reunion of ex-employees who had worked at *Rolling Stone* in its first ten years (thus the X in RSX, meaning both "ten" and "ex"), from 1967 to 1977. It would be held in San Francisco, where the magazine was then headquartered. I had been there, all right, in the early seventies, my name on the masthead as contributing editor along with Hunter Thompson and Joe Eszterhas, Jerry Hopkins, Greil Marcus, Jon Landau, Gene Marine, and the Timothys—Ferris, Cahill, and Crouse—and editors David Felton, Ben Fong-Torres, Paul Scanlon, Charles Perry, and Grover Lewis. And me. I was the only girl writer on the masthead when I landed there and would remain so for three years, until editor in chief Jann Wenner took my name off.

No question that I was going to the reunion, even though I lived in New York and I'd have to fly across the country. I had to go to LA anyway on TV business, I told myself, and San Francisco was sort of on my way. Still, I blew off college reunions, even, later, my big five-oh in May 2017; I had no interest in going, no curiosity, no loose ends. Both professors I loved were dead.

But *Rolling Stone?* I found myself yearning to be there the way you'd yearn for a long-lost lover. One you'd never really gotten over. Never thought about. Didn't want to think about, I should say. I liked telling people I'd been at the magazine in those late, great days but didn't go into much detail—not to them or to myself either—such as why and how it all ended, and I'd fled the Bay Area to start my life again somewhere else. But now here it all was with the e-vite, staring me in the face; such a high point for me, professionally and personally, and then such a low point. Why did I blow it? Did I blow it? Why did I care? What happened back there?

The party was downstairs from the old *Rolling Stone* offices on Third Street, a computer-game company by day that had been rented for nostalgia's sake, its workers gone home for the night and the dark, cavernous space now echoing with reunion laughter and cries of recognition. And it *was* weird and nostalgic to be back in that building. Also weird to find myself standing at the edge of a chattering throng of people I didn't know who were falling into each other's arms with happiness. Who were they? What was I doing here anyway? Except now, in shafts of harsh overhead light, I began to make out faces from the past I did know.

There, in fact, was Alan Rinzler, who spotted me too and was making his way to me, his Jew-fro now gone snow white, but still as greyhound-thin and handsome as the day I met him, when he was publisher of Straight Arrow, *Rolling Stone*'s book division, and I'd come here to this very building looking for a job, any job.

4

"Hey!" he said, smiling ear to ear. "Robin, meet my son. I always tell him you saved my life." (His son, I'd learn years later, was a daughter going through a phase.) Alan's attitude tonight a relief, because I'd never known how he felt about the long-ago Sunday when I'd found him a weeping, stumbling drunk in his house in the Berkeley Hills, dumped all his liquor down the sink, and driven him to the Herrick Hospital loony bin. He was a psychologist specializing in writers now and, like half the people at the reunion, it seemed, in AA or some such and drinking Perrier.

Like David Felton, who now appeared, pale and pasty-skinned as always, glass of sparkling water in hand, dressed in a shiny, garish sport coat typical of him, the man who had been my editor and whom I'd loved and slept with and run away to Chicago with—until he ditched me to go back to his wife and kids in LA—and who even now I could hardly bear to tear myself away from.

There were other girls at the party, grown-ups now, who had also been on the masthead but listed farther down the column as editorial assistants, which was pretty much all girls could expect to be in those days, especially in the boys'-club atmosphere that was then *Rolling Stone*, girls like me who'd gone to good colleges and were drawn to publishing but had landed, for one reason or another, in the wild and woolly Bay Area, where the music, and the magazine it spawned, came from.

Sarah Lazin, Harriet Fier, Christine Doudna—pretty girls then, beautiful women now, who'd risen to editorships and heads of departments at the magazine and moved on to stellar careers elsewhere and, like me, had ended up in Manhattan, Sarah and Christine in my very neighborhood. I remembered their eyes on me way back then when I'd come to the office to hand in a

5

story or meet with my editor/lover in his cramped little cubicle, regarding me with what I thought was suspicion. Did everyone know about me and Felton? Did they think I'd slept my way onto the pages of *Rolling Stone*?

I'd learn later that they didn't really know or care because pretty much everybody there was sleeping with pretty much everybody else.

Jann Wenner wasn't at the reunion. Someone told me he hadn't been invited. Was that because he had fired and/or antagonized so many of us, even gone to court with a few? Or because, as he'd told one of the three on the RSX committee, if he came it would be all about him? Which probably would have been true. Even when he hung out with everybody he seemed to keep himself separate and apart—and above—and you found yourself always holding your breath a little around him. Even when you see him today, as I did not long ago at a Bette Midler Parks Conservatory benefit in New York, he still seems bigger than life, or bigger than you, anyway, a star.

Really, it was just as well for the tenor of the event that Jann wasn't there and we could relax and have fun. As longtime *Rolling Stone* writer Chris Hodenfield said in the reunion newsletter, "Magazine write-ups all focused on Jann, but to me it was the hooligan spirit in the hallways," a vibe that sprang from hard work, long hours, and a sense that something really good was being created. It made for the genuine camaraderie so evident here tonight, all of it coalescing in the shared experience of the unpredictable: Hunter Thompson in his fishing hat and madras shorts, muttering and swilling beer and ranging around the office with his Marx Brothers stride; John and Yoko sweeping through, stopping at a desk in the subscription department to shake a clerk's hand; a new-hire editorial assistant ushered into an editor's lair, handed a short straw, offered a line of cocaine laid out on the desk, and told, "Welcome to *Rolling Stone*."

Nobody ever offered me a line of coke when I was there—not at the office, anyway—although Oscar Acosta, Hunter Thompson's *Fear and Loathing* "Samoan" sidekick and attorney, did bring a small mountain of the stuff when he came with Annie Leibovitz to a party for my twenty-seventh birthday at a friend's house in Berkeley.

We'd all been asked to write something for the reunion newsletter, published in newsprint in the tabloid format of *Rolling Stone*. Fond memories, favorite assignments, inside stories about celebrities, embarrassing incidents...

Here's how mine began:

Embarrassing incidents? How much time have you got? Having a bad acid trip and being carried out of a Sausalito restaurant [the Trident?] by Jon Goodchild, David Felton, Annie Leibovitz, and Julie Pine... Another bad trip at a birthday party for Hunter in someone's hilltop San Francisco home. But there were good trips—the Esalen editors conference, not sure what year. [It was December 1971.] I wasn't invited really, though I'd had several cover stories and was, I think, on the masthead by then. [I was.] Come to think of it, there were no women writers in those Esalen meetings, the only female being Annie [Leibovitz] to photograph.

But I was there, the girlfriend of an editor, and my fondest Rolling Stone memory is of being in the Esalen hot tubs in the side of a cliff, everyone naked in the tubs. And has anyone ever mentioned what a great body Hunter had? Swacked on mescaline as I was, he looked like some kind of god. I remember being in the back seat of Hunter's car, me and David Felton,

Annie riding shotgun and Hunter at the wheel with his bottle of Wild Turkey and his bag of little blue pills, taking the curves up Route One that night, our headlights off, "the better to see approaching cars." We were stopped by cops in a town [Monterey? Carmel?] and Annie took photographs of Hunter touching his nose and walking the line, etc. I have no idea why we weren't hauled in. But we weren't.

The incident with the cops happened, all right, but I wasn't there. It happened on the first night of the conference with just Annie, Hunter, and David. I was in the car with them on the *second* night, when wives and girlfriends and one or two girls from the office had been invited and when Hunter made that crazy ride again. But I'd heard the story many times and seen Annie's photos, so when I wrote that piece for the reunion rag, I could have sworn I'd been along that night.

My choice for best story I'd written was the very first of mine to appear in *Rolling Stone.* I'd been sent, I wrote in the newsletter, "to Dennis Hopper's house in New Mexico to see *The Last Movie,* his last for a while. He was such a beast, so cruel, so high, I was so frightened by the whole scene (though everything frightened me in those days), the piece was so good."

It *was* good. So good that it's in a compendium of "Ten Interviews that Shook Hollywood," mine listed third after stories by Truman Capote (on Marlon Brando in the *New Yorker,* November 1957) and Rex Reed (on Warren Beatty in *Esquire,* October 1967); so good that after it was published, Joan Didion, my hero, asked a mutual friend to phone and tell me how much she liked it and, soon after, an editor at *Esquire* called the *RS* office to ask, "Who's the new bitch?"

Bitch? Really? I was so thrilled about *Esquire* calling, I never stopped to think about what it meant to be called a bitch. Is that what I was? It is true that, as it happened, the Dennis Hopper story and pretty much every story I wrote from then on at the very least stung my subjects and at the most cost them their careers or landed them in prison.

Which brings me to something else that happened not long after the *Rolling Stone* reunion. I was packing up my mother's things to move her into an assisted-living complex (where she didn't want to go) and came across a photograph in a cheap drugstore frame on a shelf in her TV room: a black-and-white photo of a beautiful young woman in a bikini top, her dark hair long and messy, her flesh juicy, her smile beatific.

I'd never seen the photo before and had no memory of its being taken or of who took it, but I could see that it was a photograph of me. Who was this girl who I knew was myself but had absolutely no memory of ever being? Why was she smiling?

The photo never made it to assisted living. I took it home and put it on my own shelf, where it remained a mystery. The background was out of focus but I knew it had to have been taken on a beach, and I could think of only two possibilities: a wild hippie beach in Mexico where I'd spent a month in 1970 with a boyfriend who had a Nikon, and Canochet Beach in Narragansett, Rhode Island, where my parents had a cabana.

Finally, it occurred to me to take the photograph out of its frame and look on the back, and there it was, the reason I looked so happy: the photo had been taken by the family dentist, friend and photographer, the summer of the year my name was added to the masthead of *Rolling Stone*. I had always wanted to be a writer (maybe not a journalist, but still), and now I was— published, paid, read, praised. The year was 1971 and I'd just turned twenty-six.

Looking at the photograph now, knowing it was Canochet, brings a cascade of memories, some difficult to face, chief among them the last time I was there, a hot day in June 2012, five years after the *Rolling Stone* reunion and six months after my mother's death alone in assisted living.

My brother and I had left our spouses in the car in the parking lot across the street to read the Sunday *Times* and mind the dog, and the two of us paid to enter the public beach and went through the turnstile. We walked across the wooden boardwalk and down the steps to the hot sand, took off our shoes, and, barefoot now and in our street clothes, picked our way through the umbrellas and beach towels and sweaty, half-naked Rhode Islanders to the water's edge, where we headed north toward Narrow River on the hard, wet sand.

My brother carried a Dartmouth bookstore shopping bag that looked like it might contain a weighty picnic lunch but in fact held the crematory tin with our mother's ashes. Waves crashing to our right, we continued up the crowded public beach to the sands of the less-populated, members-only Canochet Beach Club my parents had belonged to and where the photograph had been taken, and then, farther up the beach, passed by the tony Dunes Club, where, when we were growing up, as my mother pointed out a thousand times, they didn't allow Jews like us.

We finally came to the dunes at Narrow River where it empties into Narragansett Bay and sat down on the low, muddy riverbank. Surreptitiously, because what we were about to do wasn't legal, we dug a hole with our hands in the mud of the bank beneath our knees. With little ceremony, furtively glancing over our shoulders, we took the tin out of the shopping bag, opened it, removed the plastic bag containing our mother, and emptied her oily residue into the hole.

What kind of mother gets this kind of send-off? And what kind of children give it? What kind of daughter? We told ourselves that we were burying her here because this was where she had been happiest. And that was true. My father was a greeting-card salesman with a route that sometimes took him to southern Rhode Island, and some days he would join her on the beach after he'd finished his calls. And even years after he died, at seventy-four in 1984, she'd recall how, sunning in her low beach chair near the crashing waves, she'd keep an eye on the far-away canopied Cabana Club entrance until she saw him come in, her husband, Ira, trim and handsome in a pale poplin suit that set off his hazel eyes, loosening his tie with one hand, smiling and waving at her with the other as he headed for the cabana to change his clothes.

We all loved my father—our family and the friends that always gathered around him—and we had all been happy on that beach. He'd make us gin and tonics with cut-up limes in little plastic glasses, and my mother would set out salty cocktail peanuts; there'd be laughter, jokes told, some in Yiddish, then we'd all go after-cocktail body-surfing in the bracing green evening waves. That year, 1971? Would Ronnie B., my best friend from birth whom I loved more than anyone and whose parents shared a cabana with mine, have been there that day? Or would she have been locked up again in McLean, the private mental hospital near Boston made famous by James Taylor and his brother? Why did I survive and flourish and not her? Why did I have to be the last of us who saw her in LA in 1979 on what we all afterward realized was a farewell trip cross-country in the van her parents had bought her, the very week before she put a gun to her head on the beach at Leo Carrillo State Park (named for the conservationist/actor who played the Cisco Kid's sidekick Pancho) and pulled the trigger?

After college in 1967, I left Providence and over the next few years worked a variety of menial jobs. I went from Martha's Vineyard to Boston to New York to Chicago and finally to Berkeley and San Francisco with detours to New Mexico, Mexico, and the California coast from LA to Mendocino. I lived in sin (as it was called then), smoked dope, dropped acid, and hiked with my boyfriend into the Jemez Mountains, where we slept in a cave and, naked and on all fours, grazed on the watercress that grew around a hot spring. I waitressed, made jewelry, mooched off that same rich boyfriend. In short, I was not so different than any of the other girls at *Rolling Stone*.

At last at *Rolling Stone* I finally found work that I loved and success—until it all went to shit. Which brings me back to the little piece I wrote for the reunion tabloid recounting in vague terms the end of my time at *Rolling Stone*:

> *My favorite celebrity story is one I don't want to talk about—it goes into a tell-all memoir, though I'll never write one. [I know, right?] But it's the reason I got fired, or taken off the masthead in my case. I'd been working on a story about the children of Robert Kennedy for months, never wrote it, though stuff I found out would surely have put me on a larger map. But by then I'd lost my taste for my style of irony, for telling true tales. We were in Israel—Jann was there with a bunch of people Max Palevsky [a big RS investor] had brought over to witness the dedication of a wing of the museum to his parents, and I was there on a story for Oui [which I also never wrote], and I was with Jann and the others at a nightclub and he took me out to the patio and told me if I didn't turn the story in he'd have to take me off the masthead. And I said okay.*
>
> *I was ready to go, but I also felt my life was over, in a way,*

having to go back to live in obscurity and all, that's how it felt.
But somehow, I managed to go on … and on …

What's not written there was that after Jann told me he was
taking my name off the masthead—kind of like a sergeant being
stripped of his stripes—and I'd shrugged and said okay, he'd put
his arms around me and given me a big hug and said, "But do me
a favor, will you, Robin? Never write about me, okay?"

Well, sorry, but that's part of what I have to do, write about
everything, including Jann, starting with the three minutes of our
first meeting and up to and beyond the one night I spent with
him in his room at the Sherry-Netherland (the details of which
are blurry, probably because of the quaaludes).

And I also have to write about what I said I was saving for that
tell-all memoir I'd never write, the story of why I didn't do the
Kennedy piece: because I had crossed a journalistic line and gone
to bed with an interview subject (okay, it was Robert Kennedy Jr.
in his dorm room at Harvard), and I felt I couldn't write the kind
of truthful story I prided myself on without revealing that. And I
wasn't about to reveal it. Not to a million-plus readers. Not even
to Jann as an explanation of why he wasn't getting the pages. Not
to pretty much anyone at all, except maybe strangers in bars or
at parties when I was trying to explain why I wasn't on the masthead anymore.

It's all so poignant. Also ironic and paradoxical. Because at
that point I was sleeping with everybody. We all were—women's
lib, free love, pre-AIDS, and all that—so why wouldn't I jump
at the chance to go to bed with this tall, handsome, long-haired
boy, a fucking *Kennedy*, for God's sake? Well, because you're not
supposed to. But that's the ironic paradox. Because I think it was
also some kind of journalistic curiosity and an instinct for story

that made me make that leap into a subject's bed, a leap I'd never taken before (unless you count a David Cassidy roadie, which I don't).

Because what I learned about the Kennedy male, this one, anyway (and isn't this sort of thing, like, genetic?), spending the night on that vast and undulating waterbed on the floor of that college dorm room with the falconry equipment displayed on the wall and the small bust of the slain father on the credenza, seemed to be what lay at the very foundation of the Kennedy male's power, confidence, his very Kennedy-ness.

Also, in addition to way-too-personal details, I'd learned uncomfortable truths about the kids—for example, earlier that night, I had gone with this one to a street corner off Harvard Square so he could score drugs—and I felt the Kennedys had had enough horror in their lives without my adding to it on the pages of *Rolling Stone*.

And there's more of the cruel irony. Because after the magazine moved to New York later, in the 1970s, Jacqueline Kennedy became a frequent visitor to the offices and a valued, much-vaunted pal of social-climbing, star-fucking Jann (a description even he would cop to), and no way would she have done or been so if I had fulfilled my obligation and actually forked over the Kennedy piece Jann had so wanted from me so many years before.

Ah, well, the whole thing had become a big ball of no fun anyway, both personally and professionally. After Israel and though I still occasionally wrote for *Rolling Stone* and other magazines, I was lost and floundering. Finally, in 1975, I left the Bay Area for good and went to the Iowa Writers' Workshop to begin my life again.

I didn't read *Rolling Stone* much anymore and I forgot those heady years—well, most of the time. There was one cold winter day when I was in Manhattan and found myself lingering on the sidewalk outside the building where the magazine had its offices, looking like Mildred Pierce in that movie, pulling my coat around me for warmth, hoping (vainly, as it turned out) to catch a glimpse, maybe have a conversation with Jann, someone, anyone...

And that brings me finally to the end of the reunion article, which about sums up and becomes a sort of prelude to the story of myself I didn't know I was going to need to tell but am about to.

I never saw Jann again until a couple years ago at an Annie Lennox concert. I went over and said hello, met his boyfriend [now his husband]. I told him that my years at Rolling Stone were some of the best in my life—but also the worst. And his boyfriend said, you can't imagine how many of you come up to him and say that.

Chapter One

How to Become a Journalist

It was sometime in 1970 when I borrowed my boyfriend David Leach's metallic-blue-green Pontiac Firebird convertible dual-exhaust overhead cam 6 and drove from our apartment in Berkeley, California, across the Bay Bridge to San Francisco to apply for a job at *Rolling Stone* magazine, which was then headquartered there. I'd been in Berkeley about a year, mooching off David, watching him live.

A rich man's son, David was strung along by his dad on a monthly stipend of three hundred dollars, just enough money in those days to cover the bills and buy his exotic teas, pipe tobacco, and pot. And just enough to sap him of all ambition and drive.

He'd get up late, say noon, meticulously fix himself a pot of smoky Lapsang souchong tea with sugar and warmed milk, and then, wearing only a dark green velour bathrobe, go to the living room and sit like a pasha on the elegant woven cushions of a beautiful wood chair imported from Persia, unabashedly letting

16

the bathrobe fall open to reveal his round, hairy belly, his genitals resting between his thighs, a chubby man comfortable in his own skin.

Sometimes he'd glance to the kitchen where I'd be tidying up, see me watching, and flash me his Cheshire Cat grin. He was the only child of a second marriage; his young mother had doted on him and he was accustomed to being watched.

It could be hours that he sat there, sipping tea, reading the *New York Times* and the *San Francisco Chronicle,* at some point adjusting his position slightly to begin the preparation of the first of that day's joints—crushing of buds, gleaning of seeds, sifting of pot, then the rolling, licking of paper, and producing of a perfect, thin doobie, which he'd light and toke on deeply from time to time, his head soon surrounded by a halo of pot smoke as he sipped tea and turned the pages of a newspaper, one index finger twirling a strand of his thick, curly brown hair as he read.

His was a seductive way of life. Not to have to get a job? Go to work? I don't know what roused me one morning to get up and go out and find work, but I did, hiring on as a waitress at HS Lordships, a faux-British, corporation-owned roast-beef house at the end of the street in the Berkeley Marina. David marveled that someone could do that, leave in the morning and come home with a job.

I made good money, but it wasn't long before I started to wonder what I was doing in the stupid getup they made me wear— little serving-wench outfit complete with push-up bra and ruffled apron—me with my higher education, the first generation of my family ever to graduate college, and an Ivy League one at that.

I was a talented girl, had turned down a full ride at Rhode Island School of Design to go to Brown—Pembroke College in Brown University, as the girls' campus was then called—where

I became a star of sorts, a townie with a chip on her shoulder on state scholarship who was John Hawkes's pet and who wrote poignant yet earthy short stories and skulked around campus in black turtlenecks, jeans, and black boots, a would-be bohemian made editor of Brown's literary magazine and as such the only girl on the editorial staff of the *Brown Daily Herald* that year, just as I would later be the only female contributing editor on the masthead of *Rolling Stone* during my years there and, still later, the only female writer/executive producer of *The Sopranos* for the first five of its six seasons.

Because of my editorship at Brown, I was given a room of my own in Metcalf, the singles dorm, also known as the weird girls' dorm, the only room with its own phone—a big deal in that pre-cell-phone era. A girl with a future, you'd think. Except here I was at HS Lordships working split shifts, slinging bloody slabs of rib roast to tables of leering, cheapskate middle-management types.

It was about this time that my only friend from college, from the weird girls' dorm, telephoned. She was getting married at the family home on Long Island in June and wanted me to be a bridesmaid. She also wondered what the hell I was doing with my life. She herself was climbing up the ladder in the New York publishing world. In fact, she'd been working for an editor at Macmillan, Alan Rinzler, who had just quit to go out west and be a publisher of Straight Arrow, the book division of *Rolling Stone* magazine. She would tell him about me. I should look him up.

Rolling Stone magazine? Are you kidding? I loved *Rolling Stone* magazine! Besides the *Berkeley Barb* and the occasional *Ramparts*, it was just about the only thing I read anymore and I devoured it. I remembered the first time I'd opened one up; it would have been in 1968, a year after it was founded. I was living in New York and headed back to my secretarial job after lunch break and

I was on the corner of Fifth and Fifty-Seventh waiting for the light to change. It was the issue with Eric Clapton on the cover, handsome, with a mustache and a full head of hair then, in jeans shirt and bead necklace. And there I was, waiting for the light in Midtown in a sea of men in suits and ties and briefcases, women in heels and pencil skirts.

I didn't know then that in a few years I'd make my way out to California, where *Rolling Stone* was published. And that it would have a book division. And that I'd have an in, an actual name of someone to call there.

Alan Rinzler was expecting my call and said he'd see me. I decided that for once, I wouldn't dress in the secretary disguise I'd worn for job interviews in Boston, then New York, then Chicago. This time I'd go as myself in sandals, jeans miniskirt, and tank top. Plus, I'd borrow a friend's jeans jacket that had a large patch sewn on the back of two people fucking. And just for good measure, I'd take the dog, a big black mutt called Reuben that friends had left with us on their way to Mexico. If they didn't like the fucking jacket and they didn't like the fucking dog, fuck 'em.

The sun was shining; I had the Firebird's top down, the radio blasting, Reuben on the seat next to me, nose to the wind. We drove down University Avenue in David's throaty car and took the 80 South, then swung onto the ramp to the long, grand, eastern expanse of Bay Bridge to Yerba Buena Island and from there to the western expanse of bridge, the fairyland city of San Francisco shining before us. I double-shifted down onto the first exit off the bridge and veered not to the right, where most traffic was headed, to downtown and North Beach, but to the left, a less-traveled industrial area. I soon pulled up to the converted warehouse on Third Street where *Rolling Stone* had its offices.

I set the emergency brake and looked at Reuben. Already on his feet, wagging his tail and up for anything, Reuben looked at me. This was a great dog—one ear up, one ear down, a Lab-shepherd mix with shiny black fur, a long snout, and a constant smile. (The hardest part about leaving David, as I would do in the not-too-distant future, was leaving Reuben, who had stayed with us even after our friends came back from Mexico. Reuben lived with David until he had to be put down, and his ashes were kept for years on the mantel in the living room of the house in the Berkeley Hills where David lived and sold coke and accumulated firearms and where he himself died in 2010 of a heart attack at sixty-five years old.)

We, Reuben and I, took the elevator to the fourth floor and when the doors slid open, I felt like I was home. It was a stripped-down loft with brick walls, framed posters of covers of *Rolling Stone*, big oak desk, and behind it a hip and pretty receptionist turning the pages of—what else?—the latest issue of *Rolling Stone*. (I'd learn later that being pretty was a job requirement for girls at *Rolling Stone*.) She didn't say anything like "Nice dog" or "I'm sorry, no dogs here," didn't mention the dog at all; she just, without taking her eyes off her reading, buzzed somebody on the phone, said I was there, hung up the phone, and gestured vaguely off to her right.

"You can go in," she said.

Alan's office was across the hall. When he saw me, he sprang to his feet and reached over a desk piled with manuscripts and books to shake my hand. He was another dream come true, not only handsome and hip—a whip-thin Harvard man with a Jew-fro, bandanna tied around his neck—but there in the corner also getting up to greet me and especially Reuben was Alan's own dog. He had his dog at the office! Not a mutt like Reuben, of course,

20

but a Harvard-man-worthy pedigreed chocolate standard poodle with a hairstyle kind of like Alan's.

A few years before, I'd worked as a secretary in the marketing department at the publishing house Houghton Mifflin, just off Copley Square in Boston, for six soul-crushing weeks, and I'd stealthily taken a tour through the editorial department to check it out, especially the men, to see if there was anything I liked. I didn't. The whole place seemed so hushed and oppressive, the editors (all men) frowning in concentration at their desks in their white shirts and ties, not one of them even bothering to look up and check me out.

And now here was Alan Rinzler, literate, chatty, exuding enthusiasm. He seemed delighted to see me. He seemed delighted period—nothing like the weeping, stumbling drunk he would become and whom I would one day drive to patient intake.

I told him how much I loved *Rolling Stone*, that I'd do anything to work there, just to be in its aura. I could type, I'd had experience as an editorial assistant, but also I was very organized, I could file or be a receptionist...

Alan seemed amused. Why would I want to do that? My friend from school had told him that I was a very good writer. Didn't I want to write something for the magazine?

"Write something?" I said. Truthfully, the thought had not occurred to me.

"Sure," he said. "Why not? I'll set up a meeting with Jann."

When I say that the thought of writing something for the magazine had not occurred to me, it's because the thought had really not occurred to me. Of course I knew that people wrote the articles, but it never occurred to me that the person who wrote them could be me. My thought was more along the lines that I'd get a job at the magazine and... and... I dunno, learn about magazines, about which I knew next to nothing? If I was lucky, find something I was good at? Editing, eventually, maybe? That was about as far as my thinking went.

I suppose I might have taken a journalism course or two at Brown—if they'd been offered. But there was no such thing on the curriculum from 1963 to 1967, the years I was there, or before that and for some time after. As was true then of the Ivies, it was all literature—poetry writing and fiction. At my school, students could work on the *Brown Daily Herald*, but no girls did. I was on the masthead, sure, but my literary magazine was something separate and apart—we published "art."

But though Brown wasn't registering it yet, journalism was starting to become art with the emergence of New Journalism. Harold Hayes, editor of *Esquire*, would be sending Jean Genet and William Burroughs to cover the Chicago convention in 1968, and already, real writers like Norman Mailer, Terry Southern, Truman Capote, and others were publishing nonfiction in their own strong voices and points of view in magazines. And there was Joan Didion. A woman. And one not confined to the pages of women's magazines but published all over the place right alongside the men, pieces that would be collected in 1968's *Slouching Towards Bethlehem*, writing that was as good as any man's yet completely particular to her, a woman.

This is what she wrote in the preface to that book: "My only advantage as a reporter is that I am so physically small, so temperamentally unobtrusive, and so neurotically inarticulate that people tend to forget that my presence runs counter to their best interests. And it always does. That is one last thing to remember: *writers are always selling somebody out.*"

I didn't really know what she was talking about when I first read the book and before I became a journalist myself. But I'd find out. In spades. All I knew at this point was that Alan Rinzler had arranged for me to see Jann Wenner, the editor in chief and founder of *Rolling Stone.*

I decided not to send a résumé. Instead, I got hold of a box, the kind in which you'd receive a gift sweater from, say, Saks, tissue paper and all. I put in it stuff from my life—a copy of a Brown literary magazine I'd edited, a short story I'd written, a few Marvel Comics (I'd worked as Stan Lee's secretary there; that's where I'd been heading after my lunch break that day I opened my first *Rolling Stone*)—and some chocolate chip cookies I'd made for him to eat while he went through it all.

Was this a girly thing to do? Would it charm him? Or would he think it was beyond lame? I would never know, for when I met with him, although the box lay open on the round oak table that was his desk, he didn't comment on it.

This time I didn't bring Reuben, but I had on the same outfit I'd worn for Alan Rinzler—the short skirt, the jacket with the ribald patch—although this, too, as far as I could tell, went unnoticed. Like Alan, Jann sprang to his feet. But the resemblance ended there. A baby-faced butterball of a man in jeans and shirttails, sleeves rolled up, he was all energy and eagerness. Alan had energy too, but in Jann's case, it was more a vibe of being in a hurry, like, *C'mon, I'm busy, let's do this and get it over with.*

"Sit, sit," he said, indicating a brown leather couch beneath a giant autographed photo of John and Yoko, the one of them naked, facing away from the viewer, peering over their shoulders at their self-timed camera; the picture had been the controversial cover of their recent *Two Virgins* album. But Jann, sitting opposite me at the edge of a matching leather chair, motor revving, eyes vibrating, gave me no time to gawk at or remark on or ask about it.

"So, you went to Brown," he said, teeth set in perfect prep-school lockjaw.

"Yeah," I said. I could see he was impressed by the Ivy thing. For some reason, I glanced down and noticed that his nails were bitten to the quick. I glanced back up at him. Did he see me noticing? Was that bad? What should happen now? Should I ask him something? Tell him an idea? But he was already talking.

"What was it like to work at Marvel Comics?" he said.

"What?" I said, caught off guard.

"It said you worked at Marvel Comics," he said, gesturing toward the box. "What was it like?"

"I don't know," I said. "It was okay."

I was not much of a talker at that point in my life, and up till then, no one had expected me to be. But I could see that Jann was waiting for me to say something, so I let myself say what I was actually thinking, and then I seemed not to shut up.

"Really, it was just a job," I said. "Mostly just a bunch of nerdy older people. I answered letters from pathetic fans. I answered the phone for Stan. He was nice, kind of nerdy. He wore a wig. His name was really Stanley Leiber. His wife and daughter used to swan in and out of the office in between shopping. They treated him like some sort of joke. But in the New York publishing world, he pretty much was. The superhero comic books, a joke."

I stopped, looked at Jann, who was regarding me, head cocked.

"Well," he said, "if you're going to New York anytime soon, maybe you could write an article about it."

"About...Marvel Comics?" I said, thinking but not saying, *Why?*

"If you're going."

"No, I am, I'm going in June," I said, "to be in my friend's wedding in Long—"

"Great," he said, cutting me off. "We'll pay you five cents a word." He was already on his feet and headed to his table.

"Five cents?" I said to his back. It didn't sound like very much.

"That's what we'll pay for a first-time article," he said over his shoulder. "If it's accepted. If not, we give you a kill fee, fifty percent of what you would have gotten for the article."

"Oh," I said. "Okay."

"Great," he said with a dismissive wave. "Good luck with it."

And so it was, in this random yet logical way, that I became a journalist.

I left in a daze—Had that really just happened? Did I really have an assignment to write an article for *Rolling Stone?* The white noise in my head finally cleared as I was driving back over the bridge, at least enough for me to realize that when Jann asked if I was going to New York anytime soon, what he was really saying was that *Rolling Stone* would not be paying my expenses. Well, why should it? I was a first-time magazine writer and didn't know myself if I'd be able to deliver.

Except—why wouldn't I? In college, I'd delivered when I had to. What did I know then about writing short stories? Only that I liked reading them. Brown offered courses in writing them but you had to submit something you'd written to get in, so I decided to try and write one like one that I liked. Hemingway's "A Cat in the Rain" seemed simple enough to tackle. In it, a couple is trapped in a hotel room by the rain and the husband is reading and the wife is looking out the window at a cat crouched under a dripping café table and she's feeling sorry for the cat, who was "trying to make herself so compact she would not be dripped on," of course projecting her own feelings onto the cat until finally, at the end, she bursts out in an epiphanic complaint to her husband about feeling ignored and isolated, about all that she really wanted.

So I wrote about me and my boyfriend David sitting on the rocks at Point Judith, Rhode Island, gazing out onto Narragansett Bay, him puffing his pipe, me nattering on about my happiness here by the ocean and how could he bear to leave it and go away to college in Chicago, so far from it (subtext: and me)? Not Hemingway exactly, but it got me admitted into "writer's writer" John Hawkes's fabled seminar, which eventually led to my editorship of the college literary magazine. It was advice I later gave my undergraduate students in 1976 when I was a teaching fellow at the Iowa Writers' Workshop: Copy a master. You probably won't come close but you might at least have something that works.

It was a similar approach that got me a start writing for television a decade later. A colleague from Iowa had made it big in the business and asked me if I wanted to try writing a script. My first draft was awful but after he told me I'd find the tone he wanted in Updike's short stories, particularly "Here Come the Maples," I came back with a home run, a script produced as the first episode of *A Year in the Life*, with Richard Kiley, Alan Arkin, and Sarah Jessica Parker, and the start of my twenty-five-year career in TV.

In a blissfully altered state, I drove home to our apartment in Berkeley's Fox Court, today a landmarked example of late 1920s Fox Brothers Tudor Revival architecture, a Hansel-and-Gretel-looking collection of small contiguous cottages that ran along a lushly landscaped courtyard. Ours was at the entrance to the courtyard, reached by climbing a curved outdoor staircase of rustic brick. The apartment itself was charming—a fireplace in the corner, its stones rising to a beamed ceiling so high it could accommodate a sleeping loft, which, with the help of a carpenter friend of David's, we built, and beneath the loft a space for visitors to put down cushions and sleeping bags and stay—and stay they did, for days, for weeks, forever.

This month it was Steve Ford, a friend of David's from his University of Chicago days, and Steve's girlfriend, Chris, from Ohio, which was all I knew about her, even though she and Steve had been with us when we'd camped and grazed naked at the Jemez hot springs, because she was so constantly stoned she never spoke. And anyway, in those days, any kind of small talk I might have made—*What's your last name? What do you do? Where did you go to school?*—was considered fatally uncool by Berkeley or any hippie standards. Also uncool, I felt when I got home to a cloud of pot smoke, would be any mention of the fact that I'd just gotten a writing assignment from *Rolling Stone* or, for that matter, any betrayal of professional ambition.

Steve had no job; being almost legally blind, he was on government disability and food stamps. Chris did work beside me for a time at HS Lordships in the little wench outfit, a chunk of hash installed between her inside upper lip and gum to keep her high on a shift. (A few weeks after my meeting with Jann, they would move on to the Big Island of Hawaii, find work and housing on a horse ranch—since horses could see, Steve could ride them—and then eventually break up, Chris moving home to Ohio.)

For now, however, Steve passed me a joint and I got stoned and Chris and I made Indian food for dinner from Yogi Vithaldas's vegetarian cookbook, a meal that, since there was no table, we ate cross-legged on the floor.

That night in the loft, Steve and Chris in a sleeping bag below, I told David sotto voce about *Rolling Stone* and Marvel Comics and Jann. David nodded thoughtfully. "Huh," he said.

"We could both go," I said, and since he said he was "into photography," by which he meant that taking and developing pictures was something he liked, not a career he aspired to or anything, I added, "You could take the pictures."

More thoughtful nodding, and then finally: "I could do that," he said. And he did; he came with me and took pictures at Marvel and for that brief moment he became a journalist too.

❖

Chapter Two

Face Front! You're on the Winning Team

When I opened up that first *Rolling Stone* in the spring of 1968 on the corner of Fifty-Seventh and Fifth after my lunch break, it was to my job at Marvel Comic Books that I was returning. I'd arrived in New York City that winter and, with money I'd saved waitressing in Martha's Vineyard after graduation plus some Houghton Mifflin money, I had taken a room in the Martha Washington Hotel for Women in Murray Hill, a place I thought I'd read about in the 1950s Herman Wouk novel *Marjorie Morningstar*.

I'd gotten many of my ideas about life from reading that book when I was thirteen. A Jewish girl, like me, and like other Jewish girls expected to marry a Jewish doctor, Marjorie Morgenstern changes her name and leaves the family apartment on the Upper West Side to pursue an independent life and artistic career, ending up in Greenwich Village—well, for a while. Actually, she eventually gives up the dream, marries some doctor or other, and moves to Scarsdale.

I conveniently forgot this part of the story. And anyway, that was her and this was me and it was practically a generation later and though I'd had to make an even greater leap of faith to go from provincial Providence, Rhode Island, to New York City, maybe I'd realize my dream, vague as it was. With the sky-blue vinyl American Tourister suitcase my parents had given me as a not-so-subtle graduation present—it was all but unthinkable then for a college graduate to live at home—I took the train to Manhattan and a taxi to the hotel. I checked in and was shown to my room—a heart-sinkingly small, dark pit with one grimy window looking onto an airshaft, a sad single bed, a creepy little closet, and a stain on the carpet that looked like blood. I sat down on the bed and sobbed. I wanted to be anywhere but here. I wanted to go home. I wanted to die.

At the same time, this was always the way I'd felt (and would feel) when, as a young woman, alone and on my own, I confronted any new digs: That I would die of loneliness. No one was going to come and save me. No one even knew where I was. And no one cared. *But really, so what?* I thought bitterly. What good would it even do to cry if there was no one there to see it? I blew my nose and went to the window. I tried to open it, but it would lift only three or four inches—obviously so girls like me couldn't jump out.

Not that I would have. I was not the type—too interested in what lay ahead, too afraid to go deep into despair like a real artist, like Sylvia Plath, say, or Virginia Woolf or my best friend Ronnie. In fact, my having joked to myself about the window thing was a sign that I was done feeling sorry for myself, that I was coming back to the bleak sensibility and humor that had always been me, even when I was as young as six, when my mother was called to school so my art teacher could show her what I'd produced when all the students were asked to draw pictures of their houses. Instead of using the side of a pastel-blue stick to create a pretty blue sky like the other children did, I had borne down on the tip of a black stick and created a solid black sky.

Was I murderous? Was I angry? (No one worried much about child abuse then.) It was concluded that I was neither, but it is true that sixty-some years later, I turned out to be the daughter who buried her mother in a mud bank. So maybe child abuse *would* account for the black sky, if mild psychological torture counts as abuse.

Or I might have painted the sky black because I wanted to be different. Or because I enjoyed the attention. In any case, I kept the bleak humor, and it served me well when later I took the entrance exam for the Rhode Island School of Design. They set up a wooden chair and asked us to draw it, which I accomplished ably enough. Then they took away the chair and we were asked to draw it from memory, this time placing it in an imaginary setting. I put mine in a prison cell—cinder-block wall behind it, small high window with bars. (I decided it would be too much to draw it tipped over with a pair of feet and legs dangling above, though the idea had occurred to me.) Maybe the admissions people thought the drawing reflected a trapped soul or something interesting. Maybe they let me in in spite of the drawing and it was my good grades and okay SAT scores that did it, because at that time RISD was trying to up its scholastic ante. Whatever it was, I was admitted and offered a full ride.

I didn't leave my room at the Martha Washington Hotel for Women that night—not to go to dinner or to Max's Kansas City or to a bar or anywhere. I was never one to be out after dark on my own—not then, not in Paris in my forties, not in New York City even now, except when I head out to the theater, where I actually like to go it alone. That night in my single bed, I read a dog-eared paperback Faulkner novel, slept, and then it was morning, a few strands of sun lighting up the dust motes, and here I was in New York City about to hit the streets to find a job.

I dressed in the clothes I'd laid out the night before—black Capezio flats, pantyhose, navy wool knee-length skirt, 34B white cotton bra, and light blue sweater set—and, armed with a BA in American literature and an inchoate desire to be in publishing, I walked uptown to an appointment at an employment agency, where they let me know right away that Manhattan was flooded with girls just like me and then sent me on three interviews that required a modicum of literacy and typing skills, two of them at ad agencies (I hated one, one hated me) and the third at Marvel Comic Books, where the editor in chief was looking for a new secretary. I met with the girl who was leaving and she liked me enough to send me in to talk to her boss, Stan Lee.

I didn't know who he was, had certainly never bought a comic book, though my older brother had a few around when we were kids. Still, comic-book publishing was more in the ballpark than advertising, which had no appeal at all, the personnel ladies all uptight and corporate and full of themselves and the field of advertising. And while Marvel's wasn't the tony magazine- or book-publishing world I'd envisioned, the place seemed easy and relaxed; men—and even one woman—in casual clothes at drawing boards looked up to smile as I passed through. And then there was Stan Lee himself ("Call me Stan!" he said—everything he said ended in !), likable and friendly, with a sparkle in his eye just like my dad. Stan told the employment agency I could have the job and I took it.

In the *Times* real estate listings, I found a two-room, sixth-floor sublet in Greenwich Village on Tenth Street around the corner from where Balducci's was and Citarella now is, and when that sublet ran out a few months later (I didn't renew because I'd discovered a stash of pornographic pictures in the closet and was afraid the lessor/creep that put them there would show up), I got my own place on Bleecker Street across from where Magnolia Bakery now sits, a sweet little studio with a fireplace and a beam in the ceiling from which I hung a swing and three large windows overlooking a weed-choked rear courtyard. I cried here too—the usual sadness exacerbated by the cockroaches that owned New York City in the 1960s and could be seen scurrying everywhere, including all over my toothbrush.

But this was the Village, where I'd always dreamed of living, ever since I visited as a teenager and read about it in books. Every morning I'd wake up in the heart of it, dress, and make my way through the dog shit (no pickup laws then) on Eleventh Street with its leafy sidewalks and charming old brownstones, sometimes stealing glances at the denizens within sitting at dining-room tables beneath chandeliers with their morning papers and coffee. I'd wonder who they were and how they got there, just as I'd wonder much later in LA how people came by all those Rolls-Royces and Bentleys they cruised around in, not knowing then that I'd live in my own Village town-house apartment one day and drive, in LA, if not a Bentley, a brand-new four-door BMW. These Village brownstones seemed such an impossible distance back then when I couldn't even see how my parents, so deep in debt, had managed to buy and furnish our own little house in Providence.

But it was 1968 and I was twenty-two years old, a girl with $130 monthly rent and a secretarial job that paid $120 a week, squeezing onto the Uptown E at morning rush hour, squeezing out at

Madison and Fifty-Third, stopping at the deli around the corner from work to buy a carton of milk and a Linzer torte cookie to eat at my desk. I was living my dream. Except—was I?

In the deli on Fifty-Third, I'd see the women I thought I wanted to become, with their smart suits and briefcases, heading off, I was sure, to glamorous and fulfilling jobs as editors at *Mademoiselle* or Scribner's. And the sight of them left me cold. Or, if not cold, then at least not filled with longing. If there is such a thing as destiny, I somehow knew this wasn't mine. And along with that gut feeling came feelings of self-doubt and disgust: If I didn't want that, then what the hell did I want?

In that anxious, uncertain, and vaguely dissatisfied state, I took that trip uptown, for weeks and weeks and months, to Marvel Comics. The job was okay. It was fine. The people were nice, but there was no one I saw outside of work, and no men there for me, certainly. I'd fight my way home at evening rush hour and feed the pretty black-and-white cat I'd acquired and kill some cockroaches with my shoe and make a sandwich and read and sleep to wake up and do it all over again—until the summer Friday afternoon when my old boyfriend David Leach, who blew through town occasionally, pulled up to my apartment on Bleecker Street in his shiny new blue-green Firebird convertible, top down, to take me to Montreal for the weekend.

What fun it was—the funky room with the sink in the corner, the exotic food—my first time in a foreign country, even if it was only a few hours' drive from my brother's house in Vermont. And then inevitably came Sunday afternoon. We drove to the airport in silence. I'd be flying back to New York and he'd be driving to Chicago, ostensibly to begin graduate school. (*Ostensibly* because he was only pretending to go. He'd needed the tuition check from Dad to pay the lawyer who'd gotten his pot-possession charge dismissed in New York that past spring.)

Except that when we got to the airline counter to buy my ticket home, the woman at the desk wouldn't take a personal check, not mine, not David's.

"Sorry," she said. "No can do."

David didn't want to use his credit card—his father paid the bill, and he'd blow his stack. Neither of us had enough cash and there were no ATMs then. We were stymied. Until David shrugged philosophically.

"Maybe you should come with me," he said. And I went.

I called my parents the next day and told them I had gone to Chicago with David, that I wasn't going back to New York City, and that I needed them to drive down and get my few things out of my apartment. Oh, and also go to a friend's place and pick up my cat.

They tried to reason with me—What about my job? Were we getting married? What would my mother tell her friends?—but I'd made up my mind. It was a measure of their past experience with my hardheadedness and their love and tolerance for and maybe even confidence in me (after all, I'd gone to college, surpassed them, so how could they tell me what to do?) that they borrowed a friend's station wagon big enough to accommodate my trundle bed and suitcase and box of stuff—and cat—and did exactly what I'd asked.

Then I called Stan to tell him I wouldn't be back.

"You're saying you won't be back at all?" Stan said. For the first time in seven or so months, I wasn't hearing any exclamation points.

"I'm sorry," I said, "I got hung up."

"Hung up?" he said, truly mystified.

I didn't know what more to say.

"Yeah," I said. "I'm sorry."

And that was that. Until I cropped back up again two years later with an assignment to write about Marvel for *Rolling Stone*.

"Wow, that's great! Good for you!" Stan said when I called to tell him. The exclamation points were back! "Congratulations! I'll let everybody know you're coming!"

That first article about Marvel turned out to be a love letter of sorts, showing little of the arch and ironic tone that would become my stock-in-trade. Now that I didn't work there I could see the place for what it was—nerdy and square, sure, but also a charmed fantasy factory full of sweet, self-described developmentally arrested adolescents.

Legs (that was my nickname there, because of my miniskirts and, yes, my long and shapely legs) was back, and no one seemed to hold it against me that I'd run out on them, no two-week notice, no any kind of notice. Herb Trimpe, who drew Marvel's *Hulk* comic books (and would draw a big green Hulk for the cover of *Rolling Stone* that my article would appear in and also the inside spread page. "Face Front!" it read in giant comic-book letters. "You're on the Winning Team with Stan!") told me he was really envious, that he should get the hell out of there, that he should have a long time ago. But this was Marvel-hero talk, something Spider-Man might say or any of the all-too-human, at times neurotic superheroes Stan had invented.

When David and I got back from New York to our crash pad in Berkeley, there was obviously no place for me to work, but a friend's sister—the older sister of the girl who'd lent me the jeans jacket with the patch—said I could use her place, that she was go-ing east with her little boy to Martha's Vineyard for the summer to see her folks, leaving her husband behind to write his second novel. From where I sat at her desk in the upstairs bedroom of their shingled house on Channing Way, I could see her husband at his typewriter in the converted garage below.

The sisters were East Coast heiresses, this one with Mao posters on her walls who'd met her husband in college, dropped out with him, and been arrested, but not convicted, for selling pot through the mail. His first novel had been brilliant, but now the pressure was on and he seemed miserable, blocked, chafing at his wife's goodness, her expectations, and her financial support.

It wasn't long before I repaid my friend's sister's generosity by seducing her moody husband, who, furious with himself, furious with me, wanted nothing to do with me after that. It wasn't long after she returned to Berkeley that they divorced and she came out as gay and he stopped pretending to write his book and be-came an auto repairman for many years before he started writing again.

As for me, I had my own "marital" problems with David. "Marital" in quotes because, of course, we weren't married. He'd made it clear that he thought marriage was a meaningless institu-tion (although he married someone ten years later), nothing more than a piece of paper, and I'd always accepted his opinions as wiser and deeper than mine, if I had any opinions at all. I was in that respect very much the silent 1950s girl Anatole Broyard de-scribes in his Greenwich Village memoir of that time, *Kafka Was the Rage*.

"The saddest part of sex in those days was the silence," he wrote. "Men and women hadn't yet learned to talk to one an-other in a natural way. Girls were trained to listen. They were waiting for history to give them permission to speak.... There were all kind of silences: timid silences, dogged silences, discreet, sullen, watchful, despairing silences, hopeful silences, interrogative silences."

Sign me up then for the "timid, sullen, watchful, despairing" varieties of silence with David Leach. Take, for example, when he once remarked that all I ever seemed to need was a toothbrush and a pair of underpants (pretty much all I'd gone to Chicago with); David had his pipes and pipe tobacco, exotic teas, camera equipment, shaving gear, and pot paraphernalia. Did he admire this trait or did he think I was some kind of feckless girl hobo? Or was that what I thought? Should I have been pleased or stung?

He made the remark when we were on a train from Nogales, New Mexico, to Mexico City, where we would board a bus full of Mexicans and chickens and a goat and ride over mountains to Acapulco. There we would be met by the friends who had left the dog Reuben with us and who would then drive us ten miles north to a house they'd rented with another couple. It was on a sandbar, the wild hippie beach where I thought that pretty photo of me might have been taken.

For now, though, we were still on the train somewhere north of Guadalajara, stretched out on the slept-in sheets of the bed in our sleeping compartment, watching Mexico lumber by, nothing to see really but dirt and cactus and the occasional beat-up town. Every time the train stopped, sometimes in the collection of dusty sheds that constituted a town, sometimes in the middle of absolute nowhere, weathered men in serapes and sombreros would materialize at our window with tacos and warm beer and bottles of unlabeled liquor that tasted like burning tires smell.

David had been telling me about a friend of his who had married a girl who would never go on a trip like this, a Jewish princess so uptight it was all about the hotel reservation and a decent bathroom, whereas I was ready to go at a moment's notice, needing nothing but a toothbrush and a change of underwear.

His friend's wife sounded like most of the girls I grew up with on the East Side of Providence, all of them respectable and conventional girls (except of course for Ronnie) who didn't shack up, who got married, and who expected—demanded—real toilets from life. Not like the crude wooden job in our compartment, where you could see the earth moving below when you lifted the lid to shit, which, though I tried mightily not to, I desperately had to because of the tacos, mescal, and beer, praying David wouldn't come back from wherever he was before I'd finished and the smell was gone.

I told David none of this, that I hated shitting in that toilet, that I wasn't cool at all, wouldn't even fart in front of him, that I wanted to get married, or at least wanted him to want to. Really, I don't remember telling him much of anything in those days and years we spent together, nothing, anyway, that I thought might give him a reason to disapprove of me, because I had a nagging suspicion that I had nothing and needed nothing because I was nothing.

But the real problem showed itself in sex. When I was seventeen and he was eighteen, I loved making out with David. Just the scent of his Aqua Velva made me wet. I even bought myself a bottle so I could feel that delicious desire when I took a whiff. For his part, he said that when he went home at night, he'd sniff the fingers he'd had inside me to be turned on by my smell. He had a such big, delicious mouth. When we made out, he would sometimes come. But he wouldn't go all the way with me because I was a virgin and he said it would be too much responsibility.

So, one day on my miles-long walk home from Classical High

in my flats, my light blue Dacron shirtdress with madras cummerbund, my French, Latin, and biology schoolbooks clasped to my small chest, I let Ernie, a Beatnik who hung out on Benefit Street near RISD and who I sometimes stopped to talk to, take me inside to his room. (He might have looked bohemian but, as he'd told me, he was an ex-con version, on parole from a stretch in prison for armed robbery of a grocery store.)

In no time, he was on top of me, roughly pulling at my cotton underpants, and I became terrified. I managed to tell him I'd never done this before and I was scared. Ernie reached down and felt around and then I felt a sharp pain. Noticing that my terror only grew, possibly not wanting to imperil his parole, Ernie climbed disgustedly off me and zipped up as I quickly gathered my books and shoulder bag and was out of there.

When I got home, I locked the bathroom door and saw the traces of blood on my underpants. I smiled to myself. Done. Soon David would be home on school break.

We had sexual intercourse on a daybed in his parents' sunroom while they were asleep (I hoped) upstairs. I didn't know anything about sex except what I'd read in *Marjorie Morningstar*. I thought I should be crying out. Thrashing around. Something. (Marjorie had accidentally broken a water glass on the nightstand with her flailing, for God's sake.) In truth, I felt nothing except glad when it was over—but also glad that I'd made him glad. I faked orgasm, mimicking his sounds as he came, faking it as I was to fake it every time he put it to me, which was at least once a night in the times we were together in the coming years.

I knew in my bones he deserved better, that I was a liar and a fake, but I also intuited that sex was part of the price of a ticket to go places with David—to the Newport Jazz Festival when we were kids, where we sat in the first row, so close we could see

Thelonious Monk's pinkie ring. To see Janis Joplin in New York at the Fillmore East. To Chicago, the Jemez Mountains, Mexico, and finally Berkeley.

In the end, my body outed me before I could—at the point in Berkeley when I was writing the Marvel article and fucked my friend's sister's husband, I'd gone so dry to David's attempts at entry that even faking it was an impossibility.

My Marvel story was finally finished and once again David lent me his Firebird to drive to *Rolling Stone*, where I left a manila envelope containing my article at the front desk for Jann. There were thirty pages inside. Ten thousand and a few words. I knew because I counted every one, including every *a* and *the*, and always would from then on when I finished a story. It was one of the most gratifying parts of the job.

I drove home to my untenable life. Steve and Chris had moved on, and Andrea, yet another friend of David's from Chicago, was in residence, a nervous, hypertalkative, chain-smoking would-be painter. What was she doing there? How long would she stay? The answer turned out to be years, but it wouldn't matter to me—I'd be long gone.

Sick to my stomach with anxiety, sick at heart, sick of Andrea, I waited to hear from *Rolling Stone*. And thanks be to God I didn't have long to wait because the news from Jann came right away, the next day, and the news was good. Good news seems to come fast—it would prove to be that way in television too. Much easier and more fun for an editor/producer/studio to call and say "We love it!" than for someone to bum a writer out with bad news.

And it is a mark of Jann as an editor that he'd read the piece right away and also that he sounded genuinely happy that he liked what I wrote, that he'd discovered a writer he could use. The story would be published in *Rolling Stone*. I would be paid. Ten thousand words at five cents a word—that would mean five hundred dollars, more money than I had ever had at once. And more than that, it meant I would have the possibility of a future as a writer for the magazine.

Once again, I drove to San Francisco, but this time it was to pick up my five-hundred-dollar paycheck with which I immediately bought a used car. Then I packed my few things and moved to a sixty-dollar-a-month rented room in a house in the Berkeley Hills.

Chapter Three

Good Vibes All-a Time

I found the sign for the room to rent on the bulletin board of the Berkeley Co-Op, a hippie market on Shattuck Avenue across the street from where Chez Panisse would open that very year and around the corner from the Berkeley Cheese Board and the first Peet's Coffee shop, a neighborhood that would spawn a revolution in American cuisine. But that would be some other countercultural Baby Boomer's story and this is mine.

Good Vibes All-a Time, the handwritten sign for the room read. I found a pay phone and called the number. Someone named Dennis said, "Groovy, c'mon up." The address on Tamalpais Road brought me onto verdant, winding streets in the hills north of the UC Berkeley campus, what I imagined were professors' homes, obscured by rampant ivy, cedar, and live oak trees. When I came to where the house should be, though, there was no house, only bushes and, hidden among them, a dirt path that I followed up and around through dense undergrowth, past reaching branches of live oak, into a shadowy forest of eucalyptus and California pine by which ran, I'm not kidding, a gurgling stream.

And there among the bushes and brush and trees was the house—a monster of a jerry-rigged thing, its weathered wood and batten siding engirded by metal belts, the switchback path leading up to it defined by a snaking banister like the entrance to some crazy Disneyland ride. I called hello and a forest troll poked his head out the front door and I climbed the steps to meet Dennis, a graying hippie with a trim beard and a freckled face, a constant smile plastered there. He was tightly wound, so his vibes really weren't all-a that good, but they weren't creepy or dangerous either.

He showed me through the cavernous living room, dark because of the trees and dominated by a giant's stone fireplace and hearth. From there I followed him up a few stairs, down a narrow hall, through a cramped little eat-in kitchen with cabinets painted white many times over, then up a back staircase to what would be my room if I liked it.

If I liked it? Are you fucking kidding me? It was perfect! True, it was painted an oppressive hunter green, but it was full of dappled sunlight and felt like a treehouse, a bright little aerie, especially later, after I painted the whole thing white, the bookshelves, the walls, the sleeping nook, and the desk where my Smith Corona portable electric sat once I'd retrieved it from my parents' house in Providence, a desk from which I one day looked out the window and saw, perched on a high branch of a tree like a sign of grace or a gift from God, a rare giant great horned owl staring right at me as I typed.

When I moved in, I didn't baptize the room with tears. Not this room. This would be the base from which I'd travel on assignment, where I'd transcribe my taped interviews and write story after story. This would be where I'd lure my editor to my alcove bed and learn to love sex, where I'd sleep with a housemate's famous professor father, with my and Joan Didion's semi-glamorous mutual friend (the one she'd prompted to call me to say she'd liked my Hopper story), and with a famous photographer who crashed at the house one night. Actually, that deed took place in the living room downstairs in front of the fire, but you get the idea.

There was one more tenant in the house and Dennis led me down a maze of hallways to meet him. Mark was a tall Ichabod Crane of a fellow, a graduate student in landscape architecture at UC Berkeley whose vibes weren't all that great either—he was rather quiet and dour and withdrawn—but, like Dennis's, not dangerous or even weird.

A Berkeley commune this was not. There would be no shared meals, no bonhomie, minimal chitchat. We three would simply coexist, which was fine with me. My real life would be west across the bay with *Rolling Stone* magazine.

Jann had told me that he wouldn't be my editor on the Marvel article—he'd be handing me over to one of his staff. I drove my newly acquired Nancy Drew of a car, a two-toned gray and blue 1947 Chevy coupe, through Berkeley, hippies on the sidewalk scowling at the noxious cloud of black smoke expelled from its exhaust by shot rings, and across the San Francisco Bay to my first meeting with my editor.

Jann's secretary escorted me to the office of the man who was to be my editor—it was one of a row of windowless, ceilingless cubicles with high walls and a door—and introduced me to him. David Felton rose from his chair and welcomed me with genuine warmth. Later in my life, when I was a magazine editor myself, and still later, when I was a TV writer/producer, I would come to know how he felt. Editors and show-runners are glad when they find an able writer. In fact, it's one of the best things that can happen. Finding fresh talent makes your job rewarding and exciting, not to mention easier.

But as I was to discover, there was another reason for David's warmth. I really wasn't aware of it at the time and didn't think about it much, but now that I've seen that 1971 photo of myself and heard from people who worked at *Rolling Stone* then, I can see that, with my miniskirts and legs, I was something of a babe. (But who among us wasn't in our twenties?)

I didn't know what to make of David. Pasadena-born (where exactly was that, anyway?), an Eastern Ivy Leaguer he was not. In what was probably an attempt to look rock-and-roll-ish, he looked clownish—saddle shoes and bell bottoms, a striped jacket with giant shoulder pads and outsize buttons. The cigarette holder would come later (see Rainn Wilson's ditzy portrayal of Felton in *Almost Famous*). He had a flat face, a mop of frizzy, straw-colored hair, wide-set, beady blue eyes that darted like a lizard's, and a scraggly mustache over extremely thin lips. His leap from the chair when he rose to greet me was spastic and awkward, as if his mind was a good second ahead of his body. His flesh, when he shook my hand, felt cold and dry, also like that of a lizard (and, come to think of it, very much like the hard, dry palm of my best friend, Ronnie). I probably fell in some kind of love with him right then and there.

For one thing, he seemed genuinely interested in me, both personally and professionally, and this kind of warmth and attention from any male other than my father or a professor was new to me. Also, despite his clothes, he was a grown-up, a man with talent and published books to his credit and an actual job as an editor. My editor. I had already been passed from Alan Rinzler to Jann and now to David Felton, and, looking back, I can see that what happened between us was in part because I wanted to stick with this editor, to and by whom I was both attracted and repelled, this weird and powerful man (who I would later realize resembled no one more than Beavis and/or Butthead, which would lead me to wonder if it was this resemblance that had drawn David to write for that show in the nineties. And was that why *Beavis and Butthead* hired him?).

He told me he really liked what I'd written, he had only a few notes. He asked me about myself and told me his story, how he'd been a reporter at the *Los Angeles Times,* how a series he'd written on Haight-Ashbury got Jann's attention. How he'd started writing for *Rolling Stone* and how after missing deadlines, Jann insisted he relocate to San Francisco where he could keep an eye on him—and where, even under supervision, he'd kept the slow work habits that had caused him to be referred to as "the Stonecutter" at the *Times.*

David had some new good news. They'd all discussed the Marvel story at their editorial meeting and agreed it was strong enough to be a cover. They'd commission original comic art, maybe one of the characters, maybe Hulk. I listened, stunned. My first article was going to be on the cover of *Rolling Stone?*

Well, yes, but not right away, he quickly cautioned. They'd be holding it until summer, many months away, when advertising was down and when they burned off the weaker inventory.

"Weaker?" I said, feeling suddenly sick.

"Not the article, just—business. It's a different kind of cover for us than music, and the advertisers—look, you did a great job, really," he said, reaching out to give my hand a reassuring squeeze. Our eyes met. And that's when it began, because I could see something in his eyes that set something off in me and that I continued to feel sitting with him at his desk as we went over his notes on my story, a kind of pleasant nervousness that settled in my groin. I didn't mind his notes. There weren't many and they made sense. And, besides feeling something, I was learning something.

He had told me he was married, that he had two young children, that they'd stayed behind in Pasadena. Well, maybe he was married, but it didn't feel that way. I had never really been conscious of another person's desire for me and also had never felt so palpably the desire the consciousness of his desire set off in me.

When we finally did take our clothes off and get in bed together, I had never been so present in the act of sex, had never looked into someone's eyes as we touched each other and seen his pleasure at the same time I was feeling mine.

Sex became something I craved. Instead of accommodating my old boyfriend's constant need, I was the one who got to do the wanting, to desire him when he was away some weekends tending to his family (that was how he made it sound) and when he was busy at work, which, given his glacial pace, was most of the time.

In a few years, after I'd gone to live with him in Chicago, he would leave me and go back to his wife. A few years after that, they'd divorce. He'd have other affairs at the office and an apartment in the Castro with a dentist chair in the living room and a tank of nitrous oxide nearby. In 1977, he'd move with *Rolling Stone* to New York and, in time, become the kind of drunk who passed out on the curb, had his pocket razored and his wallet stolen, before he finally gave up booze and drugs and joined AA.

But in 1971, we didn't know any of that. We'd smoke dope and have sex, drop mescaline and have sex, drop mescaline and go see *2001*, Bette Midler, Randy Newman. We'd ride up the coast in

Hunter's backseat, get naked with the whole office in the Esalen hot springs, and, that first year, when my article was finally published in the September '71 issue, go together to the printer's in Berkeley at three a.m. to watch my first cover of *Rolling Stone*, the cover with Herb Trimpe's big green Hulk, roll off the presses.

My first cover, true. But before that there were many more assignments, my byline in print for the first time, a pay hike to the princely sum of ten cents a word, and now *Rolling Stone* was paying my expenses—taxi, car rental, hotel, flight, per diem, you name it. These were my first real jobs as a journalist, and they took me into new and unfamiliar territory, unlike the story about Marvel, where I already knew and liked everybody and everyone knew me and I wouldn't have my boyfriend since childhood David Leach by my side taking pictures.

I would have, instead, the magazine's recently hired staff photographer, a big-footed and taciturn galumph of a girl in aviator glasses and baggy clothing, a Jewish air force brat (though my father had served in the army in World War II, I'd had no idea there was even such a thing as a Jewish career soldier) who'd become accustomed as a child to moving from base to base, to adjusting to and toughing out any and all strange environments. Not a cold person, exactly, but Annie Leibovitz didn't seem like the kind of gal you'd, say, confide in about how apprehensive you were about something.

It wasn't so much anything she said that made her intimidating; it was more that she didn't seem to find it necessary to say anything at all. She could wither you with a look, shaking her head sadly at the uncoolness of you, as she did at my twenty-seventh-birthday party when she gave me a twenty-dollar coupon for a Lyle Tuttle tattoo and I said thanks but no chance. And

I wasn't the only one intimidated—her subjects were too. I was there when she talked David Cassidy into taking his clothes off for the shoot—he wanted to be cool, didn't he?

Annie and I would work together many times in the two or three years to come and, mostly due to her friendship with David Felton, hang out some, but our paths would diverge. Even as Annie's star rose and rose at the magazine and in the public eye, she'd find herself sinking into a near-deadly drug addiction, and I'd drift off into my own less dramatic and decidedly less public miasma.

On this particular spring morning, April 1, 1971, however, Annie and I were flying from SFO into an unknown future. We were on a press junket to attend a private premiere of *The American Dreamer,* a documentary about Dennis Hopper, who had become a countercultural icon after making *Easy Rider* and who was now living in Taos editing his latest effort, *The Last Movie,* which would in fact turn out to be his last film for a good long while.

"The cream of the underground press," the invitation had called us, we would be flown in from all over the country for the event—though Felton had made it clear to me that *Rolling Stone,* unlike the other hippie rags, would be paying my and Annie's expenses. We would owe nobody nothing; the magazine's services as a PR tool could not be bought!

We landed at the Albuquerque airport and met up with the other journalists, a ragtag group, us included, sleepy from the morning flight but primed for whatever lay ahead, and then all of us were greeted by two men in suits from Universal Studios— young and eager Steve from Publicity and jaded Eddie from the executive suite.

While Steve ushered the other journalists to vans that would drive them the hundred and twenty miles to Taos, Eddie culled

Annie and me from the herd. If those scribes were the cream of the underground press, he let us know, *Rolling Stone* was the fucking crème de la crème, and he led us onto the tarmac, Annie with her camera bags and no-nonsense, giant's stride, me in faded Levi's with leather patches I'd sewn on the ass where I'd worn the denim through, to a plane that looked like a VW Bug with wings. We climbed inside and buckled in; the pilot fired up the engine and we bumped down the runway, then finally wobbled into the sky to fly jarringly and low over miles and miles of bumpy mesa air.

This was my first time in a private plane, my first time in a Cessna, my first press junket. I was at once puffed up by the special treatment, terrified of the turbulence, and awed by the beauty of the terrain over which we flew—raw mesa cliffs looking like some behemoth had chewed them out of the harsh red earth, hazy mountain ranges to the distance on each side, the blue gash of the Rio Grande winding through it all.

I didn't know it yet but I was flying into a nightmare—not quite up there with a Michael Herr–touching-down-in-a-Vietnamese-jungle type of nightmare, but my own personal nightmare. I was afraid that strangers would be nasty, competitive, and posturing or drunk and drug-addled and ass-kissing, and I'd find it all here: an underground press trying to be cool while they jockeyed for Dennis Hopper's attention; Eddie, sent by Universal to keep an eye on Hopper's movie editing, instead bragging about his bag of real organic mescaline, beautiful stuff, that was going to keep him blasted till Sunday; and Dennis Hopper himself. At this particular low point in his life, he was a complete and major asshole—loaded to the gills, feeling put-upon by our presence and cruelly resentful of both journalists and Universal flaks, and an absolute pig to the groupies with whom he'd stocked his house. Though I would one day get to know Hollywood some, I had never encountered it before, and now here it was in New Mexico.

The two who'd made the documentary we'd been flown there to see—Lawrence Schiller and L. M. Kit Carson—seemed like pinnacles of dignity and maturity in this setting. This should give you an idea of the environment, since Schiller was a known, if not sleazebag, then certainly a kind of ambulance chaser, having made his name chronicling the death of Lenny Bruce and, in collaboration with Susan Atkins, the killing of Sharon Tate. (He'd later go on to apply his ghoulish pen to Marilyn, O.J., and JonBenét.)

Kit was a different story. A Texas cowboy dressed head to toe in black (Schiller was all in black too, actually), he had impeccable hipster credentials, having starred in Jim McBride's cult classic *David Holzman's Diary*, a deadpan spoof of pretentious '60s cinema verité. Anybody who can spoof pretention can't be pretentious, right?

Then what could have made him—and Larry Schiller too—think a documentary about Dennis Hopper's making of his (incomprehensible and all-but-unreleasable) film *The Last Movie* was a good idea? Not a hint of irony or humor here, nothing but Hopper-worship, with Hopper philosophizing to the camera for the ninety very long minutes we press were trapped in a theater watching him say things in Kit and Larry's film like "I'd rather give head to a beautiful woman than fuck her, really…I'm just another chick, a lesbian chick" and "I don't believe in reading…by using your eyes and ears you'll find everything that there is" and "We could drop our clothes as little children and be a lot closer to the truth of life…Wanna look at my ass? Okay, here's my ass. Ass, to the world." We got to see Hopper's ass onscreen four times.

After the movie, there was a Q and A with Dennis Hopper, which was more of the same sophomoric babble, then dinner at a Mexican restaurant, where I was seated with Larry and Kit and heard them talk about their documentary, then we went out of Taos proper to Dennis Hopper's desert compound, a few of us chosen to be in Dennis Hopper's Jeep, driven by Dennis Hopper himself. Somewhere in the middle of this ride, it occurred to me that I was going to have to interview Dennis Hopper. At that moment, I probably would have preferred a Vietnamese jungle.

At the house, tequila and scotch were poured; joints, pills, and powdered peyote were passed around in baggies. Kit reminded Dennis he'd agreed to sit down with *Rolling Stone*, gesturing in my direction. Dennis was fried but shrugged and sighed and said he'd do it. We headed into the living room, a few of the other journalists close on Dennis Hopper's heels.

"Mind if we join you?" Art Kunkin of the *Village Voice* asked, meaning himself and Michael Goodwin, though they'd asked me earlier and I'd said no; the last thing I wanted was an audience at what was to be my first celebrity interview.

"Could they?" Dennis asked me. "Really, it's cool."

Now it was my turn to shrug reluctantly and soon it was a crowd scene around us on the floor: the reporters, the two guys from Universal, and Kunkin and Goodwin, cross-legged and in star-fucker heaven, hard by Hopper's side. I set my clunky Panasonic cassette recorder and microphone on the Native American carpet and pressed Record. Dennis looked at the Panasonic.

"Oh, it's one of *those*," he said. "First a tape recorder, then an ashtray," he said. "What we need is a roach clip."

"I might have been right the first time," Kunkin said to me. "You aren't going to get the interview."

"You might have been left the first time. But you were right the second time," Dennis said, then he repeated this and chuckled, Kunkin and the others along with him.

Hopper was considering the carpet. "Now, this is very strange to all you readers out there," he said, "but dig this. Is that balls and a cock on the rug? What is going on here? Readers, we'll never be able to explain this but they're all exposed here." He grabbed the microphone. "They're trying to drug me. Help, Panthers. Black Panthers listening to me, listen, brothers, help me."

It went on like that. Kunkin fetched an empty Campbell's soup can to serve as an ashtray and Hopper mused about Andy Warhol, Goodwin chiming in, until Eddie, Hopper's Universal watchdog, between pinches of powdered peyote from his baggie and slugs of scotch to wash it down, asked Dennis if he'd done what he had to do. Dennis seemed puzzled.

"Did I do what I had to do?" Dennis said. "I don't have to pee and I don't have to shit. I ate today. I drank enough. I smoked. What did I have to do?"

Eddie pointed at Steve, the young publicity guy, and gave Dennis a big stage wink. Dennis finally realized what Eddie was talking about, thanked him for reminding him, said no, he hadn't done it, and asked Eddie if he'd like to do it for him. Eddie said no, so Dennis said, "Well, okay." Then, to the group, "Watch how cool this is."

Dennis started saying something to young Steve but broke up laughing until finally, after a couple tries, he managed to get it out. "Would you leave your secretary with me tonight?" he said. "Of course, this is unreasonable, but if you would..."

We all looked to Steve, who, struggling to adopt a cool attitude, said, "Well, yeah, I'll leave her here. If I forget her."

Now Eddie and Dennis were both fighting to restrain laughter that came from knowing what was coming next.

Steve was looking around. "Where did she go, anyway?" he asked.

And now, the punch line he and Eddie had been waiting for. "To get her clothes from the car!" Dennis blurted out.

"Oh, that's terrible," Eddie said, wiping tears of laughter from his eyes.

And it was terrible. Steve looked stricken and everyone else had gone quiet, just watching and waiting. Dennis was quiet now too, studying Eddie.

"Can I tell you something, Eddie?" he said. "You're common trash, Eddie. Common trash super-pig."

"Right, Dennis," Eddie said, serious now.

"I can certainly see your point of view," Dennis said, laughing again. "But you can be used, Eddie."

"Scotch and water!" Eddie shouted, pushing a glass at Hopper. "Have some scotch and water!"

I couldn't sit there anymore. What was the point? I wasn't going to get an interview. I hadn't asked one question and, truthfully, hadn't prepared any to ask, and for all I knew, I could be Hopper's next target. I had to get out of there. Shamefaced and self-conscious, imagining the eyes of the other journalists on me, all of them knowing I'd failed, I gathered up my things—my tape recorder, microphone, notepad, and pencil—and without a word to anyone, I blindly found a door and was gone. Not such a swift move, I realized, because, though I could at least breathe out here, it began to dawn on me that I was alone in the chilly and dark desert night, miles from anywhere, from my motel certainly, with no jacket and no ride. Annie would have known what to do, but she had gotten her pictures and left the scene to go back to the motel hours before.

I was fucked and freaked out, but I'd walk if I had to. Even if

I got run down by drunks on the highway or lost and died of exposure or thirst in a ditch in the desert, it would be better than going back inside. Just then, the door to the house opened and I watched a figure come toward me, backlit by the lights inside. It was L. M. Kit Carson with his kind eyes and black clothes, blond eyelashes and cleft chin. "You okay?" he said in his aw-shucks Texas drawl. "That was quite a scene in there."

"Yeah," I said.

"Do you need a ride?" he asked. I nodded gratefully. He went inside and came back with the keys to someone's car and drove me to the motel.

"Take care," he said. I thanked him and he waited there behind the wheel until I'd unlocked my door, turned, and waved.

❖

Chapter Four

A Bitch Is Born

Before the junket to New Mexico, I had been sent on one other story, to a Bee Gees concert at the Santa Monica Civic Auditorium in LA. The assignment set the pattern for my future at *Rolling Stone*. While other writers were covering Neil Young and the Stones and Dylan, the editors had picked up an ironic tone in my Marvel piece that disposed them to send me after the lamer stuff—the Bee Gees, David Cassidy. Or the sophomoric and pretentious—Black Sabbath, say, and the Dennis Hopper/Larry Schiller/Kit Carson mess. Go be ironic.

As for the Bee Gees, the concert was undersold—the group was in a slump and what I hadn't realized was that the review of their recent album in *Rolling Stone* describing it as "banal, grace-less, trite and melodramatic" had helped put them there.

I was an avid reader of Random Notes in *Rolling Stone* and the magazine's interviews and features, but I rarely read the concert or record reviews. I wanted to listen to the music, not read about it. Besides, I wasn't the one who bought the records, my various boyfriends did.

If I had read the Bee Gee review, it probably would have saved me a trip the day after the concert to the Malibu house on the Pacific Coast Highway where I'd learned the group was staying. I might not have rung the doorbell, then knocked when no one answered, then knocked harder. Robert Stigwood, the imposing Brit they'd hired as manager when their record sales began to flag, finally came and opened the door a crack. I told him who I was and that I wanted to sit down with the Bee Gees.

"I have no intention of letting you near those boys after that stinking review your paper gave them," he said. And he shut the door in my face.

I hadn't researched Dennis Hopper either. If I had, I might have learned that he wasn't everybody's iconic hero—he wasn't a hero to his ex-wives, for instance, or pretty much anyone involved in making *Easy Rider*—that neither Peter Fonda nor anyone at the studio could stand him, that he was a paranoid and violent ego-maniac who felt he deserved full writing credit, that he'd aced Terry Southern out of points in the profits, and that, most disil-lusioning of all, he hated motorcycles.

I'm not sure even now if it was laziness in these pre-Google days or a lack of real curiosity or interest in my subjects that led me to go into their midst without research. Or maybe it was some innate New Journalism sense that I'd experience a scene more fully if I had no preconceptions. Whatever it was, I'd experienced Dennis Hopper and Hollywood-in-Taos on that junket with an open/empty mind and now, at home in my Berkeley aerie, I had to write something.

I typed up my notes and transcribed my tapes, an arduous process involving the Panasonic and a foot pedal to stop and start the thing, busywork that forestalled the inevitability of actual thinking and writing but also, I would discover, forced me to relive what I'd experienced, which also reminded me of all that I hadn't got down on tape. It helped too that I'd been blessed (and cursed) with the genetic ability, inherited from my mother, to remember every word of every incident, especially if it involved some insult and/or the hypocrisy of a rival or enemy. As a girl, I'd hear her on the phone for hours saying Lila said this and Pearl said that. And like my mother, I remembered every real or imagined injustice.

I'd suffered some humiliation in New Mexico, as well as boredom and revulsion, but what do they say—he who laughs last laughs best? They also say the pen is mightier than the sword, something I'd heard when I was a kid and thought, *Aha*. The concept landed in my psyche and stuck there. My brother was older and stronger than me, even as the undersized pipsqueak that he was then, but I could cut him with my words if I wanted. Writers who say that they don't, and that writers shouldn't, write for revenge are lying to themselves.

I decided to relate everything I'd experienced, from the Albuquerque airport to the screening of the documentary to dinner and the drive through the desert to Hopper's compound, in the third person, casting a cold eye on events as an observer, calling myself "the journalist," Annie "the photographer" (something my writing teacher John Hawkes, when I sent him the article, referred to as "my amusing anonymity").

I wrote partly to avenge my scorched feelings (and maybe young Steve the publicity guy's too) and partly, literature major that I'd been, on behalf of D. H. Lawrence, who had lived in that very desert compound, had written there, and was in fact buried on its grounds and whose tenure seemed denigrated by the dopey Hollywood freaks defiling the landscape, driving raucously through the neighboring sleeping Native American pueblos at night (with me in the car), hanging the walls of the former Dodge house with Andy Warhol posters declaring the worthlessness of reading, plus stocking the place with art like Hopper's own sculpture, the *Spontaneous Erection Machine*, an ugly white and chrome contraption that looked like an arcade game and had huge chrome balls and a phallus that rose and fell when he flipped a switch.

The last third of the article included a verbatim transcription of the "interview" on the living-room carpet, which I'd taped. It was a valuable lesson for future work: if I thought a scene might get so hairy or intimidating I wouldn't be able to remember what was said, a recorded backup was a necessity.

Using carbon paper for my copy, I wrote the article, then counted the words. This time there were only five thousand and some, half the length of the Marvel article, but since I'd been given a raise to ten cents a word, I'd still be paid five hundred dollars—that is, if the article was accepted.

Now I had a new old car, a black 1951 Chevy coupe with better rings, and I drove it across the bridge to the office, a sick feeling in my stomach—the same feeling I still have whenever I hand anything in. Writers put their *kishkes* on the table, as my journalist friend Margy says, for everyone to judge. And as my novelist/TV producer friend Barbara says, any writer who doesn't throw her stuff outside the door, ring the doorbell, and run like hell probably isn't any good.

Again, the call back came mercifully fast. David Felton loved the article; everyone at the office did. It was soon published. Not a cover this time, Peter Fonda had the cover, but it was still a game-changer for me. The editor from *Esquire* called and asked,

"Who's the new bitch?" And my name was added as contributing editor on the masthead, where, among all those guys, I was the only girl.

Where were the other *Rolling Stone* girl writers? Susan Lydon, wife of one of the magazine's founders, had written an occasional short piece, but her byline disappeared early in 1968. Judith Sims had appeared for a time on the masthead as LA bureau chief, but, though she filed an occasional short piece, she was gone from the masthead by the time I landed there.

And all the other girl writers in 1971? Back in New York, there were a lot of them writing for women's magazines, a few for the *New Yorker*. Nora Ephron was a reporter on the *Daily News* then, but it wouldn't be until 1972 that she'd be given a column in *Esquire*. As for New Journalists, at the very end of 1971, Kate Coleman would publish an article in *Ramparts* about prostitution, a piece for which she herself turned a trick so she would know what it was like (talk about embedded journalism!).

Years before, in the early 1960s, Gloria Steinem had donned a bunny suit to go undercover in a Playboy Club and written about it in a magazine called *Show*, but it wouldn't be until the end of 1971 that *New York* magazine would test the first, tentative issue of *Ms.*, written and edited by women, as an insert in its pages.

Of course, there was Joan Didion, who all through the 1960s had been proving that New Journalism could be literature—and that a woman could write it. There wasn't a new journalist, male or female, who didn't have a copy of *Slouching Towards Bethlehem* on his or her shelf. As I did, there in my room on Tamalpais Road, which was where I was the night that I got that crazy-great phone call.

"Howdy," a familiar voice said. "It's Kit Carson."

I stood there with the phone at my ear, my heart pounding. I didn't know what to expect, despite his kindness in Taos, since my article hadn't been all that kind to his documentary.

"Well, listen," he said in his slow Texas drawl in which I could hear only a smile and pleasure as he went on. "I'm down here in Malibu at my friend's Joan Didion's house. She just read your piece in *Rolling Stone* and she asked me to call you up and tell you how much she liked it."

"She did?" I managed.

"I liked it too," he said. "She's right here in the room with me now. She asked me to call you. She thought it was really good. I thought you'd want to hear that."

I must have thanked him. He must have said good-bye. He might even have said that he'd like to look me up if he was ever in the neighborhood. I truly can't remember. What I do know is that it was one of the best moments of my life and still is.

Kit did come to see me in my treetop room in Berkeley. In his forest-green Classic Morgan Roadster with leather belted hood, he took me north to a cabin on Russian River to visit Jim McBride, his director on *David Holzman's Diary*. I dropped in on Kit in Texas once and he came to see me from time to time. In 1974, after my name was stripped from the *RS* masthead and after I'd moved to a tiny house in someone's backyard on Francisco Street in the Berkeley Flats, Kit knocked on my gate with a present—a balloon full of nitrous oxide—inspiring me to write my final article for *Rolling Stone*, titled "After Acid, Wha'?"

In June 1975 and at extremely loose ends, I called Kit one night to ask advice on how to find work writing for movies.

"I'm kinda busy right now," he said, then explained that he was getting married in the morning to the actress Karen Black.

"Yeah, but still," I pressed, "what should I do?"

"Move to LA," he said.

I went to Iowa instead, to the Iowa Writers' Workshop. But a few years later I did move to LA and I did find screenwriting work, not in movies but in TV. Kit came to see me in my office at Lantana when I was writing on *Northern Exposure* with the man who would become my husband, and years later in New York the three of us had dinner in a restaurant near our house. Kit didn't look well, and he wasn't. He died soon after, in 2014, at seventy-three years old.

After the Hopper piece was published, *Rolling Stone* sent me on story after story—to write about Black Sabbath in Providence, about the filming of *The Gang That Couldn't Shoot Straight* in New York, about Tricia Nixon's marriage (a cover story, written under the byline White House Staff), plus weightier fare—the investigation of a low-rent guru in Oakland that was later reprinted along with articles on much more evil sorts, Charles Manson and Mel Lyman, in the Straight Arrow book *Mindfuckers*.

In Providence, I watched Ozzy Osbourne towel down in a pool of his own sweat backstage after a concert. In New York, I let Jimmy Breslin talk my ear off in a booth in a bar at a movie set, and later that night I opened the door of my hotel room to a fellow journalist from Chicago who had a cock of such girth that intercourse was impossible.

"Don't feel bad," he told me. "It's not the first time it's happened."

I loved *Rolling Stone*. I never really thought of working for any other magazine, though on that film junket to New York I did accept a meeting at *Esquire* with the young editor who had called the office after the Dennis Hopper article came out to ask who I was. Only a few years earlier, I would have given my right arm just to sweep the floors of *Esquire,* and now here I was, at an editor's invitation, an almost pathologically shy girl writer with a reputation as a badass.

We shook hands, sat, and settled, the editor behind his desk in his bow tie and blue blazer. He complimented my work and asked if I had any ideas I wanted to pursue for *Esquire.* This confused me. I blinked. At *Rolling Stone,* I was given all my assignments. I didn't have to, like, *think* of anything.

"Um, not really," I said.

Now it was his turn to blink. Here I'd been given a chance to move into the big time and I was looking with a dazed expression at the ball he'd tossed my way and that I'd dumbly let drop.

"Well," he said, "okay." He shuffled some papers on his desk and came up with a page. "Here's something that might be a good fit."

It was an assignment to write about a woman whose cat kept winning blue ribbons at cat shows—because it was the only cat of its breed!

"Oh," I said. "Ha!"

"So?" he said. "Eh?"

I shrugged. "I don't think so," I said. It got very quiet in there. "But thank you anyway."

"Okay, then," he said, getting to his feet. I gathered my things and headed to the door.

So much for my career at *Esquire.* Although, years later, in the 1980s in Los Angeles, I did go to work for the fabled editor who had then been the young editor's boss at *Esquire,* Harold Hayes. He had come west to edit *California* magazine and hired me as a writer and, later, an editor.

In time, we became friends, Harold and I and his wife, Judy. They lived in a charming cottage in Brentwood, the walls lined with books and hung with George Lois *Esquire* cover art and the signed work of photographers Harold had discovered, like Diane Arbus.

When I started writing for television, Harold said in his Southern accent that he was "tickled pink" and lent me his boxed set of the BBC series *Singing Detective* so I'd see that TV could be art. Years later, when I'd gotten back together with my future husband and we'd started writing TV together, I insisted he watch *Singing Detective* too. One of my biggest regrets is that he never got to meet Harold Hayes, who died in 1989, at age sixty-two, of a brain tumor. It didn't occur to me at the time, as it does now that I am in my seventies, that he had died young.

I'd lost my best friend, Ronnie; my father; and now Harold. On my weekly phone call to my mother, I told her how much I'd loved Harold, how sad I was that he'd died. "Tsk," she said, "you really have had a lot of losses in your little life." I was so struck by her rare show of empathy, I didn't think to ask what was so "little" about my life.

❧

Chapter Five

My Little Life, Part 1

The story goes that I was conceived the morning of the day my father went off to war. My mother had forgotten to apply a fresh dose of spermicide to her diaphragm for what must have been an emotional and highly charged farewell fuck. It was November 1944. My father was thirty-four, old to be called up, and with a two-year-old son at home to boot, but he didn't try to worm out of it like some men he knew. He went. He said good-bye to his family and told them not to come see him off, but as the train slowly pulled out of the station in downtown Providence, he saw at the edge of the crowd his own handsome father, tears in his blue eyes as he watched the healthier of his two sons be taken to war.

My father's older brother, Lenny, had epilepsy, had in fact suffered his first grand-mal seizure onstage at his high-school graduation while making his valedictorian speech. He was halfway through when all at once he fell to the floor, rigid and convulsing, moaning and foaming at the mouth, eyes rolled back in his head.

This happened at a time when there was no treatment, years before 1936, when the drug phenytoin (later trademarked as Dilantin) was discovered to be useful for preventing seizures. A tall, handsome, and bright young man, Uncle Lenny had been admitted to Brown University, a rare privilege for a Jew in the 1920s. He began his freshman year, but his seizures on campus were so frequent, severe, and frightening to both students and staff that the school asked him to leave.

He went home and stayed home. My father's diminutive mother, Dora, was ashamed and mortified, and she stayed that way. The family was fairly prosperous; they owned a factory that made caps, had new cars, a grand piano, dressed nicely. They took my uncle to European capitals looking for a cure but found none. This all coincided with a time when caps were going out of fashion. The business began to fail and so did my father's father; taciturn to begin with, he became all but silent now.

With their piano and nice furniture, the family moved to the top-story flat of a tenement off Benefit Street, retreating into an assimilated Jew's version of genteel poverty. My father recounted how his own father buried himself in the *Providence Evening Journal* while his miserable wife cried and raged in distress over her sick son and threatened to jump off the third-story porch.

"So jump," my grandfather would say, turning the page of the newspaper.

The year 1945 must have been a hard one for my mother, pregnant now with me, living with her immigrant parents whom she could hardly bear and who could hardly bear each other. She hated their foreign accents, their screaming fights. She hated her bug-eyed, barrel-chested, Russian-born father's crudeness, his former criminality (he'd been a gun-toting bootlegger through her childhood), and his womanizing, and she blamed him for her tall and regal Hungarian-born mother's moods and depression that sent her on occasional trips to the sanitarium for "a rest."

She often took her mother's side but she hated plenty about her too, chafing at the woman's Hungarian accent when she spoke English in public and at the Yiddish she spoke at home and with her friends.

"You fancy kike!" Grandma Rose once called her. "I hope someday you have a daughter like you!" A curse that, in its essence, if not its specifics, came true.

My mother had tried to escape life with her parents, had gone to New York City and found work with her tall and perfect size 10 figure as a manufacturer's model in the Garment District. But she grew to hate life with her immigrant aunt and cousins in their crowded Queens apartment, with hallways that she said smelled of turnips and poverty, and she hated the clothing manufacturer, who was always feeling her ass. She soon came home to Providence, where the man who would one day be my father, on a break from work as manager of a women's discount-clothing store downtown, first laid eyes on her as she was getting off the train with her high heels, long legs, white gloves, and haughty posture, a broad-brimmed picture hat framing her brunette, shoulder-length pageboy do.

In five months, in spite of the turmoil Ira Green had going on at home, the constant financial and emotional drain of it, he married my mother. Caroline Parnas eloped with this handsome, graceful man with his seeming worldliness, his to-the-manor-born airs, his half ownership of a thirty-foot sailing vessel, and his thousand-dollar debt (a fortune in those days) at the posh Biltmore nightclub downtown where he'd taken her on their first date and where the band, who knew him well, played "Hail to the Chief" when they walked in.

My mother's parents took the newly married couple in, and in a few years they had a son, and now my mother was stuck there, maybe forever, for the foreseeable future certainly, with a little boy who might never know his father, a boy who toddled around, the story goes, gripping a handsome headshot of my father in his army uniform and kepi. I know it's a true story because the very photograph my then two-year-old brother clutched in his hot little hand now hangs framed in the office on Main Street in Hanover, New Hampshire, where he now practices psychiatry, and you can see the disintegrated top corner of the photo where his fingers had grasped it all those weeks and months a lifetime before.

The morning of July 31, 1945, when my mother began having contractions, her father dropped her off on the steps of Lying-In Hospital on his way to work at his liquor store on South Main Street. Her mother, Rose, stayed home to take care of my brother. I am told that I was born quickly and without trouble.

My mother was not pleased with me. Oh, she had been hoping for a girl to complete the set, so my being a girl was fine (though she liked to joke she'd known I'd be a girl because I'd made her fat as a cow when she was pregnant with me, whereas with my brother she'd had only a neat baby bump in front). She wasn't pleased because my brother had arrived picture-perfect—towheaded and blue-eyed, a regular Gerber baby who looked like a goy, a WASP, what my mother had always wanted to be and tried to pass as—so I wasn't what she was expecting. Because now here's me, an Oscar Wilde/George Eliot/Lena Dunham of a baby.

In professional photos taken on my first birthday, I can see my mother's sad attempt to prettify and feminize me: dressing me in a frilly white dress, slicking my thin, dark hair neatly to the side, cladding my feet in stiff little white shoes. Still, even though this child's mother's heart sank at the sight of her, the toddler in the photo looks like the happiest little girl in the world.

The reason was my father, who, luckily for everybody but especially for me, came home from the war and loved me from the start. For one thing, he'd won fifty marks in a bet on my sex and birth date—I still have the German bills, encased in Plexiglas on a shelf in my office—and the timing of my birth got him home from Germany weeks sooner than he'd expected.

But more than that, when he came home, he had been completely and brutally rejected by my big brother. This was not the handsome soldier in the photo he'd been carrying around—this man was pockmarked, careworn, and haggard! This was *not*, my brother wailed, his *father!*

In my forties and into my fifties I spent eleven years in therapy, seeing my therapist through her training at the Wright Institute in Los Angeles, her master's, and her PhD and into her private practice in Glendale. Twice a week for eleven years I sat across from her and wept. The only exception was October 3, 1995, when I heard the O. J. Simpson not-guilty verdict read over the car radio on the forty-five-minute drive from my office in Santa Monica to my appointment and for the first time wanted to talk about something larger than myself.

We came, my therapist and I, to the basic conclusion that these were tears accumulated over the years that my childhood had trained me not to shed—not with anyone else around to witness or be bothered by them, that is—and that I had been permitted into my parents' presence only when I was clean and pleasant,

70

not when I was a whiny, noisy little monster with tears and snot running down her face.

"Don't whine!" my mother would wail. "I can't stand it!" And "Fine, but if you hurt yourself, don't come running to me." Along with "Don't make faces or you'll end up like Cousin Evelyn," which meant being a baby-talking spinster living with her mother and selling dresses in a little shop on Wayland Square. There was also "Don't be so sensitive" and the weird "Don't touch my face!" This last because my mother was worried that the germs on my fingers would give her pimples.

Where was my father in all this? He colluded. Sure, he loved me and lit up whenever I walked into the room (with the much later exception of when he was dying), but I'd better be cheerful and funny and bright. My brother and I didn't sit at dinner with our parents until I was seven, my brother nine; that was when we moved out of the two-family house my mother's parents had bought to accommodate their daughter's growing family (they lived in the upstairs flat, we, down) and into a single-family home of our own.

Before that, we ate at the kitchen table with Beatrice, the young, light-skinned, soft-spoken Cape Verdean my mother had hired right off the boat at ten dollars a week to take care of me and my brother. Beatrice shared a room with us, unfolding and folding her rollaway bed night and morning. When I was little, she changed my diaper (my mother didn't like that mess either) and at two years old, I tried to teach her English ("Dess," I told her, meaning the dress she was buttoning me into). In later years, she combed and braided my hair and got us dressed for school. On Sundays, she'd go to stay with her father in Fox Point, which in those pregentrification days was a modest enclave of Portuguese fishermen and their families.

My father didn't want the commotion of children at the dinner table that parents now seem to find so charming. He wanted to come home from a day at Mickler's Department Store where he'd chain-smoked three packs of unfiltered Chesterfield Kings and sold stockings and cheap underwear to the ungainly and ill-dressed, wanted to leave all that behind as he washed and shaved at the bathroom mirror for the second time that day, emerging for a martini in the living room with his wife and thence to the dinner table, where she'd serve the expected three-course meal: a half grapefruit, say, or wedge of melon in season, then a broiled protein, a green vegetable, and a starch, followed by dessert and coffee.

Beatrice would send us out in our pajamas, teeth brushed and faces washed, to say good night. There was no crying. And really, what was there to cry about? We had food on the table. We hadn't been through a depression or a war.

Upstairs, Grandma and Grandpa had the first TV on the block, a black-and-white, of course, since color hadn't been invented yet, in a blond-wood cabinet, a Philco with rabbit-ear antennas and a screen that looked like a milky convex porthole that we'd stare into, transfixed, me and my brother sitting close and cross-legged on the carpet, watching anything—fat old Kate Smith singing "When the Moon Comes Over the Mountain," John Cameron Swayze with the news and Timex commercials ("It takes a licking and keeps on ticking"), and The Howdy Doody Show with Buffalo Bob and Princess Summerfall Winterspring.

Sometimes Grandma let me come into her bedroom with its old-world mahogany furniture and heavy flowered drapes. She let me sit on the bed and watch while she patted powder on her armpits and between her thighs and dressed, let me help her lace herself into the pink-satin boned contraption that was her girdle, and once let me sit on her lap, lift one of her pendulous breasts, drape it over my head, and smile up at her, at which she only threw her head back and laughed. Once, on a summer afternoon, on the front steps of the house, she held me in her lap and I saw a rose beetle crawl into the cleavage between her breasts.

"Grandma, a bug!" I cried.

But she had already felt and seen it. She reached in, plucked it out, and flicked it away, saying, "Oy, oy, oy!" and laughing so that her whole soft body shook.

There was tension in the house. My mother began to notice that the thick cream layer was missing from the top of bottles the milkman delivered each week. She confronted Beatrice, who admitted she'd been drinking it to soothe her stomach. It was determined that Beatrice had developed ulcers.

My mother wasn't happy either in that house or in that neighborhood. She wanted away from what she called the area's schmaltzy Jews; she wanted me and my brother away from their schmaltzy kids. The sight of hairy-chested Mr. Malevsky in the second-floor flat next door eating dinner at the kitchen window in his wifebeater undershirt ate at her.

And she particularly didn't want to live downstairs from her parents anymore. She wanted a house of her own, which, ironically, was now in her reach because of the money she and my father had managed to save from the break my grandparents gave them on the rent. She thought Grandma and Grandpa should move too. To Florida.

"The winters here are terrible," she told them. "All your friends are dying. There's nothing for you here."

My own life was elsewhere. I loved school. My hand was always in the air. I ached to be called on. I knew all the answers. One Saturday morning my mother drove me to school, where I'd been called, along with the other two smart kids in my class and some kids I'd never seen before, to take a follow-up to a regular IQ test we'd been given a few weeks before.

The parents were suppressing prideful smiles. The teachers were exchanging glances. It was clearly a big deal. I finished the test. Days passed. Nothing more was said. It seemed to me my teacher didn't look my way anymore. My mother never spoke of it again. All of which told me I had failed to prove myself a genius.

Working on an essay in class one day on what I'd done on summer vacation, I got up and went to the pencil sharpener on the wall near the windows to sharpen my pencil. In a little while, I got up went to the pencil sharpener again.

The teacher looked up from her desk. "Well," she said, "somebody wants us to notice that she got a new dress today."

I felt myself burn with embarrassment. Because it was true. It was a new dress.

The evidence against me was mounting: I was a show-off, I was no genius, I wasn't pretty. There was also the matter of the drawing with the black sky I'd made. And my mother's discovery that I'd been flushing my underpants down the toilet when I went to the bathroom. Clearly Beatrice wasn't the only one in that house with symptoms.

Then, when I was seven, a new beginning: We moved to our new house on Wayland Avenue on the East Side of Providence, a leafy district of fine homes bordered by the Providence River to the east, Brown University to the west, déclassé Pawtucket to the north, and Portuguese Fox Point and the harbor south. It was the toniest part of Providence, populated mostly by *Mayflower*-type WASPS—until most of them fled to the outskirts, to Barrington and East Greenwich, in the 1950s when second-generation Jews started making enough money to move in.

Ours was the smallest house in the nicest neighborhood, just like in a Jane Austen novel, a fourteen-thousand-dollar, thirteen-hundred-square-foot, six-room white Dutch Colonial with black shutters, an apple and cherry tree in back, elm trees in front. There wasn't enough room for Beatrice, my parents said, and with the mortgage, we could no longer afford her anyway. She was gone and I never saw her again.

Gone too were my grandparents. They had sold the house and a block of land they owned on Main Street for sixty thousand dollars and bought a four-plex in Miami Beach near Ninety-Fifth Street and Collins. (Bad timing, because not so many years later my grandfather's plot of land sold for a cool million and is where the Providence Marriott now sits.)

I suppose I could have cried about the loss of Beatrice and my grandparents, but I didn't. I loved the new house and our new life there. My mother was happy. I had my own room. And I had Ronnie.

Ronnie was my best friend. She was born two weeks and six days before me, and our parents were friends so I had known her since the crib. She hadn't lived very far away before, but now her family moved to a house just two blocks from us and we saw each other constantly. We walked to and from school together, spent our free time in each other's houses, day after day, year after year, a lot of it in her older sister Leslie's bedroom listening to Broadway musicals on the record player, dancing around and singing along to *West Side Story*, *Pajama Game*, and *South Pacific* at the tops of our lungs.

Ronnie could really sing. She could sing and dance and act, and when she came to my house and I played a Mozart étude that I'd labored on for weeks on my father's mother's grand piano (which now took up half our living room; it was so big you had to crawl over the piano bench or go around through the kitchen and dining room to get to the stairs), Ronnie could sit down and pick it out on the keyboard by ear and, in a matter of minutes, be playing it herself.

Ronnie's family was rich. Her father was vice president of an advertising agency downtown. All my parents' friends were rich. One owned New England's IGA markets. One was a radiologist. Another was a dentist (the one who took the photo of me on the beach). None of the wives worked. They had their hair and nails done, their homes professionally decorated, and played golf at Ledgemont, the Jewish country club.

My mother didn't work either—she didn't want to and my father didn't want her to. My family didn't have funds for beauty shops or decorators or the club. We weren't exactly poor—we didn't live like we were, anyway. What we were was in debt: mortgage, credit card bills, overdue utilities. My father said he spent half his life digging a hole and the other half climbing out of it. Still, it was to our modest little house on Wayland Avenue that everybody came because that was where the fun was.

My father would make cocktails—the only time he went into the kitchen or opened the refrigerator door, my mother observed, was to get ice. The men told stories, the women laughed, everyone played badminton in the backyard under floodlights on summer nights, ice-skated in a rink my father made layer by icy layer with the garden hose in the dead of winter.

Under the floodlights, Ronnie and I would sing duets for the adults, belting out "We are Siamese if you please" from *Lady and the Tramp* and Irving Berlin's "Sisters, sisters, there were never such devoted sisters..."

Our whole family loved Ronnie. Her personality was so big

and dominant that, though my older brother's name was Ronnie (from Ronald, though today he prefers Ron), we all referred to him as Ronnie Green; only my friend Ronnie was just Ronnie.

She was, in her own mother's words, full of the devil. Her green eyes, set too close together, gave her an impish quality. And she was an imp, was always getting us into trouble. We were kicked out of Hebrew school for talking. Called to the counselor's tent at Girl Scout camp for telling dirty jokes in the bunk. Summoned to the school principal's office, separately, for making fun of a chubby classmate.

"You're a good girl," the principal told me, "this is not at all like you. Did your friend Ronnie put you up to it?" To my everlasting shame, I just looked away and didn't deny it.

Through our childhood and into our teenage years we were inseparable, learning to swim in the salty waters of Buzzards Bay at Mashnee Village on Cape Cod, where our parents vacationed for a week each summer, staging elaborate squid burials on the beach, and, in later years, listening to Elvis Presley. By thirteen, we were shoplifting his 45s, his and the Everly Brothers'; at fourteen we were riding our bikes to smoke cigarettes at Swan Point Cemetery (where Ronnie's ashes now reside in an urn); at fifteen we were drinking inches off my parents' gin and replacing it with water until one evening Dr. Summer took a sip of his martini and told Dad, "Ira, this thing is water." My father only laughed. He tried to chastise me but couldn't keep a straight face. I agreed not to steal any more gin.

He wasn't much of a disciplinarian. After I'd committed some infraction or other, he'd come to the door of my room and, with a serious expression, manage, "I'm very disappointed in you, young lady," and this would be enough to make me writhe with contrition. My mother did spank me once when I was four and we were living in the old flat. I'd crossed the street to play in a small forest of trees behind the corner house at the bottom of the hill and when she found me, she dragged me home and right there in the living room put me over her knee, pulled down my underpants, and paddled me with the back of a hairbrush.

She'd told me not to cross the street alone! She hadn't known where I was! She'd been worried sick!

I wriggled off her and marched toward my room, then stopped, whirled, and pointed a finger at her.

"Don't you ever do that again!" I said, and I stomped off.

She never did and liked to tell this story about me. This and another one about picking me up from first grade for a dentist appointment.

The teacher brought me out to her in the hallway. "Do you know who this is?" the teacher asked me.

I looked at my mother and deadpanned, "I've never seen her before in my life."

The teacher blanched. "You...*what?*" she said.

My mother gasped. "Robin, tell her who I am!"

Now the teacher seemed terrified.

"Tell her!" my mother snarled.

"She's my mother," I said.

"Are—are you sure?" the teacher asked.

I told her I was sure, it just—it had seemed like such a silly question, that's all. I didn't know that there had recently been a child abduction and murder in Michigan and now schools across the country felt they had to be more careful.

It was different at Ronnie's house. Her father took a hard line on everything, which only served to create a contest of wills between them. When Ronnie was young, it was easier to please him. At Mashnee Village one summer, Ronnie swam a mile clear across the bay, her father rowing a boat alongside her, and, once they were home in Providence, he had the ad agency's art department fashion a trophy out of a rock he'd brought back, commemorating the swim with her name and the date, place, and distance.

It wasn't long before Ronnie developed mixed feelings about the rock. Was that the only way she could get her father's approval, by swimming to the point of exhaustion across a choppy, one-mile expanse of bay?

We, the children of upwardly striving East Side Jews, were expected to perform—get into Ivies, become doctors or marry them—to reflect well on our parents and boost their status in the community.

We were, as Bob Dylan wrote of soldiers of war, only pawns in their game. But the times, as he also wrote, were a-changin', and it was a change Ronnie and I could feel. We began to spend time in the attic of my house, a dirty, dusty storeroom that became a kind of clubhouse where we read Beat poets, even copying one we particularly liked by Gregory Corso onto the wall:

My mother hates the sea
My sea especially
I warned her not to
It was all I could do
Two years later
The sea ate her.

Ronnie was at my side—or, more accurately, I was at hers—when we first heard Bob Dylan on the record player in Ronnie's older sister's friend Laurie Bernstein's front hall. Laurie had been living in Greenwich Village, had played an autoharp in a band behind Dylan, and brought home his first album, the one with the picture of him on the cover wearing a worker's cap and a serious expression.

I felt his music spoke right to me, but Ronnie was finding her own way into the music of protest now, soaking up Odetta, Mahalia Jackson. We'd spend long hours in her bedroom, Ronnie picking out chords on her guitar, singing "Sometimes I Feel Like a Motherless Child," "House of the Rising Sun," and "Amazing Grace," this last so soulfully it would bring me to tears—or glee, as happened one afternoon when the family's big black maid Rosa came storming into the room.

"That there's a religious song," she yelled at Ronnie, "and you is ruining it!"

Rosa stormed out. We were stunned, and then we collapsed into helpless laughter. But Ronnie was bothered. She got sad. We were moody teenagers by then, but Ronnie was moodier than most. Afraid that Rosa had heard us laughing, worried that she had really offended Rosa, she put her guitar back in its case and went to find Rosa and apologize. It was time for dinner anyway, so I went home.

When we were in first grade, most of the kids were Jewish, occasionally Irish, always white, but in second grade, two African-American girls showed up—Pat Chapman and Clarice Caldwell. Ronnie thought it was would be a good idea to bring them home with us after school for milk and cookies.

While her mother was in the kitchen fixing our snack and we four were in living room, Ronnie's half-deaf grandmother Lizzie, who lived downstairs, came in. She saw all of us playing on the floor and hurried back to the kitchen, and we could hear her too-loud, deaf-lady, Russian-accented voice saying, "Pearl! Pearl! There's *shvartzes* in the living room!"

Was this Ronnie's way of smoking out the racial prejudice she sensed her parents and their friends felt? Is this why, in sixth grade, she chose as her boyfriend Harry Bailey, the only African-American boy in class? It is certainly one of the reasons why her parents decided not to let her go to Nathan Bishop, the public junior high right across the street from their house, and sent her instead to Gordon, a private school downtown.

This was the year I began to lose Ronnie, although I never lost her completely, not even in my glory year, 1971, when I became what I had always dreamed of being, a published writer, and Ronnie was locked up on her second stay at McLean, a mental hospital outside Boston.

❖

Chapter Six

1971

The year 1971 was a glorious one all around—for rock and roll, for *Rolling Stone*, certainly for me as a freelancer, and, despite the ridiculously long hours and low pay, for everybody who worked at the magazine. Just to be part of what was going on inside the brick walls of that converted warehouse on Third Street, in those labyrinthine cubicles and copy desks and drawing boards and deadlines—it felt like being inside the heartbeat of the most happening thing on the planet, or at least in the world of journalism. It became part of our very identities.

As one associate editor at the time put it, "We were young—we were mainly in our mid-to late twenties—the energy level was intense every day, and we were putting out a word-perfect, national magazine every two weeks." An atmosphere enhanced, he might have added, by the frequent consumption of mind-altering contraband—not by everyone, not all the time, but there was an aura.

Everybody, I'd learn much later, was sleeping with everybody—editorial assistants with editors, editors with interview subjects, ad reps with celebrities, and everybody in the art department with each other.

Many of the editors and writers—males, every last one of them—had been drafted from old-line newspapers like the *Wall Street Journal*, the *LA Times*, and the *Cleveland Plain Dealer*, and most left wives and families behind (at least for a time; at least, for one guy, until his wife threatened to put her head in the oven if her husband didn't stop fooling around at work). They found themselves suddenly set loose in the epicenter of the countercultural sexual revolution, surrounded at the office by the brainy and evolved sugar candy that was the girls of *Rolling Stone*, editorial, art, ad, and production acolytes there at all hours helping bosses with the work of putting out a magazine, and also doing their filing, fetching their coffee, fucking their brains out.

One male staffer at the 2007 San Francisco *RS* reunion said, "I miss how smart everybody was, which, in my mind, was the single sexiest thing about working there."

Like the editors, and like me, the girls of *Rolling Stone* had escaped straighter fates—the publishing world of Manhattan, academia. We girls stopped shaving our legs and underarms, let the hair on our heads go wild, went braless. Picture me in a salmon-colored bridesmaid's gown at my college friend's wedding on Long Island in June 1970, poofs of armpit hair poking out. The mother of the bride was not happy.

And neither was my own mother when I'd shown up in Providence after the wedding with the clothing of a Berkeley hippie, outfits like the floor-length Indian-paisley-print wrap dress that I wore to a barbecue at Ronnie's parents' house. A few winters before, in Chicago, I'd knit a long white wool scarf, and I wore it that day as a shawl. To mock me, my mother, embarrassed by my hair, my dress, and especially my shawl, came to the cookout wrapped in a commodious white wool afghan crocheted by my grandmother.

"Robin looks beautiful," Pearl Barad scolded her. "You only make yourself look foolish."

Of course, Mrs. Barad had bigger problems. A few months before, having recently been released from McLean the first time, Ronnie had come to the family dinner dressed like a nun, confounding poor old deaf Grandma Lizzie.

"What's going on?" she had wailed. "Is she a Catholic now?"

Compared to a nun's habit, a hippie dress that looked like someone's college bedspread was nothing. Besides, I'd come east with an actual assignment to write an article about Marvel Comics for a national magazine, even if no one there had ever heard of the magazine. Shouldn't my mother be cutting me a little slack?

My success the following year, after that first assignment, served to justify everything—the waitressing, the wandering, the money spent on what seemed like a wasted education. Whereas a year ago, when someone asked my parents about me, I'd been the brunt of a joke, the two of them rolling their eyes, saying I was trying to find myself and right now I thought I might be in California.

Well, ha! I had found myself, and here I was in the summer of '71, when that photo on the beach was taken, a star! In Providence again, but this time for a story on Black Sabbath, I took my parents' friend Jane Sackett with me to their concert and then later quoted her in my article when a Cranston metalhead kept asking her how old she was and she finally saucily said, "Fuck off."

Now Jane had her fifteen minutes of fame and I was famous in my parents' circle for having given it to her, me, an East Side

Jewish girl who had made it on my own in the big world. The only other girl known to have made it out of our golden ghetto into a writer's life was a doctor's daughter, Jane Kramer. Her story was myth: Born in 1938, a private school, then a Vassar BA with honors, an MA from Columbia, and then, and then—a writer with her own column in the *New Yorker*, Letter from Europe, no less. The *New Yorker*, for crying out loud! Besides *Life* and *Time*, it was the only magazine in my house growing up. The holy magazine grail beside which my own awesome journalistic achievements would forever pale.

Jane Kramer wrote books, made documentaries, lived in Paris, married a famous anthropologist by the weird and wonderful name of Vincent Crapanzano. As fate would have it, I finally met Jane Kramer—and Dr. Crapanzano—two years ago at a party given by creative intellectual types at an apartment on Central Park West. She lived downstairs. Someone introduced me to her. My eyes slammed open.

"You're J-Jane Kramer?" I stammered. "From Providence?"

It was like meeting Gandhi or Simone de Beauvoir. Someone who inhabited unreachable realms. But now here was this tiny Jewish woman, seven years older than me and looking it, though her eyes still shone with the bright, mischievous gleam of the French-looking *gamine* I'd seen and envied in photos on book jackets and in the *Times*.

"I'm from Providence!" I said. "I've heard about you all my life! I can't believe I'm meeting you!"

She wasn't rude, exactly. She just seemed basically uninterested in hearing about Providence, in talking about it, or her escape from it, or mine. But when I mentioned later in the conversation that it was my work on *The Sopranos* that had brought me and my husband to New York, she went apeshit.

"Vincent!" she called to the little white-haired man across the room, her husband. "Come here! These people wrote for *The Sopranos!*"

I don't know if Gandhi or de Beauvoir would have had the same reaction to *The Sopranos*, but Joan Didion had and so had her husband, John Dunne, when I'd finally met them face to face at a party at their apartment on the Upper East Side years before. They'd gone completely and surprisingly and gushingly apeshit over *The Sopranos*.

But all of this was decades and a continent away from 1971 and San Francisco and the life of a girl at *Rolling Stone*. Jane Kramer and Joan Didion had grown up in the 1950s and had formed themselves in the world of Manhattan publishing and intellectual life, but we—the girls in the office and I—had come of age in the 1960s and, heeding the voices of our inner rock chicks, had lit out for the territory and landed, for one reason or another, in the Bay Area, where, in America in 1971, everything was happening.

Our cultural shift went beyond hairy armpits. We liked to smoke dope and get high and listen to music. We liked to dance to it. We liked to get sweaty. We were game and adventurous, enjoyed being desired, and were up for it—we had the pill. We were liberated—from our parents, at least, and in society, if not in the workplace.

We didn't see ourselves as victims. We were proactive in our sex lives. We were hungry for experience and beat men to it. If it was okay for men to fuck around, why shouldn't we? We sought equality in this way. We felt like we'd found it. It didn't feel like promiscuity; it felt like freedom. It felt powerful. If there was an emotional—or even professional—cost, it wasn't apparent, not then. Consequences weren't even on the radar. There was no such thing as AIDS.

In the nomenclature of the times, we were "chicks." The term was aspirational. It was cool to be a chick—a hip chick like the chicks in swinging London, a Marianne Faithfull or Jane Birkin, or the more relaxed and sartorially deconstructed hippie-chick version from Berkeley or the Haight. As chicks, we peered at the world of men from under our bangs or posed for cameras with our heads tilted coquettishly, projecting a harmless and non-threatening vibe. And we weren't threatening anything—not yet, anyway.

In this world, the world of rock and roll, men ran the show. They were the rock stars. The journalists and editors were men too. Even before that, in college, it was guys who'd been the ones to grab the microphones at sit-ins and demonstrations. A chick's mandate: to be by their sides at the revolution, looking hip.

There were three main chicks serving as editorial assistants at *Rolling Stone* in the years I was there: Sarah Lazin, Harriet Fier, and Christine Doudna. They were beautiful girls—a job requirement; Harriet told me that she'd been told that straight out at her interview—and all three wildly overqualified to be office slaves.

Sarah, who signed on in 1971, she of the pale gray eyes behind her granny glasses and untamed explosion of hair, had a master's in history from NYU, had lived in Rome, Milan, and Paris, had gone to see a boyfriend in the Peace Corps in India and then come to San Francisco for another boy who had been living in Mendocino in a tree and who, she had discovered, was strung out on drugs. They'd set up house in the Haight, but she left him in '69 after he was busted for robbery in Marin.

In 1972 came bright-eyed brown-haired Harriet, a recent cum laude graduate of Smith who, visiting college friends in San Francisco, had stumbled into a part-time night-switchboard job at *Rolling Stone* and from there into the office proper. A crew from

French television had come to film a documentary about Jann and *Rolling Stone*, and Sarah had done her best, translating with the French she knew, but then Harriet took over the task, and once Jann heard her perfect, fluent French, she was made.

Christine was next, a tall, willowy blonde who showed up in a white silk blouse, no bra, for her interview with Joe Eszterhas, who felt he needed an assistant who catered mainly to himself. Sarah, who had more than enough on her plate, remembers seeing Christine and thinking, *Oh, brother, this is all I need,* but Christine turned out to be another workhorse, one who'd pulled her weight at the *Washington Post* in Hong Kong, taught French at a university in Lagos, come to San Francisco fresh from a liberating divorce, and was out of a job when the city's short-lived incarnation of *Saturday Review* folded. There had been a second girl up for the job but it was clear that Joe wanted this beauty, though she would prove to be the rare girl there he didn't bed.

The three were adventurous girls who happened to be, like me, among the scant 10 percent female readership of *Rolling Stone* and who came to work there because they thought the magazine was groovy and it would be a groovy place to be.

I knew none of this about them then. I didn't have much to do with them. I was someone separate and apart. It was who I'd been at Brown too, skulking around the perimeters of the Ivy college scene in Beatnik black, a drawing board under my arm as I headed down the hill to RISD to indulge myself in a minor in art, the townie state-scholarship girl writer of short stories and editor of the literary magazine, a loner of sorts.

Was I shy? Socially backward and inept? Did I harbor an inferiority complex? A shame of being Jewish? Or did I think that I was better, cooler than everybody else, those smug, goofy frat boys, lawyers and bankers in waiting, and their counterparts at Pembroke, there for the sole purpose of finding husbands? All of the above. And it was simply the person I was and am. Like right now, as I enter these words into my computer, I am at a spa near Edith Wharton's house in the Berkshires where I have come for a week to write and work out in the gym and do yoga and such, and I notice that I prefer to sit not at the communal table for single guests but by myself, where I can ponder everybody else.

In those days, when I slunk (or was it strode?) into the *Rolling Stone* office to deliver a manuscript to my editor or get his notes, I imagined I could feel the cold eyes of the editorial assistants upon me, could sense their hate rays, suspicion, and dislike.

"No, we envied you," Sarah told me. "We admired you. You were the only girl writer and you were really good. And you had this gorgeous body. We wanted to be you."

Ironic, because now, looking back, I realize that while I might have felt like queen shit swanning (or was it ducking?) in and out, I felt envy too. Because those girls had one another, both in and out of the office. Sarah lived in back of a small Victorian in Noe Valley, the main house occupied by Jann's beautiful British secretary Stephanie Franklin (Jann loved her English accent answering his calls as well as the fact that she was trained in shorthand so he could dictate to her). Stephanie and her boyfriend had moved in when guitarist/heroin addict/future lover of Jann's wife Sandy Bull moved out (leaving blood on the walls).

Managing editor Paul Scanlon—a mustachioed army veteran from a straight newspaper, a lover of jazz if not rock and roll— separated from his wife, and after he'd made his way through girls in art department and publicity, he ended up with Sarah, who'd been patiently waiting. He moved in with her, and when Jann's secretary decamped for New York, they moved into that flat and Harriet Fier moved into Sarah's old place in back.

Their house—and the homes of other *Rolling Stone* employees—were party scenes. Ben Fong-Torres and Dianne, Harriet and her artist boyfriend, Sarah and Paul, and other staff members would gather even when they weren't working. There'd be potluck suppers, Charlie Perry showing up with some esoteric Arabic dish he'd made and a bottle of the good wine he'd broken out at the office. (Christine had her own scene, her and her journalist boyfriend and his colleagues from *Newsweek* and the now-defunct San Francisco *Saturday Evening Post*.) Together, they'd go to catch acts around town at the Boarding House and the Matrix, the Avalon and the Fillmore—Dan Hicks and the Hot Licks, the Dead, Steve Martin, and Bette Midler in her pre–New York Continental Baths days.

But mostly the girls' life was at the office, serving the boys—Jann and Paul and Ben and Charlie and David Felton and Grover Lewis, plus outside writers Tim Cahill, Tim Findley, Timothy Crouse, Tim Ferris, Pat Sullivan, Chet Flippo, Tom Burke, plus a string of B-level freelancers, all men, an art staff always headed by a man, male typesetters, and male bosses on the business side (except for Laurel Gonsalves), all the way on down, including people in the mailroom. The in-house testosterone levels had doubled back in 1971 when Joe Eszterhas was added to the mix, a macho man with his big Hungarian face, a pipe in his mouth, a Bowie knife (I'm not kidding) hanging from his belt, writing prose like "the great stone canyons of New York City," chronicling the seamy side—drug wars and executions, et cetera—although he'd find himself consistently out-macho'd by the presence on the magazine's pages of Hunter S. Thompson.

Hunter not only talked the talk, he walked the walk, hanging out with a motorcycle gang to write about them until they finally beat the shit out of him—hey, they felt used. What did Joan

Didion mean when she said writers were always selling somebody out?

Growing up in Louisville, Hunter had been the genuine article—a bona fide juvenile delinquent, although, with a widowed librarian for a mother, he was a literate JD, albeit one who didn't graduate from high school because he'd spent time in jail for robbery and assault. After a stint in the air force, he spent his peripatetic twenties writing for newspapers and magazines. He wanted to be a Fitzgerald or a Hemingway, but getting into bar fights in Greenwich Village was as close as he got.

He'd been sent to Las Vegas by *Sports Illustrated* to cover a motorcycle race, and when that magazine "aggressively," according to Hunter, rejected the pages that resulted, he brought them to *Rolling Stone*. David Felton and Jann went nuts. They told him to keep going, to let it rip, which he did for pages and pages that resulted in "Fear and Loathing in Las Vegas: A Savage Journey to the Heart of the American Dream," published in two parts in November. the first part as Hunter had written it, the second derived largely from taped hours of Hunter's and Oscar Acosta's muttering and raving, tapes that landed on the desk of newly hired Sarah Lazin to be transcribed. "What am I supposed to do with this?" she said to Paul. "Just do the best you can," he told her. And with foot pedal and headphones, she painstakingly typed their almost-unintelligible banter, a screeching argument with a waitress...all of it later to make up much of part 2.

It was terrific, that, all of it. Brilliant. Hunter's litany of drug talk in part 1, sure—

We had two bags of grass, seventy-five pellets of mescaline, five sheets of high-powered blotter acid, a salt shaker half full of cocaine, and a whole galaxy of multi-colored uppers, downers, screamers, laughers...and also a quart of tequila, a quart of rum, a case of Budweiser, a pint of raw ether and two dozen amyls.... The only thing that really worried me was the ether...

Hilarious. And, as I would discover firsthand, no exaggeration. But there was more than drug-addled braggadocio to his writing; there was actual thought and insight into what he saw as the failure of the 1960s counterculture.

He wrote of the sixties as a hopeful time, hope now "burned out and long gone," sunk in "this foul year of Our Lord, Nineteen Hundred and Seventy-one...Tim Leary a prisoner of Eldridge Cleaver in Algeria, Bob Dylan clipping coupons in Greenwich Village, both Kennedys murdered by mutants, Owsley folding napkins on Terminal Island, and finally Cassius/Ali belted incredibly off his pedestal by a human hamburger, a man on the verge of death. Joe Frazier, like Nixon, had finally prevailed for reasons that people like me refused to understand—at least not out loud."

His writing seemed like a new form, as close to rock itself as writing gets, unrestrained and unrepressed, wild and reckless and high as a fucking kite. Nobody was saying it better. He was thirty-four, and it all came together for him; he had found his voice and, in *Rolling Stone*, the perfect venue—a rag that came out every two weeks, neither a glossy magazine with a two-month lead time nor a newspaper with its limited space and linguistic leeway. Stories never had a chance to get stale. They could be alive and in the moment, like Hunter's writing.

Hunter in person was a different story. As with the editorial assistants, I didn't know very much about him then, his misspent youth, his aspirations, his shenanigans in Greenwich Village. I knew only what I saw when I happened to be at the office when he showed up. He was strange. Guarded to the extreme. Jumpy.

He didn't make eye contact and he muttered. I couldn't under-stand a word he said when he stopped to mutter something at Felton, by whose side I always stayed while at the office. It looked like a big put-on, Hunter's act. To protect himself, I supposed, so he wouldn't have to actually talk to anyone. Or maybe it was the drugs.

I did see him act normal once. It was in 1973, and I had gone to live with Felton in Chicago, where he was in a program for jour-nalists similar to Harvard's Nieman Foundation. Coincidentally, Hunter was slated to give an undergraduate lecture at the univer-sity, and for the fun of it, Annie flew in to stay with us on her way to or from an assignment.

She and David cooked up the idea that we would go to the lec-ture dressed as Hunter's hallucinations, so we went downtown and rented costumes—a giant gorilla head for me, a frog outfit for David, and for Annie a bird whose beak lifted to allow her eye access to her camera.

We filed into the auditorium and took our seats among the stu-dents just as Hunter was walking to the podium. He saw us, gave a slight nod, and mumbled something that Felton said later was "Will you look at that," before going on to deliver a completely incomprehensible rant that seemed to entertain the students, though it was hard to see much of what was going on through the eye slits of my suffocating and ridiculous gorilla head.

Hunter had social obligations at the university that night, but in the morning, we three picked him up at his hotel to take him downtown for a radio interview with Studs Terkel. Hunter mut-tered and ranted the whole way—bugs were crawling up his leg, this drug, that drug. We got to the radio station, and Hunter sweat and muttered to himself and paced the hall—that is, until Studs Terkel came out to greet him.

Terkel in person was just like his voice on the radio and in his writing: warm, engaging, sincere. An amused twinkle in his eye, he seemed genuinely tickled to meet Hunter. As for Hunter, I saw him instantly transform into someone else. Gone were the evasive eyes, the muttering, and the jumpiness, and in their place, someone polite and respectful. He shook Studs Terkel's hand.

"I'm glad to meet you too," Hunter said. "Honored."

"Well, let's do this, then," Terkel said, ushering him cheerfully into the broadcast booth. And in the radio interview that followed, Hunter continued to be articulate, responsive, cogent.

His was an act that would wreck him in time, his decline and suicide well documented, showing that as he grew older, the line that distinguished his actual self from the literary persona he created became increasingly blurred. In 1978, he told an interviewer on the BBC that he sometimes felt pressured to live up to the fictional self he created, adding, "I'm never sure which one people expect me to be. Very often they conflict—most often, as a matter of fact...I'm leading a normal life and right alongside me there is this myth, and it is growing and mushrooming and getting more and more warped. When I get invited to, say, speak at universities, I'm not sure if they are inviting Duke [the name he invented for himself] or Thompson. I'm not sure who to be."

You only have to go on YouTube and see him on the Letterman show or Conan O'Brien to see the physical toll this took on him. David Felton goes further to say that even while he concurs that Hunter's persona ultimately killed him, or at least played a big part in his decline, that Hunter lost sight of the person he actually was; he thinks that his suicide in 2005 was a kind of performance. He was on the phone with his wife when he cocked the gun—she heard him do it—then he hung up, put the barrel in his mouth, and pulled the trigger.

* * *

But this would be years from now, for these were the salad days, his and everybody's. Hunter was a star. He brought éclat to the magazine; he electrified the place when he came in. In addition, as I've been told since, even with the madras shorts, the fishing hat, the aviator glasses, the bowlegged gait, the jittering and muttering, he was quite the chick magnet, cutting a swath through the office that included Harriet and even Amazonian Annie. Hard for me to think of Hunter that way—that is, before late that December 1971, which was when I saw Hunter naked in the Esalen sulfur baths on the second night of the *Rolling Stone* editorial conference in Big Sur.

Or I supposed he was naked, submerged as he was from the waist down. It was after one a.m., when the baths are open to the public, and many of us had taken off our clothes and climbed into the hot sulfur spring water, but it was Hunter who stood out most distinctly, gorgeous as just himself without the ironic shirt and hat, the cigarette holder, the aviator glasses, his torso as perfect and toned as that of Michelangelo's *David*, or at least of the Oscar statue they give away at the Academy Awards. An amazing physique for someone who smoked and boozed and drugged as much as he did.

As we all did that night because, make no mistake, we were pretty much wasted on weed, mescaline, and bourbon. Enough so that earlier that evening, I'd climbed into the backseat of Hunter's rented Mustang with Felton, Annie up front riding shotgun, Hunter at the wheel. We were reenacting the ride up Route 1 they'd taken the night before, and as we rode, the three of them gleefully recounted the adventure, how at midnight. Hunter's Wild Turkey had run low, leaving him, as he saw it, no choice but to drive at dangerous speeds, as we were now, up forty-five minutes of treacherous road north to Carmel to buy more, how the California Highway Patrol had pulled them over, made Hunter get out, walk a straight line with eyes closed, and touch his nose, which he'd failed to do, how Annie had caught the whole thing on camera, including the moment he snapped his head back, causing his sunglasses to fly off, and how he caught them behind his back with one hand.

"See that?" Hunter said, shaking the shades at the cops. "That's got to count for something." And the cops had suddenly let them go, saying to Annie, "Get him out of here."

And now here we were again at midnight, purely for fun speeding north on Route 1 with the headlights off, squealing around curves and taking hairpin turns on two wheels, swigging off the fifth of Wild Turkey he held between his legs, all of us stoned on the little blue mescaline pills in a baggie perched on the console within Hunter's reach. He ate them like candy.

I wasn't afraid. I was laughing. Screeching with pleasure. We all were. What was there to be afraid of? We were on the inside lane, hugging the cliff, although Hunter did take each curve with a swing into the outside lane, letting up on the gas and then gunning around the bend, and we knew that any misstep—an animal in the road, say, or an oncoming car with its lights also off—could send us sailing over the guardrail-less edge and rolling to our deaths on the rocks below.

It occurred to me that I seemed not to care. I felt alive. Immortal. Lucky to be in that car, living on the literal edge. This, I realized, was the point of Hunter. He didn't just write this stuff; he lived it. And if we went crashing down that cliff into the Pa-.cific Ocean, so be it. What better way to die?

♣

Chapter Seven

Big Sur

We didn't die that night. We returned to Big Sur after one a.m., parked in the Esalén Institute lot, made our way down a moonlit path to the edge of a cliff, where we descended stone steps into a passageway that smelled like sulfur, like hell is supposed to smell, and soon found ourselves in a space carved out of rock where wet, naked bodies came and went in the dim light of the steamy atmosphere, like some vision of souls in hell. Had we died? Was this hell? But if it was, why was everybody smiling? Why the shit-eating grins? And would one side of a cave of hell be open, as this place proved to be, to the clean night air and the vast and beautiful black expanse of the Pacific Ocean now spread before us, its waters sparkling tonight in the light of a full moon?

We took off our clothes and hung them on hooks and joined the others in the big stone tubs, six or seven of us in each, Felton next to me, Hunter across, Annie somewhere out of sight, and Laurel Gonsalves, who ran advertising sales, beatific in the corner, steam rising around us all as hot, sulfuric mineral water met night air.

But now Jann appeared just outside the bath, naked, round, and beautiful as a cherub. We were smiling like fools.

"Hi, hey," I said, "do you want to go for a walk?"

"Robin!" he said in an admonishing tone, knowing what I was implying even if I hadn't, in my stoned state, quite realized it, his eyes finding his wife, Jane, in the next tub, watching him. She didn't look happy but strangely pinched and starved, which made more sense years later when Jann came out as a gay man.

This was the second night of the editorial conference, when wives and girlfriends (and Laurel Gonsalves) had been invited to attend. The first night and day were, other than Annie to make a photographic record of the whole thing, for men only, and though I was there on the masthead with the men, I was not on staff or retainer, and therefore not invited. At least that's what both Jann and Paul Scanlon assured me years later when I asked.

And this, of course, since I'd written like crazy that year, raises the question of why the fuck not? Which is a question everybody who'd know seems unable to answer with any certainty, myself included.

I know that I never asked to be on staff or retainer, that it never occurred to me and no one brought it up. I did for a time occupy a desk at the office—was it that year, the next?—right outside Eszterhas's cubicle in an open area that also housed Jann's secretary. I recall Jann bringing a lamp and making a show of placing it on the desk in welcome, though today Jann himself can't confirm or deny this ever happened. Charlie Perry, however, says that it's possible—writers and contributing editors often found themselves at random desks in this or that hallway in the shifting personnel and editorial tides.

Well, it's my memory and I say I had a desk, a phone, and a lamp and that Jann seemed tickled and amused at my arrival in the office. If there was sexism, it was in what felt like his delight in the novelty of having me there, a chick writer. I further remember that he invited me to attend editorial meetings—me with all the guys. And with this memory, David Felton concurs, though neither of us can remember when exactly it was. And does it matter?

It would have been some combination of Jann, Joe Eszterhas, Felton, Paul Scanlon, Charles Perry, maybe Ben Fong-Torres and Grover Lewis. They would have chewed the fat, laughed at their own jokes, sparred for dominance, and Joe, if BBC-TV footage I've seen is any indication, would have emphasized the points he wished to make by driving his Bowie knife into the conference table. Ashtrays would be overflowing, Joe puffing his pipe, everyone else, cigarettes. There would have been competitive jostling for space as editors pitched their ideas, what Harold Hayes would later tell me was the "blood on the walls" he'd encouraged at editorial meetings at *Esquire*. Jann would be simultaneously smoking, shuffling papers, jiggling a nervous knee, and talking a mile a minute, wired on either coke or speed.

This much I do remember: Jann brought up a story he wanted me to do. I lived in Berkeley and looked young enough and right enough that I could go undercover as a senior at the public high school there and then, like, write about it. I declined. I had in mind a different story about Berkeley: Hippies on government dole. Felton reminds me that he pitched them the headline "Guerrilla Welfare."

I spent weeks on the assignment, but it never ran, was in fact the only story at *RS* for which I got a kill fee. Many years later, Jann finally got the Southern California version of his high-school undercover story in the magazine with Cameron Crowe's "Fast Times at Ridgemont High." It and the movie that came after with Sean Penn were wonderful. I've never felt anything other than that the right person wrote that story.

As for me, that one or those two meetings, whenever it or they were, were enough for me, my first and last editorial meeting(s), and it would be years before another female would appear at the table. But appear she would, in 1974, brought to the magazine by John Walsh, whom Jann had hired the end of the year before as managing editor, which had been Paul Scanlon's long-held job. Scanlon elected to stay on in a lesser capacity because, as he recently put it, John Walsh looked he wouldn't last longer than a cup of coffee, which turned out to be pretty much true, though the managing editorship would never again be Paul's.

Walsh may not have lasted long, but his effect on the magazine was transformative: he hired Marianne Partridge as copyeditor and tasked her to professionalize the editorial department, which until then had been a catch-as-catch-can kind of operation.

I was mostly gone by 1974, from the magazine's masthead if not from its pages, and I didn't really know her, but I'm told she had come up through the *New York Times*, *Forbes*, and the *Saturday Evening Post*, a no-nonsense broad who didn't take shit from anybody, even Jann himself, and that she ultimately broke his heart when, after she'd risen to take Walsh's place as managing editor and had spent a few years on the job and just as the magazine was making its move to New York, she informed Jann she was leaving *Rolling Stone* to work for Clay Felker at the *Village Voice*.

According to people who were there, Jann screamed at her, "You fucking cunt!" and threw a chair across the room.

Immediately after she left, he had her office repainted, grieving for days over the betrayal.

But before all this, back in 1974 when Walsh brought her on as copyeditor, Marianne saw the brain power she had in Sarah Lazin, Harriet Fier, and Christine Doudna and put them to work, Christine as her assistant copy chief, Lazin and Fier to establish and run a fact-checking department. Barbara Downey, a new editorial girl who had come on the scene (and taken my place in David Felton's affections until, he says, she took up with writer Jon Landau, who went on to become Bruce Springsteen's manager), joined them in copyediting. They thrived. Sarah recalls that she got really interested in learning how to be an editor, that she started to see the work there as a long-term career rather than just a job and a groovy place to be.

They all took on more responsibility and, rising through the ranks and on the masthead, pushed to attend editorial meetings, pitched ideas, and organized office women's consciousness-raising groups. They called themselves women now. It was Marianne, in fact, who decreed that Detroit backup girl groups now be referred to as women's groups on the pages of *Rolling Stone*.

Landau recalls Sarah, Marianne, Christine, Harriet, and Barbara (he and Barbara have been married thirty-some years now) as great editors who improved his writing "by a factor of approximately fifty percent." Chris Hodenfield agrees, crediting them with turning him "from a chaotic hog-slopper into something resembling a writer."

Sisterhood had become powerful, and it stayed that way until Marianne Partridge took off, leaving the position of managing editor vacant. It was Sarah's thought when Jann talked to her about it that the women of editorial could run the department by committee, so it took her, Christine, and Barbara by surprise when Harriet Fier stepped up to take on the job. They felt burned; they felt betrayed, especially by Harriet's new access to Jann and the upper echelon.

By the end of 1978, both Christine Doudna and Paul Scanlon had left *Rolling Stone*, and Sarah Lazin had taken the reins of the newly formed Rolling Stone Press. Only Barbara Downey stayed behind to work for Harriet Fier.

When the second Big Sur editorial conference was held four years later in September of 1975, I had already decamped from Berkeley to the University of Iowa Writers' Workshop in Iowa City, but I would learn later that this time, in contrast to the first and in the spirit of the sea change that had occurred at the magazine, the entire *Rolling Stone* staff—editors and assistants alike, everybody in the art and advertising and circulation departments—were invited and they all went.

Howard Kohn, a staff writer from '75 to '78 who, with David Weir, published an exclusive on the Patty Hearst kidnapping and political seduction, a huge coup for the magazine, wrote about this Big Sur retreat in the fortieth-reunion newsletter.

[It was] one of those spas where you go about in a steamy half-naked state. [Notice he said half-naked.] And yet, when it came time for the class picture we were all Midwestern stiff. The photographer, kind of gawky, with glasses, wasn't so California cool herself, but finally she got us settled by the side of the pool. Standing on the opposite side of the pool, frustrated by the group's Midwestern stiffness and her inability to fit everyone into camera range, she simply jumped into the pool, several cameras round her neck, for a better shot. "Watch me," she

*said, and, with camera to eye, she took a giant step backwards
into the pool. The look on our faces! It was then I knew Annie
Leibovitz had a future in this biz.*

It all sounds kinda . . . *square*, doesn't it? At least in contrast to
the first one, when Hunter tore up the highway and brought on
the cops, when he later smashed up a wooden bench and dragged
it into his room to use as firewood (his logic being that if they put
a fireplace in your room, they ought to supply something to burn
in it), and when he later pulled his car up over the curb to block
the door to his motel room so as not to be disturbed while he—
and Annie, who was with him in there—did whatever they were
doing.

Also, this conference wasn't at Esalen, where, because of the
above antics and everyone's wee-hour carousing in the baths,
Rolling Stone was no longer welcome, and, PC and egalitarian
though it might very well have been, the conference was held instead up Route 1 at the less-hippiefied and considerably more
luxe and straight Ventana Inn.

I hadn't been happy when David Felton told me that I wasn't
invited to that first Big Sur editorial conference, not at all. He
agreed that it didn't seem fair. But that's as far as it went. I didn't
complain. And when he told me that I could come down the second night, when wives and girlfriends—and Laurel Gonsalves—
were invited, I didn't say no. Instead, on that second day, I got
in the car I'd bought from Annie—a little navy-blue Sunbeam
Alpine convertible—and drove, top down, to Big Sur.

Was that bad? Should I be ashamed? Should I have had more
pride than to go there on someone else's coattails, some *dude* I
was banging, for shit's sake? Well, I went anyway.

And if I hadn't gone, had taken some stand, had told Jann to fuck himself, I might have a brave story to tell now, but I also might have missed one of the most vivid, transcendent and beautiful moments of my life.

It happened when we were in the hot springs in the side of the cliffs at Esalen. I was naked in the cool night air, but I was all heated up from the mineral baths, so I could stand there looking out onto the ocean, feeling the ocean breeze on my body, the water evaporating from my skin. The full moon shone in the night sky, laying before it a stream of white light on the undulating black sea. The mescaline had brought everything into sharp focus and at the same time slowed everything waaaay down, so I could see what I now saw: moiling sea and, in the distance, backlit by the moonlight, shiny and sleek black creatures, preposterously huge, things big as Cadillacs propelling themselves out of the water up and into the air, then arcing and plunging back down headfirst into in the sea. They were whales, of course, a pod of them fluking one after the other on their migration south, and even at the time, stoned out of my gourd, I knew this was a peak experience—a heightened sense of wonder, awe, ecstasy, a defining moment of self-actualization, something my boyfriend David Leach had searched for since he'd read Maslow in the early sixties and had led me in his pursuit of tripping on psychedelics in Vermont, where we saw the pixelated rainbow of colors that compose the white of the snow, and later gamboling on a beach in Mexico, where a Frisbee sailed toward me sooooo slowly that I could merely reach out and pluck it from the air. And now here I'd found one on my own, my own peak drug experience, in a seaside cave in Big Sur surrounded by my luminous cronies at *Rolling Stone*.

Situated on California's Central Coast where the Santa Lucia Mountains rise abruptly from the Pacific, Big Sur is known as one of the most beautiful coastlines anywhere in the world. Its name derives from the original Spanish, *el país grande del sur,* meaning "the big country of the south"—south of Monterey, that is, then the capital city of Alta California, ceded to the U.S. by Mexico in 1848, a region all but unreachable until the 1930s, when the Carmel–San Simeon Highway was completed. Still protected and preserved, Big Sur remains isolated, rustic, mythic.

Henry Miller lived there; Jack Kerouac visited, and Edward Weston, Richard Brautigan, Ferlinghetti. I read recently that Hunter himself had worked right there at the hot springs in 1961 as a security guard and caretaker before he'd been kicked out for some infraction.

I loved Big Sur. I'd been there in the years before the *Rolling Stone* editorial conference and I would go after with the man who became my husband more than once and with my mother. But the very first time I saw Big Sur was in June 1969 with David Leach in the Firebird on our way up the coast to make a life in Berkeley. David and I had left Chicago the month before and taken the scenic route west. He was the driver and that was his way—back roads and detours and frequent stops. Me, I'd be on Route 80, blasting toward my uncertain future. Whenever I'm lost on the road, even now, my tendency is to drive faster.

Not David Leach. On our trip west, we detoured to Carbondale, Illinois, where he'd heard there was a beautiful swimming hole, then to St. Louis to see the arch. We stopped in the middle of nowhere so he could photograph a fence, and we stopped at the Grand Canyon to stand at the edge of what looked to me then, fearful of the future as I was, like too vast a vacancy. Then it was onto New Mexico, where we stayed for days and days, first in the dusty little town of Cerritos, not far from Santa Fe, to visit ex-junkie U of Chicago friends of David's, there to rehabilitate themselves and the town's decrepit opera house, to which they hoped to attract performers and artists. We slept in a sleeping bag on hard earth and woke at dawn to the sight of a stud horse in a corral not fifteen feet from us, his long, dry stud's penis hanging hugely to the ground.

Soon, with other of David's friends who were there—Steve Ford and Chris, who later showed up at our place in Berkeley—we drove into the Jemez Mountains, parked, and hiked in. Having led a denatured suburban life, I'd never hiked in the woods, never camped, never slept in a sleeping bag until days before. I'd never squatted and pissed and shat in the woods, had had no real idea we were animals.

When at last we emerged from the mountain and stopped at a dusty little general store, I caught a glimpse of myself in one of those ridiculously small mirrors they have on sunglass displays and was amazed and gratified to see how like a savage I looked. My beautiful city boots, made of fine leather and brass clasps, were shredded from the hike, and I threw them in the trash.

David and I drove on to Los Angeles and stopped for a night just off Mulholland Drive at the home of the parents of another of David's Chicago friends, the aspiring artist Andrea who would later come and live with us on Fox Court in Berkeley and who would be one of the reasons I got the fuck out of there.

Andrea's father was a director of TV shows—*Bonanza*, *The Rifleman*, *77 Sunset Strip*, shows I'd grown up on. I was awed. I'd never met anyone like that. As when the year before I'd looked longingly into those Eleventh Street Greenwich Village town houses on my way to work at Marvel, I had no idea how a person rose to these heights, this career, these sweeping San Fernando Valley views. I had no inkling that one day I'd have a career in TV and my own house in the hills above Sunset Strip with an even ritzier view, mine of the entire LA Basin from downtown past Century City to the Pacific.

When, over cocktails, Andrea's TV-director father asked me what my ambitions were, I shyly told him I wanted to be a writer—something I completely forgot I said until years later when I saw him at a party at his son's house in Hancock Park in LA and he reminded me of the conversation. At that same party, moments later, the horny bastard pulled me into an alcove, pressed me against the wall, put his hands all over me, and tried to stick his tongue in my mouth until I managed to twist away from him. I'd heard about the rapaciousness of Hollywood types, but this was my first—and last—actual encounter.

David had heard about Big Sur and after we said our good-byes to Andrea's parents, rather than blast up Highway 5 straight to the Bay Area, we instead found our way to the coast at Ventura, bypassing Leo Carrillo State Park on the Pacific Coast Highway south where in ten years my friend Ronnie would take her life.

But now, on a beautiful June day in 1969, we were heading north on California Route 1, passing Pismo Beach and Morro Bay, not bothering with Hearst Castle—of no interest to David Leach—finally reaching Ragged Point, where the coast road turned mountainous and hazardous. Top down, jazz in the console cassette player, the Firebird was in its element on this twisting, winding, unimaginably beautiful drive, the Pacific gleaming to the west, its waves crashing below against the rocky cliffs as we passed Lucia and entered the Big Sur region.

The road darkened as forests of redwood rose around us. David spotted a road to the right ahead and we followed it into the redwoods, parked, and then walked in among the giant trees, soon finding a place to sit so David could roll a joint. He set to his task, and, as always, I watched him as he slipped a single, delicate paper from the pack, creased it lengthwise between his long-nailed fingers, held it gingerly with one hand as he carefully shook perfectly cleaned pot out of a film canister along the crease, set the canister down, rolled the joint between index fingers and thumbs, placed it entirely into his mouth, then drew it slowly out between his plush lips to wet and seal it, and voilà! One perfect, tight, and compact Chicago joint.

He lit it, inhaled, and held the smoke in as he offered the joint to me. I never refused it. I thought I'd disappoint him if I did. I didn't want him to know how I felt, which was extremely ambivalent. I never knew if it would have a bad effect. Make me afraid or paranoid. I told David none of this. I simply took a toke and held it in as long as I thought I was supposed to and/or until I couldn't anymore.

This time, however, the anxiety that was always in my chest receded. I could feel myself slowing down, relaxing. We were, after all, in a really, really beautiful place, I now realized, quiet and still, the sun filtering through the tops of the tall redwoods down to us on the soft forest floor. I looked around me and saw that we had landed, literally, in clover, a carpet of clover bigger than East Coast clover, heartier and greener. And then I saw it, right there next to me. I blinked. I couldn't believe it. I reached out and plucked it from the ground.

"David, look," I said, holding it out to him. "A four-leaf clover! Isn't that supposed to be good luck?"

"Wow," he said. He took it and looked at it and gave it back to me with what seemed like a hurt or sad expression on his face. It made me want to apologize because I'd been the one to find it. I wonder now if, had I been a better person or if I'd known then how it would all turn out, that it might have meant so much to him to have received a good-luck sign, would I have somehow arranged for him to be the one to find it?

Soon, David tamped out the joint and put the roach in the film canister and we went back to the Firebird, where I slipped the four-leaf clover into the cellophane on the side of my pack of Old Gold Filters—I smoked one or two a day, though David said he didn't understand how I could stand that cheap tobacco. He never mentioned the four-leaf clover again and neither did I, but when we settled in Berkeley I bought a cheap little carved box imported from India, the kind inlaid with shell and lined in maroon felt, and kept it in there—until, in the course of moving several times in the following years, I lost track of it. It and a lot else, including David Leach.

❖

Chapter Eight

Sex, Drugs, and Rock and Roll

They say that if you can remember the sixties (and I suppose this applies to some of the seventies too), then you weren't really there. And to some extent this is true, because it all had a dream-like quality, fueled by raging young hormones and anxiety about the present and the future, also by marijuana and psychedelic drugs, sure, but it was mostly trippy because of the music then; we had "the winning ticket in the lottery of life," as one rock critic said of our generation.

Bruno Bettelheim had sniffed at us, calling what we called the counterculture nothing more than a prolonged adolescence, and maybe it looked like that to the stodgy old fart—our rebelliousness, our fuck-you attitude and stiff middle finger to it all. But we had plenty to be pissed off about, had lost both Kennedys, Martin Luther King Jr., Che, and Malcolm X. We were pissed off someone like "I am not a crook" Nixon was president, pissed off about the war and Nixon's lies about Cambodia and what we rightly saw as power turning an increasingly blind eye to Eisenhower's warnings of a military-industrial complex. And don't get me started on Ronald Reagan.

And then in quick succession, we lost Janis, Jimi, and Jim Morrison, bang, bang, bang, and it was hard not to feel they'd somehow martyred themselves for us, giving us everything with their music, which had somehow cost them their lives.

But it wasn't all anger and protest. In Berkeley especially, we were even then becoming ecologically conscious—recycling, composting, flushing the toilet only when we shat. Some of us traveled north to plant vineyards in Napa and Sonoma where there had been very few grapes grown for wine. Others founded organic food co-ops and set about inventing a new American cuisine. We lived communally. We shared wealth. We concocted elaborate vegetarian Indian feasts, mixing together our own curries from electric red and yellow spices, fragrant cloves, cumin seeds, cardamom pods, and cinnamon sticks—who had even known that the ground cinnamon in our mothers' spice racks came from curled bark like this, and that cloves were good for something else besides decorating a baked ham? We could feed thirteen people a vegetarian feast for ten dollars.

And we were artistically creative, bought anvils and hammers and acetylene torches and learned how to forge silver jewelry, took belly-dancing lessons in storefronts on Telegraph Avenue, transcending our culture by emulating the fluid hip movements and rib-cage shimmies of the Middle East.

We pored through the just-published *Our Bodies, Ourselves* to learn the stuff our mothers had been too uptight or ignorant to teach us. We gathered in women's groups on the carpeted floors of funky Berkeley living rooms and with hand mirrors and speculums looked up inside ourselves and beheld for the first time the inner walls of our vaginas and the fleshy, tiny-holed knobs of our cervixes and saw that it was not, after all, the dark and dirty place we had imagined but something immaculate and pretty, pink and pearly.

And all of the above—except for the communal thing and planting vineyards and founding American cuisine—was me. Stuff I did. How I lived my life in the Bay Area in those years.

My husband says that every generation has its own music, but was there ever one as great as ours? My music and its life and times provide a veritable template for the sentimental education of my age cohort, starting in the 1950s in Providence where I was a teenybopper—Ronnie and I danced the Locomotion and the Monkey and the Frug. Scarborough Beach had a jukebox on the boardwalk, and a summer teenage crowd would gather around Ronnie in her scandalous—to her father, anyway—pink wool bathing suit to watch her dance. She could dance white and she could dance Negro, as she would do professionally years later on a platform above a bar in what was known as the Combat Zone district of Boston during one of her temporary leaves from the loony bin, with a change of bikinis and switching a blond wig for an afro, seeming with her movements also to change race.

On a summer day in 1962, when I was walking with Ronnie down Blackstone Boulevard on our way to sit by the Seekonk River and smoke cigarettes, a fire-engine-red 1959 Chevy Impala convertible, top down, tail fins flaring out like manta-ray wings, pulled along beside us. David Leach was at the wheel, Peter Winslow, a boy I knew from Hebrew school at Temple Beth El, riding shotgun. The car stopped. We stopped. Did we want to go for a ride?

Yes, we did. Or I did, anyway. Ronnie didn't like private-school boys like them; she thought they were stuck up and shallow. Her boyfriend then was Al Shiffman, a cop's son (probably one of the only Jewish cops on the force at the time), tall and fair-haired and madly in love with her. I'd be at a sleepover at Ronnie's house and crouch by the living-room window watching them make out in Al's father's dowdy Chevy sedan, waiting for her to come inside so I could press her for details about what they'd done.

"He was just touching me down there," she said. "It was so sweet and then, I dunno, I turned my head and . . . " She shrugged and looked away into the mid-distance and shook her head.

I had no boyfriend, really. I went out with Tommy Mackinnon a few times, a redheaded jock in my class at Classical High, and Albert Taubman, a thin-lipped pharmacist's son who I sensed would be my destiny unless I got out of town, but nobody'd ever touched me, not with the tenderness Ronnie described. In truth, no one had touched me there at all. I could make myself come—I'd been masturbating since I was four. At least, that's my first recollection because of the trauma involved: my grandparents walked in while I was in the middle of it, lying on my back on the carpet of their upstairs flat, ostensibly watching TV with my brother who sat cross-legged, engrossed in whatever was on, and I couldn't stop, even with the embarrassment of my grandmother and grandfather standing there laughing at me. What a spectacle I must have been, my technique involving as it did a great stiffening of limbs and strenuous rubbing. A far cry from Ronnie's sweet orgasm—something that I wouldn't experience for a long time.

But now here was David Leach and I wasn't thinking about any of that. I was thinking about his great car, his wild reputation, and as if on cue, here he was lighting what I knew was a joint (though I'd never seen one), taking a quick sip of smoke, holding it in, and then, with the dreamy expression I'd see so many hundreds of times in the years to come, tilting his head back to let the smoke escape from his lips. Peter passed the joint to David after he'd had a toke and then David shifted in his seat and, with the joint discreetly cupped in his palm, held it out to us.

Ronnie shook her head—she could go so unexpectedly prudish—but I saw it as a challenge and I saw my future in it if I accepted. I knew who David was by reputation. His friends referred to him as Party Chairman on those occasions when some of us were at Peter Winslow's house late at night after someone's party or after the movies making sautéed mushroom sandwiches. The guys would all be watching the door, hoping the Chairman would show up.

Which I saw him do once just after I'd left Peter's to walk the three blocks so I could be home by midnight curfew. David didn't have a curfew. He didn't have much supervision. He was the product of a second marriage, born to a father in his fifties and the pretty young Portuguese girl who'd waited on him in a department store downtown and had converted to Judaism so he'd marry her. They lived in what seemed to me a kind of exile in Lincoln, a far suburb of Providence where no Jews anybody seemed to know lived.

I'd seen David Leach before when I was a little girl at the Conservative Jewish synagogue we belonged to for a minute before we joined the swanker Reform one near our new house. Half Portuguese, half Russian Jew, with his curly hair, smiley crescent eyes, and plush lips, he didn't look like anybody else, not then and not that night as he got out of the flashy red car and, with another boy and a six-pack of beer, headed up the walk to Peter's house.

I knew somehow that David Leach was my ticket into the big world and I made it my business to go after him, somehow knowing too that I could have him if I did. I did the unthinkable for a girl in those days—I called him. His mother answered. She asked who I was, then yelled to David somewhere in the house that I was on the phone. He answered, "Hello?" I said hi. Then, after a short moment, he said, "Ma, hang up the phone." There came a soft click on the line to tell us she had done as he'd asked.

David was cool. His Moses Brown prep-school friends were cool. Through him, they opened musical worlds to me. Joel Zoss, barefoot boy with guitar, played Leadbelly and Big Bill Broonzy in the local coffeehouse when we were kids, going on in life to open shows for B. B. King and Etta James and to perform and record with Taj Mahal, James Taylor, and Howlin' Wolf. Rick Turner also played blues, then went on to build guitars for Jackson Browne, David Crosby, Lindsey Buckingham, and Ry Cooder, to name a few, and to help engineer the Grateful Dead's "Wall of Sound." (Vinnie Decesares would have turned out to be cool too, if he hadn't wrapped his Morgan around a tree and perished at seventeen. But everybody has a classmate like that, right?)

A few weeks after my decidedly unladylike phone call, David took me to the Newport Jazz Festival, where we sat in the very first row, and the music continued in our time together in Chicago, where he took me to jazz clubs and we sat feet away from Charlies Mingus and Parker and, at home in David's South Side Hyde Park apartment, played Miles Davis and John Coltrane, Herbie Hancock and Keith Jarrett vinyls on his top-of-the-line stereo. And, of course, rock—Cream, Traffic, Otis Redding...

In Berkeley, at our apartment in Fox Court, we dropped mescaline, got into the Firebird, and headed to San Rafael to see the Grateful Dead at the Euphoria Ballroom. We never got there. The mescaline came on as we were crossing the San Rafael Bridge and we realized we were getting *way* too far into euphoria already and headed home.

We saw Jim Hendrix and Janis Joplin with Big Brother and the Holding Company at the Fillmore East in the winter of '69 and that December saw the Rolling Stones at the Oakland Coliseum, where ten thousand people seemed then like a scary-big crowd. Even Bill Graham looked frightened as he patrolled the aisles, trying to keep us from rushing the stage. Or had I OD'd on pot brownies and imagined this?

We lived in Berkeley and missed Woodstock but we did make it four months later in December '70 to Altamont, where, though we were unaware of the hit-and-run death, the LSD-induced drowning in an irrigation canal, the stolen cars, and the actual Hells Angels' knifing and stomping murder of a man stage-side, we were more than aware of the prevailing bad vibes. They had begun even as we drove to the venue in heavy free-concert-going freeway traffic through the scorched, radioactive Livermore hills, parked in a broiling sea of cars, and tramped with the others through the hazy heat to the concert site, where we spread our blanket on what space remained on trampled brown grass high on a hillside, vying for room with decidedly un-peace-and-love hippies pushing and shoving and stepping on said blanket to claim their own patch of dirt with a view of the stage far below.

In David Leach fashion, we were late, had missed Santana, the Flying Burrito Brothers, the Jefferson Airplane, but Crosby, Stills, Nash, and Young were playing, filling the late-afternoon air with their music, or they would have been if they hadn't been drowned out by the war-zone sound of arriving helicopters bearing the Rolling Stones. It was announced that the Grateful Dead would not be going on—we'd learn later they were concerned about security for the vulnerably low stage—and the crowd, already restless and bellicose, grew even more so waiting for the Stones, who, we'd also learn later, were, with questionable logic, themselves waiting for dusk with the thought that darkness would calm everyone down.

But then a wave of sound as three hundred thousand people cheered and whooped when they saw Mick and Keith and Charlie Watts and Mick Taylor and Bill Wyman—the Stones at their height—finally come onstage. They took up their instruments, and a bare-chested, caped Jagger strutted and shouted, "All roit! All roit!" into the mic. They launched into "Jumpin' Jack Flash," and it sounded great, even over what David said was a shitty sound system, though from where we sat Jagger himself appeared so minuscule that, stoned as I now was on purported Acapulco Gold, I decided to go down to the stage for a closer look. Others had the same idea but I did get close—close enough to a stark-naked fat man flailing around in the middle of the crowd in a crazy dance, close enough to see Hells Angels beating back a man who was trying to mount the stage, close enough to see that Mick Jagger was, in fact, actually minuscule—and, as the band launched into "Carol," I made my way back up to our dusty blanket. A few songs later, somewhere in the middle of the evil strains of "Sympathy for the Devil"—not exactly a song designed to bring calm—when the commotion around the stage caused the band to stop playing again and again, Mick begging everyone to be cool ("Be cool, people!") before they took it from the top, David decided it would be good to beat the traffic, so we gathered our things and got out of there.

When I heard about the Hells Angels murder, I imagined the victim was the fat man, but it was, in fact, some meth-head with a gun.

In Providence when we first got together, David was an elusive boyfriend. If he would not accept discipline from his parents, he certainly didn't want to hear anything like it from me. Anyway, I considered my father so denatured by my mother that David's intransigence seemed manly. And, conversely, since my father had been a man about town, a regular boulevardier before he met my mother and she domesticated him, maybe deep down I thought that's what I should try with David Leach.

In any case, yearning for someone was a new sensation. It felt like what I thought love must feel like, the thrilling if painful unpredictability of him and the helpless feeling when I couldn't stand waiting another minute for him to phone or appear in front of my house, the sweet sensation of giving in to an urge I shouldn't, borrowing the family car to buzz his hangouts, cruising in and around places I thought he might be just to know where he was, just to get a glimpse of his red Impala.

He moved according to his own rhythms, would not be hurried. Me, I could be ready to go and out the door in minutes, but David could take hours just to get out of his own house for the day, even when he wasn't stoned. He wanted to be sure that he'd have everything he'd need—who knows when he'd make it back home? It was basically the same stuff he'd always need—sunglasses, contact case, cleanser and eye drops, a spare set of the contacts themselves, pot, rolling paper, a tin of Balkan Sobranie cigarettes and lighter. The pipe and camera paraphernalia would come while he was away in college and would slow things down even more.

Sidebar: I once watched him give my mother an empty Balkan Sobranie tin after he'd smoked all the cigarettes, telling her maybe she'd want to keep bobby pins in it or something. When he was out of earshot, my mother leaned in and mouthed, *Watch out for him, he's cheap.*

He didn't seem cheap. I felt like we lived large, driving around with the top down, me sitting hard by his side on the bench seat cars had then, the Party Chairman's moll. Feeling like a moll wasn't entirely fantasy. One of David's close friends was Raymond Patriarca Jr., whose father, known as Big George—in the same way, I suppose, that the U.S. president is called POTUS— was boss of the entire New England Mafia.

Double-dating with Ray Jr. and his girlfriend (one of his girlfriends, anyway) Rosemary, we were treated like royalty at Middle Street Café, a pricey, clubby, hidden little downtown steak joint patronized by my parents and their friends, served cocktails though we were clearly underage. It was a scene out of *Goodfellas*, though that movie wouldn't come out until 1990 and this was 1962, a full ten years before the first of *The Godfather* movies, eight before Mario Puzo's book on which the films were based.

It was all so romantic, so picaresque. Ray Jr. had an XKE, a Vincent Black Shadow motorcycle, the first Volkswagen bus anyone had ever seen. He went to Provincetown; he went to Miami Beach and came back with an illegal pet ocelot for Rosemary. And he had bodyguards—Zeke and Hillary, contemporaries of his who'd been to "college," aka prison, and had been assigned by Big George to keep an eye on his son. The coffee table in Rosemary's basement studio apartment had in fact been made by Zeke and Hillary in the prison wood shop.

Picaresque but also faintly dangerous, as when David and I drove Raymond up to Boston to deliver a message from his dad to someone in a nightclub in the Combat Zone. We pulled up and immediately a limo with tinted windows materialized behind us. Ray got out and got into it and the limo drove off. We waited. A big mook came out of the nightclub and stood there watching us. But soon, here was the limo again behind us. To our relief, Ray got out, nodded to the mook, got into David's car, and we went home.

Not that Ray was then all that involved in the family business, though he would take over as boss after his father died in 1984 (peacefully and at home after a stretch in the pen for conspiracy to commit murder) until his own incarceration in 1992 for racketeering. But for now, he was only a bright young man in Brooks Brothers button-down shirts on his way to URI, the University of Rhode Island in Kingston, to study prelaw, just like Michael Corleone, except there was no Michael Corleone yet.

The Patriarcas lived in a modest house in an unassuming neighborhood off Hope Street not far from where we'd lived downstairs from my grandparents. Ray's mother, a sharp-mouthed little woman, made Ray Sr. smoke his cigars outside in the backyard. You'd see him there, even in the rain, under an umbrella. Standing at the kitchen table wrapping Christmas presents for Ray Sr.'s crew, his wife cursed the task, cursed Christmas. And when, in that same kitchen, David's Russian-immigrant father, Jonah, asked in all innocence, "So, what does your husband do?" Mrs. Patriarca looked incredulously at David and said, "What is he, kidding?" (Which with a Providence accent is pronounced "kitten.")

All of the above about Raymond and more, like the times I'd stay at Rosemary's apartment my first year at Pembroke and see her relationship with him more intimately—served as fodder for a racy and poignant short story about the two of them and also about Zeke and Hillary, Junior's bodyguards, the story that put me on the map at Brown and, years and years later, informed my work as a writer and producer of *The Sopranos*.

It was during my first year on *The Sopranos* when we were in Down Neck filming an episode my husband and I had written, a flashback to Tony Soprano's childhood in that Newark neighborhood, that I began to think about my Russian grandfather who had begun his American journey in Down Neck and remember snippets of stories I'd heard about him, that he'd worked in a butcher shop there, that he'd been married, that maybe he'd shot someone—his wife? And that he'd had to come up to Providence to start his life again, and here the stories I'd heard became concrete: How my mother's family had lived for a time in the coastal town of Wickford, Rhode Island, where under cover of night he and his crew would unload barrels of illegal booze off boats from Canada, how at home they'd all siphon the liquor into bottles with Gordon's Gin labels they'd glued on, how they'd moved thirteen times in my mother's childhood, and the story of how on his delivery rounds in Providence her father would use her as a beard so he'd seem like a man out for an innocent Sunday ride with his little girl—a scenario we used in *The Sopranos*—and how my mother waited in the car for him, sweat pouring off her, knowing she and her father were doing something wrong and frightened to her core they'd be caught and put in jail. I began to realize that Grandpa had been a gangster—not on the level of Raymond Junior and his father, certainly, but a tough-Jew-with-a-gun-to-defend-his-turf rumrunner during Prohibition. A photograph I had of him now made sense—the double-breasted suit, the cigarette dangling from his lips, the thuggish gaze—and with that realization came a deeper understanding of my mother's disdain of him.

I graduated from high school in January 1963—January classes being a temporary measure to accommodate the enormous postwar influx of Baby Boomers—and, to save money for college in the fall, I spent six months working at the greeting-card factory my father now repped for, punching in at eight, half-hour lunch and two ten-minute coffee breaks, punching out at five. The hands on the clock seemed barely to move. Time slowed to a crawl. To make it go faster I filled orders at demon speed, so fast that the owner, who was our next-door neighbor on Wayland Avenue, came onto the floor to cite me as an example of how fast the work could be done. It was then I realized, in no small part because of the way my co-workers looked at me and rolled their eyes at each other, what an asshole I was, because I knew then what they already knew, that there would always be orders, incessant and endless, so what was the rush?

I was miserable at work and bored and lonely at home. My brother had gone to college and left a void in the house, and David Leach was also away at college. I took to my room, drawing self-portraits of my miserable self, until one day I stopped sketching for some reason and wrote my first short story right there on the drawing paper on the drawing board about a man with no legs escaping to Florida.

I'd all but lost track of Ronnie. I was now at the college-prep public school and she was at Hope High, a peg or two down the academic ladder. I heard that she had broken up with Al, that she hated school. I heard that she was drinking a lot and driving her mother's Nash Rambler station wagon with her left leg hanging out the window. And that at someone's house down the beach she dived drunk into a swimming pool that was only half full and broke her nose.

Things had already begun to go bad for her. The year before, we had started hanging out with boys at Rhode Island School of Design. I learned to drive that year, the year my father had come home with a white, two-door 1960 Cadillac (last year's model, a real steal), a Jew-boat, as we young people so adorably called it. My mother, embarrassed by the nouveau riche Jewiness of the car, with its bulbous body and sleek, sharp fins, said he should get a license plate that said IRA and pull the thing around on a string.

I loved the car, partly to spite my mother, but mostly because

I felt so competent handling something so big so deftly. I loved to act the ironic limo driver, ferrying the RISD boys around in the backseat. I knew Ronnie loved one of the boys, but I didn't know exactly what happened between them, learned only later that when he refused to return her physical affection, confessing to her he might be gay, she slit her wrists in the upstairs bathroom of her house, wrote his name all over the walls in blood, and left a trail of it for her parents to follow, out of the house, down Taber Avenue, and up Doyle, planning to find the boy and die in his arms. It was her first trip to a mental institution, this time to the newly opened psycho ward at Butler Hospital on Blackstone Boulevard next to Swan Point Cemetery, where we used to sneak cigarettes and where her ashes now sit.

Over that year and those to come, I didn't see Ronnie much. I visited her at a basement apartment in Boston when she was briefly at Emerson, a performing arts college. I visited her at McLean, the psych hospital outside of that city made famous by James Taylor's and his brother's times there and fictionalized in the 1999 movie *Girl, Interrupted*, with Winona Ryder and Angelina Jolie. It was a breakthrough role for Jolie, who stole the show—and the Oscar. And though Ronnie was, like Ryder's character, a girl from a privileged family at odds with her parents and their mores, sad enough for a half-assed wrist-slash-suicide attempt, she resembled Jolie more—wild and soulful and ballsy and bursting with anger and life force and, as we'd all later understand and before her illness had the name bipolar and better meds to treat it, in horrible mental pain.

It was grim when I went to see her in her locked ward. She was on the edge of tears. She didn't want to meet my eyes. She seemed ashamed of herself. All she would say, over and over, was that she felt dead and empty. I didn't know what to do or say. When I left that day, I felt that I had failed her. At the same time, I couldn't wait to get out of there.

I never visited her at McLean again, not that time or the second time she was locked up there. I heard that when her parents no longer wanted to pay or could no longer afford its hefty price tag, Ronnie was transferred to what she later referred to as Mass Mental—the psych wards of Massachusetts General Hospital located in Boston on, true fact, Fruit Street.

I didn't see her again until 1973, when she was out of Mass Mental and living with Richie, a boy she'd met there. I spent a few days with them at the third-floor flat they shared in Eastie, or East Boston, in its pregentrification days, an area at the edge of Boston Harbor and in the shadow of planes landing at Logan, connected to Boston proper by, fittingly for Ronnie, the MTA Blue Line. I'd see Ronnie only twice again—at Canochet Beach with Richie in 1977, and then again in Los Angeles in 1979, two weeks before she shot and killed herself.

At that time, the third-to-last time, I was east researching the story about the Kennedy children, the one that would pretty much end my time at *Rolling Stone*. But that would be later. Now it was 1972; George McGovern was running for president and I'd write a few things about that for the magazine plus my next two cover stories, and I was still the girl in the photo on the beach with the shit-eating grin—unlike Ronnie even then, juicy and healthy and productive and riding high.

❖

Chapter Nine

Poison Pen

"Drive over to the Hippopotamus," Henry instructed, the Hippopotamus being then a slick Upper East Side nightclub in New York City and Henry being Henry Diltz, celebrity photographer, telling the driver of our Lincoln limo where to carry David Cassidy, the girl with him, his friend/valet, plus Henry and me late one night in the spring of 1972. The quote was the lede of my cover story on Cassidy, in town to perform a sold-out show at Madison Square Garden the next night. But when we got to the Hippopotamus, the guy at the door wouldn't let us in, in fact had absolutely no idea who David Cassidy was, which was pretty much the point of the ten-thousand-word cover story that would follow.

Cassidy's PR man had approached *Rolling Stone* about doing a story. David was getting old for *The Partridge Family*, a TV sitcom in which he played—and then became—a teen idol. *The Partridge Family* was getting old period, and David now wanted to be considered an adult talent. Since the media had created the teen heartthrob he was in the first place, it seemed logical, I supposed, to call on the media to transmogrify his image. And what groovier vehicle than a cover of *Rolling Stone?* So we gave it to him.

And I was the one assigned to do it.

If the PR man or Cassidy himself had taken the time to read anything I'd written in *Rolling Stone,* we could all have been spared a whole lot of trouble. The *Esquire* editor hadn't called me the new bitch for nothing. I can see now that I was, in much of my writing, at least, on a one-woman crusade to out the pretentious, the phony, the self-deluded, the boorish, the cruel.

David Cassidy wasn't any of those. He was merely lame. He wore his heart on his sleeve. He and the industries from which he sprang were such easy targets. I wrote the shit out of the thing, not just about him in his little androgynous white jumpsuit, but about the teen-magazine, poster, and lunch-box businesses that profited from him.

Still and once again, other writers were traveling with the Stones, the Dead, Dylan, and here I was for five days in New York City and then Bangor, Maine, with this kid and his stepmom, Shirley Jones, who always seemed to be somewhere around.

After the article was published in the May issue, there was fallout for Cassidy. The PR guy got fired; endorsements dried up; Cassidy himself retreated to Hawaii for a while. But what I wrote wasn't even half of it. It was Annie's naked photos, both on the cover and in the center spread, that finished the job.

"It pissed off everybody that was really profiting from the business of David Cassidy," Cassidy later said. "I had fan letters that came to me—and there were hundreds of thousands of them, literally—in defense of me by fans of mine that said, 'Oh David.

I know that you couldn't possibly have done this because I know that you would never have posed nude for photographs.' And the fact was I had, had willingly done so, had thought about it. I scratched my head and thought, You know, this David Cassidy business has really gotten outta hand."

He'd told this to an interviewer in 1992 on the occasion of the publication of a book of iconic *Rolling Stone* covers. But I was there that day in 1972 at his house by the pool when the photographs were taken, and I had seen Annie coax him into it—he wanted to be hip, didn't he?

Well, sorry, I guess. I can't speak for Annie, but in those days, I didn't think much about the damage anything I wrote might do, how it might hurt feelings, careers. It comes back to what Joan Didion wrote about our brand of journalism in the preface to *Slouching Towards Bethlehem*: "People tend to forget that my presence runs counter to their best interests. And it always does."

In November, I'd have another story on the cover, "Joe Conforte, Crusading Pimp," about the owner of a legal brothel outside Reno, Nevada, an article that resulted in a grand jury investigation and then a prison sentence for Conforte for tax evasion: in the wee hours of the morning, I'd watched him oversee the burning of the night's receipts in a backyard and make a joke of it.

I'd spent a day and night in the brothel (a collection of interconnected trailers in a compound surrounded by chain-link fencing topped with razor wire), hung out with the prostitutes in a snack room overflowing with sugary treats, stood by in the dank double-wide-trailer parlor to observe them as they lined up in their bikinis so the customer could choose the one he wanted to follow back to her little cubicle in the trailer.

Annie flew in to photograph the scene, and the two of us spent a few nights behind the walls of Conforte's garish home in Sparks and joined him on his rounds—to a party at the governor's mansion in Carson, to the county seat to see about a vanity plate for his new custom car, to a nightclub he owned a piece of. He relished showing up with an entourage, trotting us out, but it wore on me, all this putting my own self aside to enter somebody else's life, with Conforte at the whorehouse and even before that, with David Cassidy, with Victor Baranco, with Dennis Hopper.

It wore on Annie, too, when she went on tour with the Stones, and instead of maintaining her distance, she began to think she was a Stone, taking up their lifestyle and habits, including the cocaine addiction that almost did her in.

For last year's Victor Baranco and Morehouse story, I'd gone undercover, pretending to be just another lost soul enticed by a cult that, in this case, was kind of the low-rent, Oakland version of the Mel Lyman celebrity-filled and decidedly more ominous pre–Jim Jones Boston cult covered by David Felton's story in *Mindfuckers*. Baranco had devised a scheme whereby he bought decrepit houses and then recruited runaways and refugees from the Haight to fix them up so he could sell them at a hefty profit; at the same time, these recruits were paying him two hundred dollars a month each for room and board and the companionship of others at loose ends, a setup so lucrative Baranco had begun to franchise it, and he was soon known around the Bay Area as the Colonel Sanders of the commune scene.

In addition, his Morehouse Institute of Human Abilities offered pricey if low-watt classes in the bullshit philosophies he'd developed, like Basic Sensuality, a course on pleasuring another person; it involved practice sessions with plaster-cast replicas of penises and vaginas. "Doing" the other person was "a sure-fire way to a perfect orgasm every time."

I didn't live in a Morehouse; I was a day student. Even so, it was hard not to feel kinship with the other young people around me, harder and harder to hold myself apart as an observer. Also, it was hard not to be brainwashed. More than once, David Felton would pick me up after a day of classes and take me to my treetop room and to bed and talk me back to myself.

It was difficult in this way at the whorehouse too. I felt such sympathy for the women, even as they played me, fabricating obvious lies about themselves. But I felt like a liar too, sure that as professionals in the field, they could see through me, could tell that I was an inauthentic human being, a sexual fake who didn't know who or what I was or what sex was.

I'd made some progress since my days and nights of fakery with David Leach, beginning with the night I found myself in the loft bed at Fox Court with Andrea while David was off driving a taxi—the one job I'd known him to have. It didn't last long, what with the peanuts he felt he made for the hours put in and the fact that the Zodiac killer was on the loose and was thought to have murdered a cabdriver.

Sex with Andrea was wonderful—to touch her breasts and feel what a man must feel when he touches yours, her clitoris too, and mine when she touched it, wonderful to know that you were giving as much pleasure as you were feeling (see Morehouse sex class, above). That was as far as we went that night in the loft bed, but at least it was something to go on. And I had gone on to love sex with David Felton in much the same way.

But fucking remained a mystery. Clitorises were becoming all the rage; vaginal orgasms were declared a myth, and clitoral orgasms "the feminist orgasm." Still, here was Germaine Greer in her 1970 *The Female Eunuch* saying otherwise. Masters and Johnson, she said, and their Reproductive Biology Research

Foundation promulgated dull sex for dull people. Real gratification, she said, was enshrined not in a tiny cluster of nerves but in the sexual involvement of the whole person.

"If women are to avoid this last reduction of their humanity, they must hold out not just for orgasm," she wrote, "but for ecstasy."

This sounded exactly right to me. Still, how exactly is a girl supposed to go about finding it?

Ms. Greer had also cautioned against the Jackie Collins model of sex. "Women who understand their sexual experience in the way that Jackie Collins writes of it," she said, "are irretrievably lost to themselves and their lovers."

"He took her to the bedroom and undressed her slowly," Collins wrote, "he made love to her beautifully. Nothing frantic, nothing rushed...took her to the edge of ecstasy and back again...She floated on a suspended plane, a complete captive to his hands and body...He had amazing control."

In college in 1965, though I had been among the first in line at the infirmary for birth control pills, I was very conscious of wanting to keep the number of guys I slept with to a minimum: David Leach, Bumpy (my Greek-American townie boyfriend when David was away at college whom I dropped like a hot potato whenever David came home), and a black-leather-jacket-wearing hipster at Brown named Teddy something, one of the first dope smokers on campus, who became interested in me only after I became known as the Girl Writer.

After that, in Boston's Back Bay after Bumpy and I broke up, a one-night stand with the Brit in the next apartment, a traveling wallet salesman with white nylon wash-and-wear dress shirts dripping dry in the bathroom; another one-night stand in New York with a junior editor I met at the deli where I got my Linzer torte cookie; my friend's sister's husband in Berkeley. Then, in the year after I left Fox Court, a sexual tear that included just about every male that crossed my path—Felton; L. M. Kit Carson; Kit's brother in Texas; my Tamalpais Road roommate's famous anthropologist father; the photographer Danny Lyon, who was crashing at the Tamalpais house for a night; Jann Wenner.

Jann, I went to bed with when I was in New York for the David Cassidy story. I was staying at the Plaza and he called from his room at the Sherry-Netherland across the street to ask how the tour was going. There was a pause on the line and then he said, "You want to come over?"

I went. It was weird and weirdly uncomfortable in that posh room, a weirdness explained when he came out as a gay man years later—for once the lack of passion and engagement hadn't been entirely mine. He took a phone call, I did some yoga on the carpet, we dropped quaaludes and went to bed. He managed the act: missionary position, striving for orgasm (his), followed by a drugged sleep. Sometime before dawn, I got out of bed and went back to the world's smallest hotel room across the street. No mention of the incident was ever made by either of us again.

In going to bed with these men, I was looking for something, but I didn't know exactly what. Whatever it was, I didn't find it with Kit. Kit's cowboy brother, however, proved to be no ex-Jesuit.

I was on my way back from New York and David Cassidy when I decided to make a stop in Dallas to see Kit. After New Mexico, Kit and I had had a relationship of sorts. We'd gone to bed in my treehouse room; we'd gone on a trip north in his Morgan sports car to visit Kit's director on *David Holzman's Diary*. When I called from the Dallas airport, Kit's mother said he wasn't home—he'd gone to Austin for some kind of film festival—but I should come on over, he'd be back that night.

When I got to the motel-like apartment complex in Irving where they lived, everyone was busy with his or her Sunday morning. Kit's father was out tending cattle he kept on some land outside of town, a kind of hobby, Kit's mother explained. She was making sandwiches that Kit's brother would bring out to him after he dropped his own wife and kids at church. Maybe I'd want to take a ride out there with him, keep him company and see some of Texas.

Kit's brother and I sped down the highway at Texas speeds in his family station wagon. It was hot and I had the window down. Kit's brother looked over at me in my leather sandals and jeans and little white peasant blouse.

"C'mere," he said. "Sit closer."

I did. Dark and wiry and rangy, he looked nothing like the ethereal Kit. He gave me a sideways glance and smiled, almost to himself. He reached down and unzipped his fly and took out his already-erect penis. He put his hand behind my head and held it there, with a nod indicating what he wanted me to do. Which I did, bending over and blowing him, and it happened fast—he came in my mouth going ninety miles an hour. I was so surprised I sat up and swallowed.

We got to the land where Kit's father kept cattle and there he was among them on horseback. He waved and Kit's brother got out and climbed a fence and gave him his sack lunch, then pointed me out to his father, who smiled and gave me a wave. Kit's brother got back in the car and asked if I knew how to ride a horse.

Soon we were in some woods on horseback. It was hot and I was sweating. Kit's brother said I'd be a lot cooler if I took my blouse off, so I rode bare-chested and, as I went in those days, braless.

"Let's take a break," he said, so we stopped and tied the horses and had some water. Then he unbuttoned my jeans and pulled them and my underpants down. He pressed me against a tree, had his hands all over me. But I didn't respond. I was frozen—not frightened, just at a loss. He stopped and look at me and in that instant knew something about me that I didn't know myself, for he grabbed me by the wrist and started to pull me somewhere.

"Wha'? What are you doing?" I said, tripping along after him. He didn't answer, just continued pulling me by the wrist, and because my pants were down around my ankles, I could take only these tiny, mincing stops. It was embarrassing and humiliating. And then it occurred to me.

"Hey!" I called to him, "Is this bondage? Is that what this is?"

He just yanked me harder along with my frantic tiny little steps until the embarrassment and humiliation changed into something else—something like anger—and I rose up against him to...what? Fight him, I guess, and I have to guess because now I wasn't at all in my head anymore, and he was inside me and we were madly fucking in what felt like midair, all of which I realized only when we were done and I had landed panting and breathless on the ground. I had come.

Well, my, my. So that was arousal. And fucking. And coming while fucking.

It is only now that I look back that I can see some humor in the situation. Me mincing along with my jeans around my ankles. With a student's brightness and eagerness asking, hey, was this bondage?

We drove wordlessly back to the apartment complex and he dropped me off. Kit was home. We had dinner with his parents and Kit and I went to bed in his room. We had sex and I faked it like I always did and Kit didn't seem to notice or mind. I said nothing to Kit about what had happened with his brother, and I didn't say anything about it to anyone else for a very long time.

Besides the longer pieces and cover stories, I was assigned other stuff. Again under the byline White House Staff, I compiled from various newspaper items an account of Nixon's visit to China, the first by any U.S. president, accurately if sarcastically quoting him as saying of the Great Wall that it "looked like a postcard" and was, indeed, "a great wall." (Ironically, and weirdly, Nixon's trip to China and what might have been his attraction to the place would prove to be one of the reasons I fell in love with my husband. But that would occur years from then.)

I was also, under my own byline, sent out to cover local Democratic caucuses proposing delegates to the party's Miami convention in April, which I dutifully reported, though I have absolutely no memory of having been there, not even when years later I came across the article I wrote about it. My heart just hadn't been in it. I was no political reporter, and I would prove this on my next assignment in May, when Jann sent me to cover a fund-raising concert at the San Francisco Civic Auditorium for candidate George McGovern.

This story I did remember doing. Jann was there because stars were there volunteering to perform and usher on McGovern's behalf. Judy Collins, Merry Clayton, Chicago, and Mama Cass were set to sing, and Goldie Hawn, Jon Voight, and Michelle Phillips were among the ushers greeting concertgoers in the foyer. And—

"Look, there's Jack Nicholson," Jann said. And there he was, lounging against a wall outside a door to the auditorium.

"Oh, yeah," I said. "Wow." I'd seen *Easy Rider* and *Five Easy Pieces* and now there was Jack Nicholson, in person, mere steps away. I stood there gaping.

"Well, be a reporter, go talk to him," Jann said with his usual impatience. "Go on. Ask him why he came out for McGovern."

I steeled myself and walked over. "Hi," I said. "I'm reporter from *Rolling Stone* and I was wondering if you could say what brought you here tonight on behalf of George McGovern?"

Jack Nicholson gave me a level Jack Nicholson look. Then he said in his flat Nicholson voice, "Gimme a break, okay?"

What could I possibly say after that? I was wondering what in the fuck I should do next when all of a sudden Warren Beatty, who'd been talking to Jann, made a beeline from Jann to me.

"Hey," he said, "I wanna talk to you, come on."

He took my hand and pulled me along into the auditorium, down the left aisle, and to the stage. Everyone seated could see me, Robin Green from Providence, Rhode Island, being led backstage by none other than Warren Beatty himself from *Bonnie and Clyde* and *McCabe and Mrs. Miller*, arguably one of the foxiest guys on the planet.

We went up some stairs and behind the curtain, and while a band was setting up, he sat me down on a backstage sawhorse and sat himself down inches away facing me and proceeded to talk to me, or at me, rapid-fire and practically spitting in my face, about McGovern, about why he had come out in support and why he had convinced these stars and more like them to do the same, here and at six venues around the country, that it wasn't just about money from the concerts, it was about signing up young people to go out and knock on doors, and how important it was, how absolutely imperative, that Nixon be defeated.

Meanwhile, a backstage door to the outside opened, and Julie

Christie, his then girlfriend, appeared and hung there, a limousine behind her in the fading California light, calling in a plaintive English accent, "War-ren, c'mon, the driver's here."

Warren Beatty held up his hand to signal he'd be a minute and continued his harangue against Nixon.

"C'mon, War-ren," Julie Christie said, "we're going for Chinese food."

Whereupon Warren Beatty told me that he lived at the Wilshire Hotel in Beverly Hills and if I were ever in LA I should give him a call and come over and we'd finish the conversation.

Warren Beatty left. I sat there for a moment watching as he joined Julie Christie and they slipped away. What does it say about me that I much preferred Jack Nicholson?

I never ran into Jack Nicholson again, and I didn't feel anything like his vibe until September 1976, in my second year pursuing an MFA at the University of Iowa Writers' Workshop and my first year as a teaching/writing fellow for which I'd been tasked to instruct undergrads at the university in the art of writing fiction.

I'd asked my students to come to my office individually so I could learn a little about them, and this one kid came in. He wasn't a kid, really, he was older than the other students and rougher-looking, had been late to class that first day, had come in sweating and out of breath and taken a seat behind me, and I could sense him breathing there and I was nervous enough teaching my first class of anything ever without some sweaty grown man breathing down my neck—and now here he was in my office for a student/teacher conference.

"Hi, c'mon in, have a seat!" I said in my briskest teacher-y voice. He sat down in the chair beside my desk, lounging more than sitting, like he was home in an easy chair watching baseball. I learned that he was from Cedar Rapids, about twenty miles north, and was attending the university on the GI Bill, having been newly discharged from the U.S. Army. It had been the tail end of the Vietnam War and he hadn't seen battle; he'd been stateside for two years, guarding a safe in a small, locked room in a motor-pool office in Texas.

"Still," I said brightly, "the army! You should have plenty of interesting things to write about!"

He regarded me levelly, as Jack Nicholson had, like he didn't know who to feel sorrier for, me or him. "Lady," he said, "nothing interesting happens to you in the army."

I was pretty much done for right then. His name was Mitch. He'd been living in his car. Before the army he'd worked in a Wilson meatpacking plant in Cedar Rapids and also for Quaker Oats, loading fifty-pound sacks of oats into freight cars. I didn't know it then, but this was the man I would one day marry.

❖

Chapter Ten

A Big Journalistic No-No

The year 1972 was drawing to a close. The Dow Jones average was 1,020. The average cost of a new house was $27,550. A gallon of gas, fifty-five cents. In September, eleven Israeli athletes were murdered by Arab terrorists at the Munich Olympics, and in November and despite Warren Beatty's efforts, Richard Nixon defeated George McGovern in one of the biggest landslides in U.S. history.

Then 1973 dawned, a year in which the Dow and gas prices would fall, housing costs would rise, Israel would defeat the Arabs in the Yom Kippur War, and Watergate would send Richard Nixon away in disgrace.

My year also proved to be a mixed bag. It was a year in which, with four cover stories and a bunch of other work in *Rolling Stone* to my credit, I'd be sent off on a prize assignment, one that had real potential for national notice. A year in which I'd pack my few belongings, leave Tamalpais Road for good, and run away with David Felton. A year in which I'd travel the country and the world. Sleep with who knows how many more men.

It was also a year in which I'd blow the prime assignment, lose my place on the masthead, blow an assignment for another magazine, break my leg in a bicycle mishap in Providence, and, trapped upstairs in my parents' house with a plaster cast from groin to foot, discover that I had the crabs, an affliction that would have led my mother, were she to find out about it, to burn the sheets, my bed, and possibly the entire house—with me in it.

But that would be the next July and now it was fall of '72 and Jann was asking me to write an in-depth article on the children of Robert F. Kennedy. There had been ten zillion stories about John-John and Caroline after Jack Kennedy was killed—the public couldn't get enough of it. But who knew anything at all about these kids of Bobby's? There were eleven of them then (one of them later died of a drug overdose). The youngest had been in Ethel's womb when Bobby was murdered.

More than four years had passed since RFK had been shot three times in the head at the Ambassador Hotel. Who were his kids? Had they seen the TV footage? How were they doing? How were they coping? There'd been talk—the older boys had been in and out of trouble, one kicked out of school for fighting, the other arrested for pot possession, and the younger kids were said to be allowed to run wild in the neighborhood, both at Hyannis Port on Cape Cod and Hickory Hill outside DC.

The kids were all back east, Kathleen and Bobby Junior in college, but Jann could arrange for me to meet Joe, the oldest boy—the one who'd been kicked out of several prep schools for his temper and who, after a year at UC Berkeley, had recently dropped out but had remained in the Bay Area. (It wouldn't be until after he'd gone back east the following summer that a

Jeep he was driving overturned, fracturing one of his brother David's vertebrae and permanently paralyzing David's girlfriend, for which he was charged with reckless driving and had his license suspended.)

For now, however, he was just a big, affable twenty-year-old with a mouthful of big white teeth, kind of goofy and vague and lost. We'd agreed to take a long walk through San Francisco, and we met in North Beach on a sunny afternoon. I had thought I'd probably be intimidated and nervous no matter what kind of Kennedy he turned out to be because he was a Kennedy, after all, and the Kennedys loomed large in my psyche, in every American's. I'd seen Jack Kennedy himself once from a distance as he stood on the steps of the Providence City Hall addressing the crowd and I'd been awed at how, even from far away, he was so vivid—the blue eyes, the shock of auburn hair, the expensive-looking dark blue winter coat. And I also vividly remembered that November day in 1963 when I'd driven to Boston to see my townie boyfriend Bumpy who was working in a parking lot there and I was in a sea of traffic inexplicably stalled in Copley Square and I looked over and saw that the burly driver of the taxi next to me was crying like a baby and I turned on the radio and learned that Jack Kennedy was dead. All of us who lived then remember that day.

For the walk with Joe, I did what I always did when I was afraid I'd be so thrown off that I wouldn't be able to remember what was said: I hid the big Panasonic in my pocketbook, pressing Record before I met up with him so I'd have it all on tape.

We walked and talked about nothing in particular—that is, nothing that I would remember afterward when I sat down at the desk in my aerie room on Tamalpais Road, pressed Play on my tape recorder, and was horrified to hear only noise, cars and horns all but drowning out the muddled sound of our own voices, Joe's and mine, the whole clangorous mess punctuated by a rhythmic thud that I realized was the sound of my pocketbook, heavy with the useless tape recorder, hitting my leg with every step I took.

Shit. I tried, but I couldn't remember much about him at all, hardly a word he said—except for one thing when we came to the end of our walk. We were at the water's edge in the San Francisco Marina; spread before us were neat rows of small craft at harbor. Joe looked out over the boats. He was silent for a moment, then asked, "Do you sail?"

Did I sail? I lived in a sixty-dollar-a-month room. I couldn't even pay for insurance on my (used) car. I proceeded to blather about everything I could think of connected to sailing. That my father had sailed. That he'd been part owner of a sailboat until he married my mother and she'd made him sell it. That I'd taken sailing at college for the brief moment it took me to crash the little boat into the rocks along Seekonk River.

Joe Kennedy wasn't listening. He'd lost interest in the question, in my answers. We had come to the end of our time together and said good-bye. I hadn't asked him about his father, about how he felt when, at sixteen, he learned he'd been killed, about what effect he thought it had had on his life to lose his father in this way, at that age. And I wouldn't ask Kathleen when I met her either. Or Bobby Junior.

It's possible Joe would have wanted to be asked. Would have even expected to be asked. Maybe they all would. But these weren't questions I could bring myself to pose, not even a few months later when I lay on the waterbed that covered practically the entire floor of Bobby Junior's freshman dorm room at Harvard, taking in the falconry equipment displayed on the wall and the small bronze bust of his father on the credenza, an object that surely could have provided a natural segue into the subject.

I had been to Hyannis Port and talked to passersby and shop-keepers in the area and learned that it was all true—the Kennedy kids ran wild, played pranks, begged money from neighbors. But would it be fair to write gossip about children? Or would it be of interest to readers of *Rolling Stone*? And anyway, would their mother even let me anywhere near them?

I decided I'd narrow it down to Joe and the other two Kennedy kids launched and out of the house—Kathleen, a senior at Rad-cliffe, and Bobby Junior, in his freshman year at Harvard. Instead of trying to contact them—I was afraid that would make it too easy for them to put me off—I decided I'd simply go to Cam-bridge and track them down. Which I did, asking around campus to find out what dorms they were in.

I started with Kathleen. No one answered when I knocked on her door, but just as I was about to leave, she came home. She didn't want to talk to me but I pleaded with her and she reluc-tantly agreed and let me into her room, a suite, really, with a living room and fireplace. I sat; she didn't.

She was a guarded and stern girl, or she was with me, and who could blame her? I tried to draw her out about herself—what was she majoring in, planning to do after college? She answered but grew increasingly impatient. She really had to study. She didn't have time for this. She had a paper to write. She shut down com-pletely and so I thanked her and left.

Outside, in the cold Cambridge fading light, I felt ridiculous. What a weird, oddly desperate thing to do, to lie in wait and im-pose myself on someone who clearly wished I'd go away. But what else could I have done? I had a job to do. I steeled myself and headed across campus to find Bobby Junior's dorm.

I didn't have to lie in wait for Bobby Junior, since he was leav-ing the building just as I was walking up. He wasn't surprised when I stopped him and introduced myself; Joe had said I might be coming to see him. He wasn't preppy-looking like Joe. He wore worn jeans and his hair was long and he was taller and lankier, with a crooked smile and a distracted air. Something like thought seemed to go on behind his Kennedy-blue eyes, which just then were at half-mast. Which made sense, as this was the Kennedy who as a young teen had been busted for possession of pot.

He said he couldn't talk now, he was supposed to meet somebody. He scratched his head and pondered, then shrugged and said maybe I could come with him, it wouldn't take long.

We walked through campus and out onto Harvard Square and then went down a side street to the next corner, a doorway from Hazen's Diner, where, in 1965 when I was attending Harvard summer school to make up the only course I'd flunked at Brown (poli sci—I'd handed in a blank exam book, hadn't even felt like bullshitting my way through an essay, had taken the course only because it was David Leach's subject), I'd had my first waitressing job. That was where, for the first time, I heard the Stones' "Satisfaction" and then "Get Off My Cloud." When someone played either one on the jukebox, the whole place stopped and listened in awe, everybody looking at each other with expressions that read *What the fuck is that?* because nobody had heard anything like it before.

But now it was 1973 and Robert Kennedy Junior said for me to give him a minute and he went over to a guy and they made some kind of furtive exchange. When we got back to Bobby Junior's dorm room, he explained about the falconry equipment, something he used to do, hunt wild quarry with these kind of trained birds...then he shrugged and trailed off.

I asked him what he'd scored, and he said it was Dilaudid. This is maybe where I could have asked why he was resorting to such a powerful painkiller and referenced the little bust of his father. It might have opened up a whole world of discourse about his feelings and his loss. But I didn't. Instead, we took our clothes off had sexual intercourse on the waterbed.

A big journalistic transgression I know. But I slept with almost every man I met in those days, so why wouldn't I have sex with this gorgeous Kennedy? Well, because I was pretty sure it was an unwritten rule that you weren't supposed to have sex with the subject of an article you were writing.

Still, it could have been—maybe it really was—a kind of journalistic instinct for the story that led me to it. Because what I found out on that undulating waterbed could have been key to understanding the Kennedy male. It wasn't just his command of the situation—he told me it would go better if I braced myself against the undulation of the waterbed—but what he looked like naked when he knelt before me.

How to say it delicately...okay, I'll just say it. The guy was hung. Probably halfway to his knees. I had never seen anything quite like it before. And wasn't that sort of thing, like, genetic? Were they all this way? Was that where the confidence, the drive, the very cockiness came from? What must it be like to go through life with something like that banging against your thigh all day? How could you keep from thinking about anything else?

Well, journalistic instinct or no, the act made it seem impossible to write the Kennedy piece. Because how could I, who prided myself on honestly depicting what I saw and experienced when I covered a story, how could I write anything about the Kennedys without saying what I'd done? For a long time, I didn't tell anybody—not Jann when he eventually threatened to take my name off the masthead if I didn't turn the story in, no one, except maybe strangers in bars and at parties to explain why I wasn't on the masthead anymore.

Well, I did tell one person, David Felton, when I got home to Chicago where we were living in a sublet near the university while he was on a journalistic fellowship there. Feeling I'd backed myself into a corner, I wanted reassurance, advice on how to write the story anyway. Instead I was hit with what felt like the retaliatory news that while I'd been away, he had bedded one of the students in a seminar he was teaching. I went nuclear. He'd cheated on me? What I'd done wasn't the same thing at all! I'd done it for science! What he'd done, he'd done in the middle of our life together! Did everybody know about it?

I huffed off to bed and the next morning woke to find him packing. I'd scared him. He thought I was crazy. He was going back to his wife and family. From our second-story window, I watched him and his suitcase go down the front walk and into a waiting cab. I retreated to our bedroom and knelt on the bed, rocking and keening like an Afghan widow. It was the first time I'd felt that kind of pain. The first time anyone I was so physically tied to had left me.

After a while, however, I came to the end of it. I got up and went to the mirror above the dresser to take stock, I suppose, and have a talk with myself. *Well, well*, I thought. *That's done.* And I'm ashamed to say I saw a sly smile cross my face. Because I was actually relieved. I had never really expected—or wanted—to live my life with David Felton. And now I was rid of him. I was free. And without guilt or possible regret because he was the one who had left me.

Then I did what I always did and would do when I was at a loss—I looked for work. Ever since those first successful short stories in college, writing had become a lodestar, the one sustaining constant in my zigzag journey forward. Since it seemed unwise at that point to ask Jann for another assignment, I called up Jon Carroll, whom I knew from San Francisco and who was now here in Chicago editing the new *Playboy* knockoff *Oui* magazine. He said he'd see me that afternoon.

Jon Carroll's office was downtown in a glass tower that looked west onto a brilliant pollution-red sunset. Jon was his jolly self behind his desk, flush with his big new job, one that came with lots of money for freelance writers. I told him I was basically homeless, that I could go anywhere. He pondered.

"Israel," he said. "Robin Green in Israel. Write whatever you want."

I had no idea what he meant, but he was the editor in chief and he was offering me a way out of town and airfare and enough up-front expense money to last a month, the way I lived. So I went. It wasn't until much later, when I'd returned to Berkeley after the episode in Providence with the broken leg and the crabs and was trying to write the story, that the Yom Kippur War broke out. I called *Oui* and left a message for the new editor (Jon Carroll having been fired), asking if the war changed anything, if they still wanted the story—and also asking about anything Jon might have said about what the story was about anyhow.

The new editor wrote back. Robin Green in Israel? Yes, they wanted the story. And as for what they were expecting: "Did you get laid over there? If so, how was it?"

Did I get *laid? Excuse me? What business*...After I got over being indignant, however, I realized that this was, after all, *Oui* magazine. Why should their interest in sex shock me? And, to be perfectly honest with myself, my relations with men were, in large part, how I experienced the world, and my interactions in Israel—the men I'd met and "getting laid" by some of them—were no exception. I did, in fact, have stories to tell: about the soldier who had lost his leg in the 1967 war, whose stump above the knee I had been curious to see (it looked like a huge innie belly button, the flesh somehow gathered into the center like the fabric at the end of the arm of a couch), whose Israeli macho bravado left no room for consciousness of his country's dependence on the United States for its very existence and from whom, on that bare mattress on the floor, I'm pretty sure I got the crabs; about the playboy parliamentarian in a pink shirt who gave me a tour of the Knesset and bought me lunch there, a man who I didn't go to bed with; about the Arab who looked just like my older brother—same face, blue eyes, fair hair—with whom I also didn't sleep but with whom I walked for hours around Jerusalem while he assured me that the Arabs would see the Israelis gone, if not in his lifetime then eventually, as the Arabs always had, squatting patiently in the sand until the day their enemy disappeared into the sea. "Just look at the name of the cigarettes the Israelis smoke," he said. "They're called Time."

There was also a Canadian waiter at the American Colony Hotel in Jerusalem where I stayed for a while who said I seemed lonely and took me home to have tea, who wanted not sex but philosophical conversation that veered into a weird religiosity that soon made me realize he was a brainwashing Moonie trying to recruit me into Sun Myung Moon's South Korean Unification Church and who, when I said I had to go, became very angry and berated me and yelled at me, trying to intimidate me into staying.

And last, a sociology professor from UC Berkeley with whom I traveled for a week to Tel Aviv, Haifa, and the Caesarea ruins, where he bought me a necklace of jade stones, the sight of which infuriated a couple he knew that we had drinks with, as they were friends with the professor's wife back home.

He and the disapproving couple and a bunch of other people, including Jann Wenner, were part of a party flown to Israel and put up at the King David by Max Palevsky, an LA art collector who early on had made a zillion dollars in computers and who had rescued *Rolling Stone* from financial ruin in 1970 by buying a substantial share of the stock and who was now a director and board chairman of the magazine. He'd brought everyone there to witness the dedication of a wing of the Jerusalem Museum to his deceased immigrant parents, Izchok and Sarah.

Jann had learned that I was in Israel—"not the best Mediterranean climate," he called it—and he telephoned me at the American Colony to invite me to join him and few others at a club that night.

It was there, at a nightclub somewhere in Jerusalem, that the issue of the Kennedy story came to a head. We had gone outside to the patio to get some air and have a smoke (cigarettes). He asked me, after all the time I'd taken, not to mention the expenses I'd racked up, where the hell the story was. I was sorry, I said, but he wasn't going to get it.

As he absorbed this, he turned away and blew a stream of smoke out of the side of his mouth, then looked at me and shook his head sadly. "You realize," he said, "if you don't write it, I'm going to have to take you off the masthead."

I said that was okay. And, really, it was. I was, in fact and again, relieved. Between my lack of any real commitment to journalism and my misgivings about being some sort of journalistic hitman, with this story in particular, the whole thing had become kind of a drag.

And as time would prove, it was lucky for Jann I didn't write the article, because when *Rolling Stone* moved to New York a few years later, would he have enjoyed such a happy relationship with Jackie Onassis, a much-vaunted and valued friend, if, my own questionable behavior aside, I had exposed the dirt about any kids of Ethel's?

"Okay?" Jann said that night. "You sure?"

I said I was and we hugged and that's when he asked me to please never write about him.

A young British couple I'd befriended at the American Colony Hotel offered to let me stay in their London apartment for two weeks while they finished their tour of Israel. I'd never been to London, or anywhere in Europe—and what else did I have to do?

They lived in a lovely book-lined flat in Hampstead Village. I walked the wild heath and tried to eat the food at a pub in the quaint little town—scotch eggs, bangers and mash. I went into the city to Harrods, had tea and crumpets in a little shop on a side street, dined on the Strand, stopped outside the gates of Buckingham Palace to watch the changing of the guard. I walked through Hyde Park, where I saw secretaries strip down to their underwear to bask in the first thin sunlight. No one bothered them. No one bothered me. It was all so civilized, especially after Israel, where everybody ogled and catcalled, pushed and cut in line.

It was all so *English*. It was just like the England in the books I'd read, all cultivated and refined. I told the young couple when they came home that I thought I might stay in London forever. *Rolling Stone* had an office in the city; I'd pay them a visit. I was sure they'd have a story for me to do or that they'd at least let me use a desk and phone.

The young couple had a friend named Earl, an editor at a publishing house. The garden apartment of his house was vacant; maybe I could live there. Earl turned out to be handsome, erudite, charming. He seemed to like me too—an American girl on assignment, tanned and wearing a jade necklace. He read *Rolling Stone*, thought he might even have read me.

I came to his house with my suitcase. He had made a picnic for me in the garden—the greenest, neatest lawn and hedges I'd ever seen—and had a blanket spread with sandwiches from the deli, a bottle of wine. We drank to my future in London.

It was my first night in the sparsely furnished garden apartment. It had nothing but a mattress on the floor, but Earl said he'd help me fit it out later. I invited him to stay. Which proved to be a mistake because afterward he couldn't get away fast enough. In his polished British accent, he politely excused himself (manuscript to read, early appointment the next day), and went out and upstairs to his house, his disappointment and even revulsion palpable.

I lay there feeling I'd ruined everything, that I'd soured London and anything that might have happened between me and Earl. And I soon realized that I had fouled this nest in more ways than emotionally. There was a bad smell, and I realized it was me. The end of my period, maybe. Or maybe I was malodorous from the pubic lice I didn't yet know I had—though I could have gotten them that very night from Earl or Earl's mattress.

In the morning, embarrassed and humiliated, I fled. I didn't want to stay in London anyway. It was too tame. Too confining. I belonged in the wilder, freer, less judgmental California. But first I went home to Providence.

My parents, as always, were glad to see me. And yet. Was it me or was it them? Do parents really want an almost-twenty-eight-year-old daughter showing up in their midst? My mother had told me how wonderful it had been for her and my father to have the house to themselves again after my brother and then I left; "Like velvet," she'd said. She told me of an evening when she and my father were in the living room and he was watching television (a black-and-white—he wanted to wait until they perfected color to buy a new set) and she was feeling ignored, and, on the couch just out of his line of sight, she stealthily shed every piece of her clothing so the next time he glanced her way, she was stark naked.

"What did he do?" I stupidly asked.

"What do you think?" she said smugly.

Well, now I was home again, plopped down in my old room with no clear plan. A little R and R and pampering, someone to do my laundry and feed me. Daytimes, I rode my old Schwinn around the leafy East Side Providence streets like some big, overgrown child, once pedaling clear out of town into the exurbs, ending up finally at Kirkbrae Country Club, a kind of second-tier club with a mixed membership—Irish, Italian, Jewish—and one my parents went into further debt to afford.

My father loved it there. He'd taken up golf late in life; after suburban shopping malls killed downtown Providence and his job at Mickler's along with it, he'd found new freedom in outside greeting card sales, joined the golf club, gotten a hole in one, and was so well liked he was elected president, a formal portrait of him mounted on the wall.

He didn't seem all that glad when I showed up at the club. I sensed I'd invaded his space, so I beat a hasty retreat from this male lair, and it was the next day that the wheel of my bike twisted under me as I slowed to take a corner and I fell, landing on my knee and fracturing the tibia just below it. Now in a cast from hip to toe, I was the *Man Who Came to Dinner* and I was in bed in my old room when I reached down to scratch a terrible itch in my crotch, and instinct made me examine my fingers; that's when I saw tiny red crabs scurrying around there, waving their tiny little crab claws.

❖

Chapter Eleven

Bankruptcy

After London and Providence, I went back to Berkeley and tried to write the article about Israel, or at least tried to think about writing the article about Israel, but I really didn't want to think about it, about any of it, particularly about the fact that when Jon Carroll said "Robin Green in Israel," what he meant was "Robin Green and men." Did I have some sort of reputation? How? David Felton was one thing, but could Jon have heard about Kit Carson or his brother or Jann or any of the others? That one thing with the reporter on that movie junket to New York, maybe. He lived in Chicago...

I never wrote the article, and the new editor who had asked if I'd gotten laid in Israel never called again. I figured they'd blame the failure on Jon Carroll and I turned again to waitressing—not at a low-end-of-the-high-end restaurant like HS Lordships in the Berkeley Marina now but slinging pizza at a Persian joint on Telegraph Avenue, then working the graveyard shift at a Copper Penny on University Avenue.

At the same time that the girls of *Rolling Stone* were coming into their own, both in their office lives and out, I was becoming increasingly unglued and alienated. Basically homeless now, I lived in one converted garage and then another, one of which happened to be the garage of Timothy Leary's house in the Berkeley Hills, though the man Nixon called "the most dangerous man in America" wasn't there, having gone to prison for pot possession, escaped with the help of the Weather Underground, lammed it to Algeria under Eldridge Cleaver's increasingly oppressive protection, then escaped him and was now in Switzerland or Afghanistan or somewhere fighting extradition to the United States. His kids, Susan (who ultimately committed suicide by hanging) and Jack (who didn't), needed money. So they refurbed the garage and rented it—to me.

On off-hours, I tried to live the life of someone with inner resources—like the Beat poets I'd read about or as Patti Smith would do in a few years in New York City—and I frequented hip coffeehouses in Berkeley and San Francisco, but I only felt more acutely, self-consciously alone. Although one day at Caffe Trieste in North Beach, Jerry Rubin, who was an original Yippie, founder of the Youth International Party along with Paul Krassner and Abbie Hoffman (and who later became a successful businessman and, still later, in 1994, was hit by a car as he was jaywalking across Wilshire Boulevard and died soon after), recognized me and sat down at my little marble-topped table. He had read my articles in *Rolling Stone*, couldn't understand why I wasn't writing anymore, and for that brief chat, the girl I had been lived, the one who had been on the masthead and written things that people read, the happy girl in the photograph just a few years ago at the beach.

I did finally find a real place to rent in the Berkeley Flats—a little cottage with its own gated yard behind someone's house on Francisco Street. I would settle down and make a life for myself. It wasn't just a room of my own; it had a kitchen and a living area where I would set up a desk. I invited friends over for a painting party, among them the heiress friend's older sister, who had forgiven me, and her little son as well as David Leach, Andrea, and Mark (who had returned from Mexico, moved into David's Fox Court studio, divorced his wife, Vicky, and taken up with Andrea, whom he later married and still later divorced).

I planted a garden, my first, growing and harvesting tomatoes and zucchini. Freelance writing work came my way from publications such as *City Magazine*, the *SF Examiner Sunday Magazine*, and the *Boston Real Paper*, whose editor called and asked me to write an article about Inez Garcia, who had become a feminist cause célèbre after killing a man who she said had held her while another raped her. The story was complicated and I told it that way, feminist cause or no. A while after it was published, Gloria Steinem herself called, wanting my permission to reprint the article as a cover story of *Ms*.

One afternoon I was surprised to see Kit Carson appear in my yard holding a balloon that turned out to be filled with nitrous oxide—a way to get high that was a new craze in the Bay Area that he thought would make a great article for *Rolling Stone*, and when I pitched it they agreed. It was funny and smart and five thousand words long. It was also the last article I'd ever write for *Rolling Stone*.

Because even though I was productive again, I was miserable. You can see it in the photographs David Leach took of me in the backyard of my little cottage on Francisco Street sometime in 1974. I'd put on weight. I looked homely and chastened, like one of the twin girls in that Diane Arbus photograph (a large signed print of which hung on the wall of Harold Hayes's house in Brentwood), identical twins, dressed alike in little dark dresses with big white collars, except that one little girl is pretty and the other homely, both reflections of their inner feelings about themselves.

As Joe Conforte, the crusading pimp in my *Rolling Stone* article, said of his housekeeper who was serving Annie and me breakfast in his kitchen in Sparks, Nevada, "Look at her. Her nose is so big it would keep a cigarette dry in the rain. But she is beautiful. You know why? Because true beauty comes from inside and she is beautiful inside."

I wasn't and hadn't been beautiful for a while—since London, since Providence, since the morning I found lice in my pubic hair and to deal with the little bastards, had waited for my mother to go out on errands and then called Hall's Drugs and told the pharmacist that the Rid anti-lice shampoo wasn't to be delivered until after eleven (when a friend of my mother's was picking her up to go to the beach).

That day, my plan was to sit and take the stairs down one by one, just as I had come up, backward, the day before, then crutch it to the front door to wait for the delivery. My mother's friend was, of course, late, and from an upstairs window I saw the pharmacy van pull up. In a panic, I started making my way downstairs on my ass, rounding the corner to see my mother take a small paper bag from the deliveryman. She turned to face me.

"What's this?" she said, holding up the bag.

"None of your business," I said.

She smirked at me. "I know what it is," she said. "It's cigarettes, isn't it?"

With a scornful and superior look, she handed over the bag just as her friend Dottie honked the horn out front.

"You think you know everything, don't you?" I said in a tone that suggested it was, in fact, cigarettes.

I never told my mother or father about the crabs and I didn't tell them, six weeks later, after they'd waited on me hand and foot, after they'd wrapped my cast in plastic and hauled my sorry ass to the beach, after the bone in my leg had knit and the plaster cast had been removed and my crutches exchanged for a cane, that I was going back to California. I just went.

They had gone out to dinner with Ronnie's parents and I had a rare evening to myself. I sat on my bed and looked around my little room in the little house on Wayland Avenue, the smallest, cheapest house in the nicest neighborhood. My bedroom was just big enough for two twin beds, a cheap white wicker dresser, and the window seat/hope chest my father had built for me, really more of a plywood box than the chintz-upholstered, crown-molding-edged window seats in the bedrooms of the girls I knew—Ronnie and Lynnie and Jackie and Susie and Jill—all of which had been designed and carpentered by professionals.

My father had tried. He'd found affordable white vinyl floor tiles ("You can hardly see what makes them seconds," my mother had said) and installed them himself and installed the white louvered closet doors too, both jobs sadly uneven, black gullies appearing between many of the nicked white vinyl tiles and a closet whose doors formed a long X when shut.

I'd spent hours, weeks, months, and years in this room, as a teenager feeling especially marooned, deserted, and hopeless after my brother went off to college—alone with my parents at the dinner table, alone upstairs while downstairs they talked and laughed with Frank and Pearl and Raymond and other friends, alone at the window, watching rain, alone in front of the mirror, sketching myself and then writing my first short story about escape.

I'd made one big escape and now it was clear to me, although with no specific plan, that it was time to escape again. My father's aunt Frances, who had herself fled Providence for Manhattan and a semi-glamorous life as a saleslady at a swanky Park Avenue dress shop called Polly's, a swanky Park Avenue studio apartment, and a miniature gray poodle with a rhinestone collar named Chico, told me once that I was the only one in my family with ambition. (Apparently, in her mind, my brother's becoming a physician who spent his life teaching neuroscience at Dartmouth Medical School didn't qualify, maybe because he'd never gotten out of New England.)

Was it ambition that drove me that night? Or was I simply on the run from myself? Or both? Whatever it was, I left that very night. I wrote a note to my parents, called a cab, and soon limped on my cane into the Greyhound station and boarded a bus for Logan Airport in Boston, where I got on a plane to Oakland.

What a little shit I was not to think of how my parents would feel when they got home and found me gone. Of how hurt they'd be that I'd deprived them of a proper good-bye scene. Of how worried they'd be that I'd behaved so rashly. But if I had bothered to think anything, it might also have occurred to me that they'd be happy to have the house to themselves again.

After I left Providence and flew back to Berkeley and before I started living in garages, David Leach, Andrea, and Mark took me in. They'd moved from the Berkeley Flats to the north Berkeley Hills into a house they'd bought with proceeds from their work in waterbed sales and also from David's new business dealing coke in what he described as small quantities to friends. Cheek by jowl with other houses on the hillside, it was a cozy little place with sweeping views of Berkeley and the bay and San

Francisco—the whole shebang—and there were David's Persian chairs by the fireplace, his expensive sound system, and Reuben the black dog wagging his tail and glad to see me.

The woman David eventually married, his widow now, still lives in the house today and when I went to see her she showed me the deck David had had built with a rustic outdoor shower that was his pride, pointed out the plot in the garden below where he had finally buried Reuben's ashes. The Persian chairs still sat by the fireplace, their cushions now covered in beautiful cloth woven by his widow, an artist whose medium is fabric.

I had been in touch with Mark and learned that on David's death, in addition to figuring out how to deal with an arsenal of firearms that David had stashed around the house to protect himself from a real or imagined cocaine-dealer threat, my old boyfriend's widow was coping with what to do with contents of the basement closet that had served as his darkroom and that was filled with photographs and contact sheets and negatives, all of it neatly labeled, though now mildewed and moldering from years of his neglect. She had agreed to let me take the material from his and my time together off her hands.

I'd had no idea there was so much stuff—not just of me, but all that he had photographed in his life. Had he been an artist? He had never given himself credit for being one and went to his death feeling, as he had felt all along, like a failure. When I spoke to Mark recently, he told me a story about David, how David had called him weeping one night not long before he died and said that he had to tell him something he had done, something horrible.

Between sobs, David managed to tell Mark that old friends from Providence had called and said that they were coming to the Bay Area and wanted to see him but that he'd lied and said he'd be out of the country. The old friends continued to press—could he at least tell them about himself? He had been so interesting and brilliant; they had always admired him and wondered what he'd done with his life.

Still sobbing, barely able to talk now, David said that he'd told his old friends from Providence of Mark's life—his accomplishments and travels, his life abroad working for the World Bank, the many languages he spoke—that he'd told them of Mark's achievements as if they were his own.

But David's death would be years away, in 2010. When I returned to Berkeley from Providence, it was still 1973 and David's life in the new house was the sybaritic, hedonistic affair it always was, except now, in addition to the liter a day of Johnnie Walker Black, the Lapsang souchong tea, Sara Lee pound cakes, and pot, there was cocaine, lines and lines of it, making for nights that lasted until dawn and days spent sleeping.

People came and went—dealers, buyers, friends. Andrea played "Angie" over and over on the stereo, swaying to the music, entranced. Mark sat cross-legged on the carpet, endlessly proselytizing Werner Erhard's EST. David drank, smoked, snorted. An old friend of his visited one day and announced that he was moving in with his girlfriend and did I want to stay in the converted garage he rented in the flats near the Oakland border while he saw whether the relationship was going to work out or not?

I did. I lived in that garage and then the Leary garage. I still had the little Sunbeam Alpine I'd bought from Annie and I drove it one night to San Francisco to a Victorian house in the hills above Noe Valley where someone from *Rolling Stone* was having a birthday party for Hunter Thompson. I went alone. David Felton wasn't at the party; he was in LA—with his family, I supposed.

On the baby grand was a glass bowl filled with little blue pills—mescaline. I took some and soon I was tripping.

I'd had a bad trip before, the one I'd written about in the reunion newsletter, at the Trident Restaurant in Sausalito with Annie and Felton and Jon and Julie from the art department. That time I'd felt unable to walk and they'd had to haul me out of there. They were laughing and happy and tripping as they carried me outside, and then in someone's car we drove to Jon's house, where I took off all my clothes and got into someone's bed and writhed and whimpered and hallucinated that I was an infant until I finally came down.

You would think that I'd have known better than to try it again. If anything, this time was worse. I felt paranoid; I felt crazy; I had to get away. I found my way into the backyard and crawled into the bushes, where, kneeling in the dirt, I watched the party from between the branches. I knew I couldn't stay there forever and somehow got through the party and outside to my little sports car parked perpendicular to the curb on one of the city's steepest hills on an angle that made it a struggle even to open the door and get in. Somehow, I backed the car out and somehow I managed to drive back to Berkeley—down the hill, through San Francisco, over the Bay Bridge, and up Wildcat Canyon Road to Tilden Park.

In a catatonic state, I sat unmoving in the sand at Lake Anza. The sun came up. People walked into the park. A woman let her Weimaraner off the leash and it came to where I sat immobile, sniffed me, then lifted its leg and peed on me.

Is this low enough? Is this miserable enough? How about this: Days later, distracted by thoughts, I was driving in the Berkeley Hills and didn't see a car coming around a bend in time to avoid embedding my little car in the front of hers. Fortunately, she had insurance, because I didn't. My car was totaled and I took to hitchhiking around Berkeley.

And finally this: After I'd moved into my lovely little backyard cottage in the flats and harvested a season of tomatoes and squash from my garden, I befriended the woman who managed the laundromat on University Avenue where I washed my clothes. She told me she and her boyfriend were gleaners—they went to the fields east of the Bay Area and gathered crops that had been left behind, onions, potatoes. I thought it might be something to write about, so I went with them. We shared a motel room and it was all benign enough until a few days later, when the boyfriend, hulking, furtive, showed up at my little cottage behind the house on Francisco Street.

He said if I ever needed protection back here against intruders or anything I should let him know. He told me he had a gun. He took it out to show me. I told him thanks but I was fine. I somehow got him out of there. But I had the impression he was casing the joint, and I felt very strongly that he'd be back.

I called David Leach's house. Andrea answered the phone. "I think I'm in danger," I said. "I have to leave here. Can someone come get me?" It was from David Leach's house in the hills that I telephoned Kit Carson the night before his wedding to Karen Black and he told me that if I wanted to write for Hollywood, I should move there. Which I would do. But not for another three years.

❖

Chapter Twelve

Fields, Fields, and More Fields

In August 1975, I decamped to Iowa City, to the University of Iowa Writers' Workshop. The younger heiress, the one who lent me the jeans jacket with the patch of people fornicating on the back that I wore to interview for a job at *Rolling Stone*, had married a poet who had gone there. It sounded so classy. And so cushy. A writing workshop? Nothing to do but read books and maybe write something? And the last place I'd felt safe, much as I'd wanted to flee from it, was academia.

I sent in a short story to apply and was put on some sort of waiting list. I later learned that one of the readers, the novelist Allan Gurganus, found my material "thin." I wrote John Hawkes, my teacher at Brown, who hadn't found my writing thin, to ask if he'd put in a word for me. We'd kept in touch a little. I'd sent him my *Rolling Stone* article about Dennis Hopper and later had dinner with him in Palo Alto when he came west to speak at his friend and colleague Wallace Stegner's writing program at Stanford.

In what was probably an effort to seduce my old writing

teacher, I dressed provocatively in black crepe pants and a midriff-baring red satin top that tied under my breasts. When I went to the Stegners' grand hacienda to pick him up, the Stegners were at dinner. It was a memorable tableau, the dignified couple in their formal dining room, sitting kitty-corner at one end of a long table, in front of each a glass of red wine and plate on which sat a single serving of Stouffer's macaroni and cheese, still in its tin. (In those days, this frozen product came in a tin that you heated in an oven and got this nice, caramelized cheesy crust; today it's microwavable plastic, faster but, alas, no crust.)

Mr. Stegner raised his eyebrows at my outfit, then gave a hubba-hubba look to Hawkes. We left and had steaks and our own glasses of red wine someplace in town, and somewhere in the middle of dinner, I realized the futility—and unseemliness—of trying to seduce this man, something I'd tried in college, staying at a party at his house after the other students had left and his wife had gone up to bed. We'd sat close, cross-legged on the floor. He put a hand on my knee and then, with a sigh of what seemed like amused regret, gave my leg a dismissive pat and said good night. I hadn't read his novels then and didn't until Iowa, but when I did I saw that he was a strangely, if brilliantly, perverse son of a gun. Still, he wrote a letter of recommendation to John Leggett, the workshop's director, and they let me in.

I found a room to rent in a big, creepy old Victorian house—like something Charles Addams would draw—hard by the railroad tracks at the edge of town. Not fifteen feet from my window as I lay sleepless in the saggy iron-framed single bed, the trains would come to a stop outside in the black Iowa night, sounding for all the world like a herd of giant mechanical buffalo, clanging into each other one by one by one, all the way down the line ad fucking infinitum.

My landlords were out of Charles Addams too: hardscrabble Iowans, the fat middle-aged matriarch careening around in a baggy housedress with stockings meant to be knee-high falling down around her ankles, her Jack Sprat husband in worn-out farmer's overalls, and their useless lummox of a son, a grown man who spent most of his time in front of the TV (they all did) and whom I once saw amusing himself by pinching his little nephew to the point of tears.

My room was in the back and had its own entrance, so I rarely saw them. I was busy reading seven volumes of Proust and discussing it in seminars and trying to write and discussing that in seminars and also working—for money, that is, to bankroll all this erudition. In Berkeley months before, I'd answered an ad in the classifieds: *Writers Wanted!* I'd telephoned for an appointment, borrowed a car, and driven across the bay to lovely Sausalito—and then to the address they'd given me, which proved to be a grubby strip mall just outside of town.

The office was above a doughnut shop, and the job was rewriting porn. They'd send you a paperback book with the cover torn off and instructions like *move location from city to countryside* and *change dog to baby bull pet.* You kept as is the dirty parts— paragraph upon paragraph of taut nipples, straining shafts, pink pearlescent slits, and shooting jism. It was a bit illegal, they said (like being a little bit pregnant), so I should keep the job to myself.

You had to have good grammar and spelling and you'd better be able to type because each manuscript came to about two hundred and fifty pages, for which, after you mailed it in and it was accepted, they mailed you back an envelope with another book to write and a note that said, *Mayhaps this will help,* referring to the enclosed check for two hundred dollars. The beauty was that you could mail it in from anywhere, where was where I now was.

Fields, fields, and more fields were all Jenny Fields could see, I was typing one night—rejigging a porn novel to have its protagonist lured from the city by an Iowa corn farmer who proved unable to satisfy her sexually but who gave her a baby bull pet that did— when there was a hard knock on the door that connected my room to the landlords' quarters. I opened the door to find the landlady there, all fury and righteous indignation.

"I need to talk to you," she said. "I came in today to check the radiator and—are them dirty books you writing?"

I allowed as how they were.

"Well, I can't have that here," she said.

I packed my few things and moved in with a couple girls from the workshop, then one of them left and it was just me and Nancy in the apartment. A Nebraska girl, fresh out of Mount Holyoke College, Nancy didn't smoke, but she drank—she kept an awareness of how much bourbon was left in the bottle in the cupboard, much as I knew how many brownies remained on the plate above the fridge—and she was still a virgin, which seemed perfect for me, as I wanted to become one again too.

The second year, we were both awarded prime teaching/writing fellowships, which paid tuition and a stipend, and we shared an office in the English building as well. She was at her desk when Mitch came in for the first student/teacher conference, and she was there when he returned again and again as weeks went by. She could tell he had a thing for me. Once, when we heard his heavy footsteps in the corridor, she turned to me and mouthed a Stanley Kowalski *Stella!* and then the door slammed open and in came Mitch.

He threw himself down in the chair beside my desk and handed me a new short story and I could see on his face that he knew he'd hit it out of the park, epiphany and all. He was a wonderful writer with a voice uniquely his own that, when it evinced itself in an essay he'd written for an undergraduate rhetoric class, led his teacher to suggest he take a fiction-writing class. Rushing to class that first day, sweaty and out of breath, he got the room numbers wrong and came into my class by mistake, changing both our lives forever.

He remembers what I was wearing that day—jeans and a long-sleeved white thermal undershirt with a rainbow printed across the front that I'd bought from a street vendor on Telegraph Avenue. My hair was short and prim like Nancy's and I'd slimmed down to my fighting weight. Mitch says he remembers thinking, *Now* there's *somebody for me.*

On the last day of class that December, he was conspicuously absent. I knew he worked at Epstein's, a bookstore in town—I'd seen him there when I went to a poetry reading one night and I remember his eyes on me when I left with the African poet who'd read. What can I say? I'd never been with a black man before, let alone an actual African.

I went straight to the bookstore.

"You didn't come to class today," I said. "I wanted to make sure you were all right."

"I had to work," he said.

I nodded. He nodded. We both knew we were lying. (He confirmed later that he'd stayed away hoping I'd come.)

We were standing close. I felt like I couldn't breathe. I felt like I was about to jump off a cliff. I met his eyes.

"I'm going to California for Christmas but I'll be back right after," I said.

"Okay," he said. "I'll pick you up at the airport."

"Okay," I said. He reached out and gave my white wool scarf—the one I'd knit in Chicago and that my mother had mocked—a little adjustment against the cold outside. When he touched me, I felt like I might faint.

True to his word, he was there in the Cedar Rapids airport when I got off the plane from Oakland. My heart sank at the sight of him, his soon-to-be twenty-five years to my thirty-one years, his scraggly beard and mustache, his cheesy, nipped-in-at-the-waist, double-breasted gray wool coat. He held a bouquet of red, white, and blue carnations—because it was 1976, he said. I had a gift for him too, a small ceramic fried-egg pin I'd bought on Telegraph Avenue, which I fastened to the overwide lapel of his coat.

We drove to Iowa City in the 1970 Ford Montego he'd "bought off" his dad. It was yellow save for a Bondo-patched fender painted blue, and it had a hole in the floor on his side through which the frigid air of Iowa winter blasted in. We went to the one Italian restaurant in town and he didn't know what to order, didn't seem to know what anything was. It was as if he'd never been to a restaurant, let alone taken a girl to one.

He drove me to my apartment on Dodge Street. Nancy was still in Lincoln. We were alone. We went to bed and I would like to say that bells rang and so on, but it was, for me at least, an awkward, detached, and uncomfortable act. It was also the beginning of a sexual relationship that would span, off and on, forty-some years, a relationship in which an entire Italian city's worth of bell towers would come to ring.

His apartment was a few blocks away: waterbed on the floor, little kitchen, and, in the living room, a decorated Christmas tree he'd "drug in" from a friend's apartment across the hall. Naked on the carpet by the Christmas tree, we again had sexual intercourse. I remember pine needles stabbing me in the ass from when he'd "drug" the tree in.

He learned then that I had no feeling for or history with Christ-mas. I'd learn he'd met only one or two other Jews in his life. We'd both learn what we did have in common: We both used Oral B toothbrushes. I got up in the middle of the night and went back to my apartment and he let me know the next day that I'd better not do that again.

Now it was New Year's Eve. We lay on the couch in my and Nancy's apartment in each other's arms making small talk. There wasn't even enough conversation to last until midnight. We fell asleep. The next day, I said I thought the whole thing was a bad idea—the age and cultural differences, the fact that I'd been his teacher. He put on his awful coat and headed out the door.

"Where are you going?" I said.

"Home," he said.

"Please don't go," I said.

"What?" he asked, incredulous.

"I don't want you to go," I said.

He looked at me like he thought I was crazy, but he came back in.

I was awarded my MFA in June, but I stayed in Iowa another year to wait for Mitch to earn his BA in history. He was on the GI Bill; that was why he'd joined the army. It was the end of the Viet-nam War era and he'd figured he wouldn't be sent somewhere to be killed, and even if he was, it would be better than load-ing oat sacks onto freight cars or slogging through pig blood in the slaughterhouse/packing plant where he'd worked after high school.

That last year in Iowa, he found a pretty little apartment for us on Dubuque Street with lots of windows and good light. I hung a large Divan Japonais Toulouse-Lautrec poster on the wall and cooked us Indian food that so pleased him, he took pictures of it. The army paid him three hundred dollars a month, which covered his tuition and the rent, and I got a secretarial job at the university medical center in a residential treatment center for autistic boys.

My boss, Alan Horowitz, ran the treatment center. A wide-assed Jew with a medical degree from Harvard—this was who I was supposed to be with, not some Iowa undergraduate hick. He invited us to his house for Passover dinner. I felt awash in shame: Ashamed of Mitch, the ultimate goy. Ashamed of myself for being with him. If I had only known then that in twenty years, Dr. Alan Horowitz would earn a ten- to twenty-year sentence for molesting children in his Boy Scout troop and that when he got out, he'd skip parole, flee to India, and be captured as one of America's most wanted sex offenders. He was probably molesting those poor autistic boys at the center even then.

"Iowa's most dissolute couple" was how Jack Leggett referred to us when Mitch waited on him at the bookstore. It didn't sound like a compliment. Together, we looked it up in the dictionary. *Dissolute (adj.)*, it read. *Lax in morals, debauched, decadent, intemperate, profligate, wild, promiscuous, drunken.*

Were we any of those things? All? It was true that we drank, were thrilled to party it up with Ray Carver in his bad old unreformed days, that we caroused at the workshop morel-mushroom-hunting picnic at Vance Bourjaily's house (carved in the fireplace's stone mantel: DOLCE FAR NIENTE), Mitch running around with me riding piggyback, the sexual heat between us there for all to see.

We couldn't get enough of each other. When I picked him up at Logan Airport that first summer to take him up to my brother's house in Vermont, we didn't make it an hour out of Boston before we had to pull off the highway to find some woods and privacy, mosquitoes eating our bare asses as we rutted on a bed of old leaves on the hard ground.

Other than the African poet, I'd been chaste at Iowa, even when given the opportunity, such as the morning in the student union that I saw Anthony Burgess, esteemed author of *Clockwork Orange*, sitting alone and went over to tell him how much I'd enjoyed his lecture the night before, how much I loved his books. He invited me to sit and shortly asked if I'd like to come to his room for a drink. It was eleven o'clock in the morning. I said I had to be in class.

In that same cafeteria, I was having coffee with Henry Bromell, the writer who'd led the seminar on Proust and who, at twenty-four, had won the Houghton Mifflin Literary Fellowship Award for his short-story collection *The Slightest Distance*. An Amherst grad, he was the son of a high-level CIA operative who, now retired, manned a kiosk in the Boston Museum of Fine Arts lobby, demonstrating the art of putting little ships in bottles.

I'd never met anyone with so exotic an upbringing, someone who had lived in such places as an Egyptian compound, where helicopters landed within its walls to whisk his father away on secret missions. He was so WASP-y, wore expensive-looking sport coats ever so casually, wrote with such a delicate sensibility.

I didn't know then that I'd know Henry all his life, that we'd work together on TV shows, that he'd go on to run *Homicide* and *Homeland*, to write and direct movies, to write more excellent, literate books, or that we'd find ourselves one afternoon in 1991 in my office at the CBS show *Northern Exposure* where we worked, Henry lounging languidly on the sofa, the sleeves of his blue oxford shirt rolled up just so on his perfectly shaped forearms, and he'd say, "Robin, what's to stop us from fucking right here on this couch right now?"

"Ha!" I said. "Everything!"

And we both laughed and let the moment pass. It came up once again twenty-one years later, in February 2013 at a party at the house in Santa Monica where he lived with his third wife, Sarah, and their infant son. I'd flown from New York to LA to attend a WGA event at which Josh Brand and John Falsey, who had given me my start in television, were to be honored, and Henry was throwing a bash for the guys the night before.

"I guess I'm just a Mrs. Dalloway at heart," Henry said.

"I'm sorry," I said. "Mrs. Dalloway?" I knew it was a book by Virginia Woolf but couldn't remember anything else about it.

"She liked to throw parties," he said, shrugging. "C'mon, a bunch of us are in the library."

We went back to the elegant writer's lair he'd built in the garage and had drinks with Josh and John before joining everybody in the house. It was a great party, Henry's young wife padding around in bare feet, so many people we'd worked with over the years. I was saying good-bye to Henry and his old friend and fellow producer Ian Sanders at the door, and I guess I must have looked pretty good that night, or happy, or flirty, because Ian asked, apropos of something that had been said, "How about you two? Did you ever…"

Henry and I looked at each other, big smiles coming to our faces as we simultaneously remembered the moment in my office we'd let go by so many years before.

Henry died of a heart attack only a few weeks later, at the age of sixty-five. Ian died three years after that, at sixty-eight.

But for now, we were young, and Henry was my teacher—in a writing seminar as well the Proust course—and he seemed way out of my league, mostly consorting with lady poets with last names like Pendergrast and with a WASP-y element in the fiction workshop as well—Jane Smiley and her pals.

That morning in the student union, Henry and I looked up from our coffee to see the famed Argentine writer Luis Borges moving by, old, blind, being led by a small young Asian woman he had introduced at a seminar the day before as his translator. Henry gave me a look that said he was wondering the same thing I was wondering, about what was really going on between her and the great man. Now, however, she was simply carrying a tray with his breakfast and they sat and she opened his small box of Kellogg's Corn Flakes and poured its contents into a bowl and we watched him carefully spoon the dry cereal into his mouth.

"Amazing," Henry said.

The day before, a small, worshipful group of us had gathered at Borges's feet to hear his answers to our questions.

"Tell us, Mr. Borges," a young male student finally worked up the courage to ask, "why is it that you only write short stories, not novels?"

As his pretty young translator spoke in his ear, Mr. Borges nodded thoughtfully, looking blindly into the air at God knows what, like Stevie Wonder.

"Becuss," he finally said in his soft Argentine voice, "the novel, it is too long."

It was moments such as these that defined Iowa, moments like Leonard Michaels's diatribe in class on *Catcher in the Rye*: "What kind of asshole," the edgy New York writer said, "hates a nun because she's carrying a crappy suitcase? What does that even mean?"

Talks by John Irving and Robert Coover and John Cheever— it seemed like every writer in America passed through Iowa City. You'd get to hear what they had to say and then drink with them in some bar or at a party at somebody's house.

I didn't write much, just enough to make Lenny Michaels

like me, just enough to complete the pages needed for an MFA. Maybe I was dissolute after all. Though I was an early adopter in Iowa to the jogging craze that was gripping the country, running miles on the lunch break from my secretarial job—well, not running, exactly, more like trotting.

I ran, or trotted, in Iowa City's first 5K run in 1978. Nervous and excited at the starting gun, I began with the pack but very soon fell far behind. So far, in fact, that I finally lost sight of them minutes later, after we'd left town, and found myself trotting past cornfields (not corn for humans, mind you, there was no corn for humans growing around there). Now there wasn't a runner in sight, so I decided to head south toward the river where I'd at least know where I was, soon arriving back in the civilization of the Iowa City suburbs. A man was mowing his lawn.

"Excuse me," I yelled as I trotted by in the road, "but have you seen a bunch of runners?"

He shook his head. "Runners?" he said. "No."

I trotted on, cut through campus, and finally met up with the others as they headed en masse for the finish line, joining them somewhere in the middle of the pack.

I was thin as a whip then. It was June 1978; Mitch had graduated. I wanted to go back to California, to LA this time, as Kit had suggested. I probably harbored vague notions of finding work in the film industry, but it wasn't something I consciously admitted to myself or anyone else. We'd befriended a few other people who were going out west: a fellow workshop student, Michelle Huneven, who was returning home to Pasadena, and a couple she'd introduced us to who were to become lifelong friends, T. C. Boyle and his wife, Karen.

Michelle and I scoffed at Karen because she was a mere writer's wife, whereas we two were actual writers. Lost on us then was the fact that she held a master's in special ed and held a job with which she supported Tom the long years he worked toward his PhD in literature, all the while typing short stories on his Olympia portable at the small desk in their bedroom, the wall in front of which completely plastered with pink rejection slips.

Tom would publish ten acclaimed novels and more than a hundred short stories, win the PEN/Faulkner Award, and become a tenured professor at USC, but he didn't know that in 1978 as he headed there to take a teaching job. And Karen didn't know that her instinct for buying and selling the homes they lived in would take them from a tiny tract house in Tujunga to one with a pool in Woodland Hills and finally land them in a Prairie Frank Lloyd Wright house, which they meticulously restored, in a butterfly preserve walking distance to town in Montecito.

Mitch and I didn't know what would happen to us either.

"Should I go to California or do you think I should stay here?" Mitch asked me one afternoon when we'd stopped on a street corner in Iowa City, heading back to our apartment from the bookstore.

I didn't know what to say and I said so. "That's something you have to answer for yourself," I said, but I was and remained plagued by the question. Was this the price I paid for getting involved with someone who had been my student, someone younger? Would I be responsible for his fate and future if he came with me?

Should I have told him to stay if there was any doubt in his mind? If he had stayed, would he have become the great fiction writer he'd shown signs of being? Like Dubus or Faulkner or O'Connor or any of them, was home soil more likely to bear literary fruit?

I remembered watching Mitch once when he didn't know I was looking. He was sitting in the window of a bar in town, by himself with a beer, reading a paperback. That would have been his life if he had stayed here, a lone wolf in a weird gray coat, drinking and, maybe, writing.

His father was a drinker, and a mean drunk, the way Mitch described it. I'd first met the family when Mitch took me home for Thanksgiving dinner. We'd gone up to Cedar Rapids the night before, and, having been told Lloyd Burgess liked a drink, I'd brought him the gift of a bottle of scotch.

"Bad idea," Mitch said.

"Why?" I asked. "That way we'll have something to drink before dinner tomorrow."

When we came back the next day, I saw what Mitch meant. The bottle was empty. His father had drunk the whole thing in the night.

The family lived in a tract of small homes built after the war— World War II, of course. The little yellow, white-trimmed house, with its one bathroom and three tiny bedrooms, seemed small for the nine people who had lived there before the oldest three girls had gone off on their own, then Mitch, then his younger brother Bradley. Bryan and Becky still lived at home and were there, along with Bradley, for Thanksgiving dinner, which we ate in the kitchen, as there was no dining room.

Mitch had shown me the room he'd made for himself in the cellar of the house behind the area that housed the boiler and the washer and dryer.

"Let Jeff Melvoin or Matt Weiner start off in the cellar and see how far they got," Mitch would later say more than once of our TV colleagues whose fathers had gone to Harvard or who had been physicians and raised their boys in posh neighborhoods and paid for their college tuition.

Mitch's father was a welder at a crane manufacturing plant,

now defunct, like all such manufacturing in Cedar Rapids. He worked the night shift, a good thing, Mitch said, because the kids didn't have to run into him much.

In my house growing up, my brother and I would jump up and down with glee and say, "Daddy's home! Daddy's home!" when we heard his car pull into the driveway after work, but at Mitch's house, the kids would say, "Daddy's home!" and run out the back door in pure dread as he came in the front.

I liked Mitch's father. He was a handsome man of Welsh descent, trim and of medium height, with flashing blue eyes and sharp features—unlike Mitch, fleshy-faced and tall, who more resembled his mother, née Virginia Colbert, whose ancestors had come from Alsace-Lorraine to be farmers in Iowa.

Mitch's father was from Birmingham, Alabama. His mother had died of appendicitis when he was a baby, and his father, also a drinking man, had placed Lloyd and his sister with his own sister, who was married to Jimmy Morgan, the mayor of Birmingham, where he was unhappy and unloved and a behavioral problem. He joined the Marines when he was underage and spent the next seven years fighting in the Pacific. He met Mitch's mother at a canteen in Washington, DC, where she'd gone to help serve the war effort as a secretary and also to see the big world, have some fun, and, as it developed, find a husband. "Ginge" was the promise of home to Lloyd and he returned with her to Iowa City and her big family.

Lloyd was smart and quick—everyone at the table was, all of them book and newspaper readers, people with opinions who didn't mind sharing them. It was a challenge to keep up with them in conversation. Still, years ago, at this same kitchen table with many of these same people, Mitch had put his cigarette out in his mashed potatoes, his mother had asked him please not to do that again, Mitch had told her, "If you don't like it, don't look at it," and the next thing he knew, his father had taken a fork and stabbed Mitch's hand clear through, pinning his hand to the table.

However, it was also this same father Mitch had so beautifully and therefore lovingly described at the beginning of a novel he was starting, his father coming home from work at the factory, sitting at the kitchen table, and, with a paring knife, paring the black grime out from beneath his fingernails, the black crescent moons falling into the ashtray below. He never wrote the novel. Instead, we bought his brother Bryan's two-door, blue-and-white 1971 Chevy Impala with a modified steering wheel a foot in diameter and packed it up and drove it west on Route 80, over the Continental Divide and down through a moonscape of California desert into the smoggy sprawl of Los Angeles. We had nothing but each other, the thirteen hundred dollars we'd saved, and a two-hundred-dollar car.

❖

Chapter Thirteen

Ronnie

Our first few nights in LA, we stayed with one of Mitch's older sisters who was house-sitting a lovely apartment at the edge of Hancock Park, a place with Mies van der Rohe chairs and a mauve velvet couch. The first thing she asked was what kind of car we were driving and when she saw the Chevy, she just shook her head. It was clear she thought we'd be losers here.

We drove around looking for apartments to rent and quickly found a one-bedroom on West Knoll in West Hollywood—a home run away from Beverly Hills, as Mitch would come to say— one of six units in a white stucco, terra-cotta-tile-roofed Spanish Colonial Revival building set in palm trees, our own little sitting porch crawling with magenta bougainvillea. Inside, we sanded and varnished the blond-wood floors and made couches and chairs from industrial pallets and foam cushions for which I bought fabric and sewed covers. We acquired a gray cat Mitch named Bob.

Our Iowa cohorts would come for Indian feasts and copious amounts of gin and tonic, and we'd sit on the cushions on the floor arranged around a door that served as a banquet table. In this kitchen, I'd lie down by the stove so I could see my parathas puffing up under the broiler. Or we'd go out to Tujunga or Pasadena and laugh and drink into the night with the music blaring.

We'd see John Falsey occasionally—he and I had been in the same writing seminar in Iowa one term and he'd become a basketball buddy of Mitch's. John had published a short story in the *New Yorker* that year, a rare feat in those days, that had attracted a Hollywood agent who'd found him TV-writing work on *The White Shadow*, a show about high-school basketball. John was raking it in. There was no furniture to speak of in his Westwood apartment, but he had a brand-new Alfa Romeo outside. There was a gas crisis that year and he laughed and said the best part of making money was he didn't even have to think about how much a gallon cost.

John would go on to partner up with Josh Brand, a fellow writer on *The White Shadow*, and together they would create *St. Elsewhere*, *A Year in the Life*, *Northern Exposure*, *I'll Fly Away*, and more. When we'd been in class in Iowa together, our avant-garde seminar leader Rosalyn Drexler didn't think much of John's short story, a delicate suburban tale of a family in Darien, Connecticut, an alcoholic mother. "*So conventional*," Rosalyn had sniffed. I'd passionately defended it, a good thing as it turned out, because in eight years, John would try me out on one of his and Josh's shows, the beginning of my twenty-five-year TV-writing career.

But for now, I was broke. Mitch and I were both broke. I'd wanted to start my life over and now I had, and, as with the first

179

time I'd started my life, that meant from scratch. The difference was that the first time, when I packed my suitcase and went to New York on my own, I knew my parents had my back, that if I got in trouble, they'd be there for me, that if all else failed, I could at least go home. Actually, my father had said as much.

"You realize you don't have to do this," he told me, "you can stay home and eat bonbons," implying, it seemed to me, that that was how he thought of my mother, as some useless beauty like Zsa Zsa Gabor who just lounged around all day eating chocolates. Once, when I complained to him about my mother's lack of purpose and engagement in the world, he said, "What you have to understand about your mother is that she is completely dependent on me." And yet that was how he—like all of the men in their circle—wanted his wife to be.

Now, however, going home was not an option. I was thirty-three years old, living with this rough young hick from Iowa who, on a visit east, wouldn't look them in the eye, they said, and they wondered why not. They didn't understand what I was doing in Los Angeles. They didn't understand what I was doing with Mitch. And I knew they probably sensed that I didn't understand entirely either.

Now there was no David Leach's father's money coming in or, for that matter, money from the GI Bill. People with money, even a little money, like ten thousand dollars in a bank somewhere that some grandmother had left them, or even five thousand, or three, don't realize what it is like to have absolutely no money. And no credit card because you have no credit. What if your car breaks down or gets towed? Now you simply have no car and no way to get around or get home.

That first December, we spent the night in Pasadena on a friend's couch after a Christmas party. They lived in a historic

California Craftsman courtyard bordering a ghetto. In the morning when we went to our car, we discovered that someone had helped himself to a Christmas present of the headlights and alternator of our Chevy Impala. The car looked blind, its eyes plucked out. It took all the money we had to fix it.

I probably say all this to try to ameliorate what comes next, which is what happened when my old best friend, Ronnie Barad from Providence, and her boyfriend Richie, from the Massachusetts state mental hospital, showed up in our lives in LA. Maybe I'm hoping that it might help explain why I acted the way I did. We all felt responsible when Ronnie killed herself, but of all us, I was the last one to see her alive.

Mitch and I were working out of a temp agency, which seemed like a way to make money and at the same time give us access to the inner workings of our new city and even, hopefully, a way inside Hollywood. Mitch was sent to work in the stockroom at A and M Records on La Brea. I was given a job in the office of an independent movie-production company on Sunset. I, who had been a writer of cover stories for *Rolling Stone,* who had flown around the country first class, who had hobnobbed backstage with Annie Leibovitz and Jerry Garcia, was now the lowest of the low, being instructed by some haughty little pipsqueak ten years younger than me to go out into the glaring noonday LA sun and pick up her lunch. I said sorry, not in my job description. She called the agency and I was gone.

The agency next placed me, chastened, in a job filing and typing and Xeroxing at a bank in Westwood, then at a law firm, then at a small public relations company in Century City, where Mitch soon joined me. It was at that PR firm one afternoon in November 1979 where Ronnie called me.

She was crying. She told me that she was in Los Angeles, that she and her boyfriend Richie had driven cross-country, that their van had broken down. They'd made it to a gas station and she had her father's credit card so the van would be fixed, but they had two big dogs and the motel wouldn't take them and she didn't know what to do. The gas station was on Franklin and Argyle Streets, under a freeway exit to Hollywood and Vine. I told her to hang on, that I'd be there as soon as I could.

I told my boss I had an emergency. She wasn't happy but she let me go. I told Mitch and then I left work, hurrying out of the building and down to the Santa Monica Boulevard bus stop. To save money on parking, Mitch and I took the bus to work; we were usually the only non-Hispanics on it. The bus stopped a block from West Knoll, and there I picked up the old Chevy with its tiny custom steering wheel and headed for Ronnie.

It had been a long time since I'd seen or spoken to Ronnie. I'd visited her at McLean when she was first there and in Boston proper, where she lived briefly, but there were long stretches when I was waitressing on Martha's Vineyard or being a secretary in New York or Chicago or someplace when I didn't see her at all. I'd heard she gone back to McLean and then to Mass Mental, where Richie was a fellow inpatient.

In musical therapy there, she and Richie and some others formed a band, Richie on bass, Ronnie singing and playing fiddle. They called themselves the M. T. Heads, a play on *musical therapy heads* and also *empty heads*. (Em Tee Heads—get it?) Under supervision, they were allowed off the ward to play gigs, driven in a hospital van that backed up to the venue, an old folks' home or sometimes an actual club, where they'd offload their equipment, set up and play, then be escorted back into the van and to the hospital again.

Ronnie had told me all this on the sunny June day when I did finally see her, at the flat she and Richie had rented in East Boston after their release from the psych ward. The flat was in a part of Boston I didn't know except to drive past on the way to Logan Airport, but this time I took the sharp right that led into the working-class neighborhood of two- and three-story tenements and housing projects, looking then in its pregentrification days as it had years before when it was a starting-off point for waves of immigrants—Russian Jews, Italians, and Irish, the early Kennedys among them. The ones who hadn't made it into the suburbs were left behind.

Ronnie buzzed me in and I climbed the rickety staircase to her top-floor flat.

"Hey, Rah-Bin!" she sang-shouted down into the stairwell in a throaty alto. And then there she was: Ronnie, not the dead-and-empty version I'd seen at McLean, but a beaming and excited Ronnie with her arms out in welcome. A dance-y, manic Ronnie. It occurred to me it made her nervous that I was here.

"This is my apartment," she said, indicating with a sweep of her arm a long, barren space, equipment for the new band they'd formed piled at one end near the bed/sofa I'd sleep on that night. Ronnie's artwork was on the walls, and by that I mean *on* the walls, pastel swirls and flowers and the vague faces of blond girls painted right on the basic tenement white.

"And that's Richie," she said of a man in a plaid shirt who sat at the front window looking out. A slope-shouldered, sad sack of a man with a receding hairline and dead-flat affect, Richie turned in slow motion and held up a hand.

"C'mon," she said and I followed her down a hallway to the back of the house. "This is the kitchen," she said when the room opened up. Which it was, an old kitchen with a white four-burner stove, a Formica table and chairs, and a door that led to a back porch from which you could see over the tops of the East End projects at Maverick Square clear to the Boston Harbor. Or you could have if there had been a porch. But you had to content yourself with merely getting a glimpse of the view through the window because, as the hand-painted sign on the door read (instead of DANGER, DO NOT OPEN!), PORCH ISN'T THERE.

"It's not?" I said, loving the words on the sign, knowing that only she could have written it.

Ronnie shrugged and smiled at me with her pale, too-close-together eyes. She knew she had me again. And I realized that maybe I was the one who'd been nervous, and, now that we were back in our old dynamic, I remembered why. I was always wary around Ronnie because I knew could see through me, was always on the lookout for phoniness or high-handedness, both of which I had plenty of. Of the two of us, she was the more righteous. More alive. And dominant.

When we were little, we had a game we played in her parents' living room in Providence. Ronnie would sit regally in one of the chintz-upholstered wing chairs, and I, and her little brother when he was old enough, would dance for her or sing a show tune and she would watch us, and then at some inevitable point—and we always knew this was coming but we always danced and sang for her anyway—she would press an imaginary button on the arm of the chair.

"Into the room of shit!" she would declare. And we imagined that the floor beneath us yawned open and dropped us into a shit-filled room below.

Ronnie always sat in the chair. We believed—and she believed it too—that she was the one true artist, the one who felt things most fully, good and bad. When she sang, she sang with such

Billie Holiday/Janis Joplin depth of sadness and beauty that people in the audience would be moved to tears, as my parents' friend Jane Sackett was the night she and her husband and my parents saw Ronnie and her band play in downtown Providence. Jane's hands were black-and-blue the next day from applauding.

"She defined for me what real music felt like, what real feeling felt like," her little brother, a Harvard-educated psychiatrist, later said. "She showed me heaven and hell and told me I would never have what it took to live in either, that I could only see it, live it through her. I was destined for the vat of shit."

"You look like Elvis Presley," Ronnie said to me then, in her kitchen in East Boston. It was Elvis's fat-cheeked, Vegas phase and she was right, I did, in a way. My flesh was juicy; I was bursting with health, especially compared to her. She seemed slighter than she had been, her skin and hair drier from all the years of hospitalized suffering and psychotropic drugs.

"Hey," she said, "let's go get a meatball sandwich."

"It's three o'clock in the afternoon!" I said.

"I love you, Robin," she said with a small note of pity. "Richie!" she called into the living room.

Richie got up and followed us obediently to a dark bar up the street for meatball sandwiches and Cokes. Richie didn't speak, just watched Ronnie with his mournful eyes, the way my dog watched me, alert for cues. Ronnie talked. She told about the M. T. Heads, about her job go-go-dancing at a bar in the Combat Zone where we'd go that night, about her and Richie's sometime work with a team of lawn-care specialists in the Boston suburbs.

"Tell her the joke you made up," Richie finally said.

"Okay. What did the dog with the harelip say to the other dog?" Ronnie asked me, and when I didn't know she told me. "Bark mulch?" she said.

I laughed and so did Richie, or he tried to. It was more like the sound of a car engine that can't quite turn over.

"*Je m'appelle* Hank!" Ronnie called out once when she, my father, and I were downhill-skiing on a day trip to Mount Sunapee.

"*Je m'appelle* Hank!" we all started declaring every time we passed one another on the slope. We "*Je m'appelle* Hank"-ed on the two-and-a-half-hour drive back to Providence and then at my house at dinner. My mother didn't understand why we thought it was funny, and it wasn't funny, it was stupid, but what is love if not stupid?

We all loved Ronnie, my brother, Ronnie Green, included, and when he was a nerdy sophomore at the University of Rhode Island, he invited her to homecoming weekend. She said she would go out with him only if he smoked cigarettes, so he took it up. At the dance, the Ronnie-who-was-my-brother drank too much, probably trying to keep up with Ronnie, and Al Shiffman, her old boyfriend who was still in love with her and who was also there, had his friend Louie Najarian waylay my brother and drive him out to a country road and dump him there, crying and puking. This was the year before my brother, Ronnie Green, who never smoked again, dedicated himself to the study of medicine and met the girl who would be his wife and still is fifty-some years later.

"Good, huh?" Ronnie said of the meatball sandwich. And it was delicious and I realize now that it is one of the very few things I can remember eating in all those long-ago years. Today, food is a major part of my life—my friends are chefs and food writers; I was even a restaurant critic myself for a while—but back then I didn't think or care much about it at all.

More than anything, food was a window into other cultures, as when David Leach took me to Zum Deutschen Eck in a German neighborhood in Chicago, where I had goose for the first time, with red cabbage in goose fat and boiled potatoes—and I've been searching for the crisp skin and juicy dark meat of that goose ever since. Or like my first time at a Middle Eastern restaurant eating pita bread with raw onion and baba ghanoush in Boston. Or like learning to mix bright spices to cook Indian food in Berkeley.

When I was at *Rolling Stone*, editor Charlie Perry took me out to dinner at the Poodle Dog, then San Francisco's oldest and fanciest French restaurant. I don't remember what we ate, I just remember a discordant feeling that going out to dinner in places like this was something my parents and their friends did, which I thought then was an obscene waste of money.

I do remember that in my little backyard cottage in Berkeley, the one I escaped to Iowa from, I picked the last green tomatoes from my garden—the ones that would never ripen—dredged them in a little beaten egg and flour, and fried them, and that was truly delicious. But before that, I remember no food—not on Tamalpais Road or in either converted-garage room.

But I remember that meatball sandwich in that dark bar with Ronnie Barad at three o'clock in the afternoon—too late for lunch and way too early for dinner—as one of the most satisfying meals I've ever eaten.

That night in Boston, we went to the bar in the Combat Zone where Ronnie go-go-danced. We watched her on a high platform, first in a blond wig and tiny aqua bikini dancing like a white girl, then becoming black in an afro wig and little silver bikini. She looked like two completely different people. The crowd loved her, just as the locals on the boardwalk at Scarborough Beach had when we were teenagers and she'd danced for them in her pink wool bathing suit.

When her sets were done and she had dressed and come to our table, it was clear that her mood had soured. "I want to go home," she said to Richie.

"What happened?" I said. She just shook her head.

"It's no good" was all she would say.

I saw her once more after that in the summer of 1977, when she and Richie came to the beach at Canochet, bringing with them from their neighborhood two stray children who had never had a day at the beach. Ronnie was skinny, strangely wizened from the drugs, and over-cheerful as she horsed around and mugged, manic. And now, in November two years later, I drove Mitch and my Impala into the gas station at Franklin and Argyle, and although I didn't know it, I was about to see her for the last time.

The van was parked in the gas station, the back doors open, its messy innards emitting the powerful scent of patchouli oil. Richie and Ronnie were across the street with two more strays she'd picked up, dogs this time. They approached across the busy thoroughfare and I got a look at her, and I had to put my sunglasses on so she wouldn't see the pain and sadness in my eyes at the sight of her.

Her complexion was sallow, her face a mask of tics, her jaw working, forehead creasing—what my brother would tell me later was tardive dyskinesia, uncontrollable facial movements resulting from all those years of Thorazine, Stelazine, Haldol, and other antipsychotic drugs that had been pumped into her. She and Richie both looked rough and haggard and, well, crazy.

I managed what I hoped was a welcoming smile, but I don't think it fooled her. In any case, she didn't smile or look at me as she told me the van would be fixed tomorrow and the man at the gas station had said it was okay for them to sleep in it tonight.

I said to at least come home with me and take a shower if they wanted, have dinner. They said they'd come but they couldn't stay long, they had to feed the dogs. They put the big mutts in the van and Richie got out a heavy rucksack and the two sat silent in the Impala on the drive back to West Knoll.

They disappeared into the bathroom with the rucksack and came out after a short time in a change of clothes, their hair wet from the shower. Ronnie sat on the couch and let out a sigh, looking more like herself. Richie sat close beside her. They told me about their trip cross-country, how her father had bought them the van, how they'd stayed with Ronnie's great-aunt Fanny in Providence, how she'd left some of her paintings with Fanny "for safekeeping."

Their plan was to visit people they knew along the way, see the country, and end up in Los Angeles to try to get into the music business. They'd spotted the Capitol Records tower from the freeway and taken the exit toward it when the van broke down, and they'd pushed it into the gas station.

And then, out of nowhere, Ronnie said, "We bought a gun in West Virginia." At which Richie started and gave Ronnie a stern look. My eyes found the rucksack.

"I can tell her," Ronnie told Richie. And then to me: "Because of the bears."

"Bears?" I said.

"In the campgrounds," she said, "where we stayed sometimes."

"Wow," I said. "Right." But all I could think was *I've got to get these two out of here*. Mitch would be home from work any minute. Would he see what I had when I first saw them at the gas station? Crazy desperadoes? Who were, as I now knew, armed.

"Hey, you know what?" I said brightly. "Why don't you take the car and go get some food and feed the dogs and whatever you need to do? Really. We don't need it. I can come get it tomorrow."

They looked at each other and Richie slowly nodded, and they did, they took the keys—and the rucksack—and drove away in the old Chevy. When Mitch got home, I told him what I'd done and he understood. We didn't hear from them at all the next day, but Ronnie called the day after that.

She said she was sorry about the car. She said it was in the parking lot of a grocery store on Fountain and La Brea. She said that while the van was being fixed, she and Richie had driven to the market to get some cereal and some food for the road and left the dogs in the car and that when they came out, they saw that the dogs had destroyed the Impala's front seat, completely tearing up the cushions.

"Oh, Ronnie," I said.

"I'm really sorry, I'm so sorry," she said. "Please forgive me."

And, to my everlasting regret, I didn't say, *Of course.* Or *I love you.* What I said was "What choice do I have?"

"I'm sorry," she said, and hung up.

Mitch and I got the car from the supermarket parking lot and drove to an auto shop, where we bought a fitted blue nylon cover for the front seat.

A week or so later, Ronnie's mother, Pearl, called to tell me that Ronnie was dead. That she and Richie had been camping in Leo Carrillo State Park and she had shot herself under the chin but survived and that Pearl and Frank had flown out but that Ronnie had died in the hospital. She said Richie had disappeared, they didn't know where he was, and no, there were no dogs. She wanted to know if I wanted the van. I didn't.

I was afraid for a long time that Richie would show up at our apartment in LA and kill me. I thought I deserved it. I worried that Mitch might get hurt. I wondered if Richie had been the one to shoot Ronnie. I decided that if he had, it would have been because she had asked him to.

Ronnie's younger brother, now a sixty-five-year-old man, says he thinks her whole trip across the country was a farewell tour, though he didn't know who else she had seen along the way besides Aunt Fanny. He also thinks the whole thing was his fault, that something he'd told her had set the trip in motion. He told me things I didn't know, how she had called him nearly every day for years and how every day he had to talk her out of killing herself, telling her that she could do it tomorrow. He said he tells people she had trained him for his profession as a psychiatrist.

What he had told her that he thinks set her off was that he was getting married in February of 1980, and it might have been the last straw, the thought that she was losing him.

My brother, also a psychiatrist, told me that mental pain is real pain, pain that can become unendurable. He thinks that Ronnie was in pain. He says that's why she killed herself. My brother also told me that months before she died, Ronnie had called him out of the blue, after years of silence. She said she wanted to tell him that she had discovered the secret of great sex: Artane! Which is one of the drugs given for the Parkinson's-type side effects caused by the antipsychotics.

He said that he remembers exactly where he was when he spoke to her: standing up against a counter with the telephone to the left of him in the kitchen of the first saltbox in Vermont he and Sue had built, the one in which we all celebrated his son's bar mitzvah. He said it shows how weird the call was, that he remembers it like the Kennedy assassination.

She stays with me too. I tell her story to every new friend. Is it a story to warn people that I won't be a good friend? Or is it that Ronnie, even from the grave, is making it impossible for me ever to have another best friend besides her? Everything reminds me of her, but that was true even before she died. When at Iowa I read Kafka's "Hunger Artist," I thought of Ronnie and how, like the Hunger Artist starving himself in a straw-filled cage, drawing an audience, she was the true artist, and we—her friends and family and everybody else—were her audience. And how, as with the Hunger Artist when the audience lost interest and moved on to other things, we all somehow abandoned her. And when the Hunger Artist was finally abandoned even by his handler, who had always forced him to eat at some crucial point, he was free now to starve as long as he wanted, withering to nothing in his cage, his hand only "a small bundle of knuckles" (even this reminded me of her, her small, dry hand in my warm and fleshy one when we were children), until the Hunger Artist all but disappeared into the straw, and, as he had become to his handler, she had become dead to us. And then she actually died.

I didn't mourn Ronnie then. I don't know if I have completely yet. At the time, however, I was about to learn that I had problems of my own. I was pregnant.

❖

Chapter Fourteen

Therapy

In the winter of 1983, I climbed off a man named Brian and into therapy. Brian was a philosophy professor at USC, refined, erudite, soft-spoken, whom a friend had introduced me to the day before.

"So, you're from England," I'd said when I met him.

"New Jersey, actually," he said with a dimpled, self-deprecating smile, "but I studied at Oxford. I must have picked up the accent."

Like Kit Carson (and Jerry Brown too, for that matter—what is it with these guys?), Brian had once studied to be a Jesuit priest, and his monkish apartment in Westwood reflected it—polished wood floors, Persian carpets, desk, books, reading chair. We were in his sparsely furnished bedroom and I was astride him on the bed, going through the motions.

"You're not at all engaged," he said in his English accent, looking up at me. I admitted I wasn't and climbed off. He told me,

193

in a kind way, that I really should see a shrink, and when I said I couldn't afford it, he told me about a place that trained therapists and offered patients sliding-scale fees.

I'd been to a shrink a few times before. Once was at the clinic in college, where I told the doctor I was unhappy, and when he asked me what I thought he could do to help me, I had no idea and never went back. The next time was in Berkeley, a few months after David Leach and I returned from Mexico and I had smuggled back a hundred Valium, which you could buy there without a prescription, and I popped them like popcorn, loving the release from anxiety they brought.

I wasn't much of a druggie—diet pills in high school doled out by a quack above a five-and-dime in Warren, Rhode Island; Miltown in Manhattan (a mild tranquilizer) procured from a friend of David Leach's. Mescaline, LSD, and other hallucinogens were more than recreational, they were instructional, mind-expanding, showing you the colors that, as the song says, were really there. They facilitated conversations with God—well, only one, actually, and we had a good laugh, He and I, and, yes, He was a he.

Then came coke and it was everywhere and stayed that way. I loved the exclusivity of it, the clubby-ness and hipness of being invited to do a line. But not so much the drug, which seemed to make users edgy and mean and superior in their attitudes toward the square nonuser. Timothy Leary himself, on the pages of *Rolling Stone*, posited a future in which only the psychedelically evolved would be allowed aboard his spaceship to a safer planet when humans destroyed this one, and I remember thinking: *But then my brother won't be allowed on.* I wanted off.

I like to joke that I was lucky no one ever offered me heroin because I would have loved it. I loved downers, loved junkie music—the Cowboy Junkies, the singer formerly known as

Antony who sang with the Johnsons, Chet Baker. But the truth is, I was too straight for heroin, too square even to be around it. Lightweight that I was, ten milligrams of Valium was as far down and chill as I wanted to go.

The trouble was that when the hundred Valium ran out, the anxiety they relieved returned tenfold and with it an even more acute paranoia. I felt crazy. Not right in the head. I went to the outpatient clinic at Herrick Hospital and was assigned to a pudgy fledgling, a Freudian wannabe complete with tweed sport coat and goatee. He was mainly interested in how I masturbated, and when I demonstrated my hand position, he told me that the way I held two fingers of my right hand in my left fist indicated penis envy and the fact that I wanted to be a writer—the pen being a phallic symbol—did as well. He freaked out when, on the second visit, bored, I got out of my chair to check out his bookshelves.

"You can't do that!" he said. "Go back to your chair!"

I sat in the chair for a few minutes and then left, never to return.

Christine Maginn, studying for an advanced degree in psycho-analytic psychotherapy at the Wright Institute in Los Angeles, the place Brian recommended in 1983, was a different story, a soft, warm, poised, and pretty blonde I was to spend the next eleven years sitting across from twice a week, through her Wright train-ing, following her into a private practice in Glendale.

Mostly, I cried, spilling thirty-some years of unspilled tears and untold woes, and Christine watched and listened and nodded with complete patience and empathy, holding out the Kleenex box as I blubbered on week after week, year after year, explaining to me in time that it sounded like my mother—and my father too—were okay with me as long as I was cheerful and pleasant but that I'd been banished at any sign of upset so that I'd learned to keep it all in.

Well, now it was coming out, all those backed-up years of whining and whimpering and complaining. I don't know how Christine stood it, but she gave me a comfort I'd never known. She re-mothered me and I was grateful. It must be a feeling like this, I thought, when people say they love their mothers.

"I don't *do* shit," my mother had said on the phone one day after telling me about an incident with my father who was slowly withering away in their bed at home from prostate cancer that had spread to his bony skeleton, rendering him unable, finally, to make it to the bathroom. He had shat the bed and she had had to strip the sheets and then lift his diminished legs, hold them up in one hand by the ankles, as you would an infant, then, with the other hand, wipe his ass while my father, my handsome, immaculate, sweet father, even morphined to the gills as he was, wept in humiliation. It was the day my mother called in hospice.

She didn't do baby shit either, which was why she'd brought home a new immigrant from Cape Verde named Beatrice Gomez and paid her ten dollars a week to change my diapers, to keep me clean and neat, to get me ready for school each morning, brushing and braiding my hair into pigtails. I can still remember the sensation of running my fingertips over those tight, perfect braids, the Braille of love.

As therapy went on, I began to understand my mother, even to feel sympathy for her and appreciation for her struggles, et cetera, to realize on some level that she had done her best in raising me and to admit that I had come out mostly all right, things had eventually worked out for me. But even in that regard, even after my professional and financial and marital success and even after all those years of therapeutic re-mothering and counsel, I still resented her, still bristled when, as a very old lady in assisted living near my-brother-the-doctor in New Hampshire, she would for the thousandth time get all smug and say, "Look at my two kids, look how well you both did, better than anyone else's" (meaning anyone on the East Side of Providence), which would be followed by the inevitable self-congratulatory lip-smacking: "I must have done something right."

This is a woman who had told me when I set out from Providence again and again that only losers left town, but I had left anyway, and now, in LA with Mitch, broke and barely making ends meet and pregnant, I had proved her right.

The abortion was performed in an office building on Sunset on the border of West Hollywood and Beverly Hills that then housed a Hamburger Hamlet, where Dean Martin, who was said to live nearby, ate and drank at night. In the waiting room of the abortion clinic upstairs, a young woman wept softly into a balled-up tissue as the woman next to her, probably her mother, sat unmoved. I was called to a cubicle and asked if I had thought this through, if I was sure this something I wanted to do.

I was shown into a small operating room, where I changed into a hospital gown, and the procedure was explained to me as I was positioned on the table, feet in the stirrups, knees up and wide apart, and given anesthesia. I awoke in another room with other woozy girls, one of them, a different one, crying softly. I felt only a mild throbbing below, like period cramps. Three months later, I discovered I was pregnant again. Talk about being a loser.

I didn't want another abortion. I didn't feel I deserved it. Even though I had the same misgivings—that I was in no position to bring a child into this world, financially or psychologically—I decided I'd go through with the pregnancy. But what felt like my martyrdom ended a month later in an explosion of blood and tissue in the toilet of the bathroom on West Knoll.

The doctor who examined me at that same abortion clinic explained that the fetus was still inside me and there was a possibility the pregnancy was still viable. Still, I was cramping so violently that my only thought was to get rid of it. I was saved another abortion only because the fetus spontaneously aborted right there and then on the exam table.

Years later, Mitch and I landed a job rewriting a Showtime movie about abortion, which aired as *Critical Choices*, and in the course of our research we went to a demonstration in front of a downtown LA abortion clinic—placard-carrying Right to Lifers chanting and praying, red-faced with fury, met by a line of counter-protesting red-faced women, screaming and yelling back at them.

And I saw what I'd already thought, if inchoately—that they each had right on their side, that the issue was complicated, that the entities of church and state, kept so guardedly and rightly separate in our democracy, met squarely right there, or right here, I should say, in a woman's womb. I am and was pro-choice, but as a practical matter; women, myself included, were going to choose to have abortions anyway, always had, always would, no matter what their beliefs, so shouldn't they be able to have them legally and safely? Amen.

Mitch and I moved from West Knoll to a nice little side-by-side Spanish duplex with its own backyard a few blocks away on La Jolla. We worked full-time at the PR agency now. Mitch ran the computer department and I'd started writing press releases. Home and office computers were then in their infancy, and we were helping introduce MS-DOS to the world, floppy disks and all. Bill Gates was one of the agency's clients, his privately held company then worth a mere fifty million dollars.

I was good at writing press releases and it felt good to be writing again, even something like that. Someone at the LA Weekly, an underground rag, knew my byline from Rolling Stone and I wrote something for them and that felt good too.

Things at home were not so good. I'd started a conversation with myself: If I didn't want this man's baby, if I didn't have that kind of faith in him, in the relationship, what was I doing with him? Maybe it was myself I didn't have faith in. Maybe I had work to do. To become a person. A nonloser. A writer again. Maybe being with him was holding me back. I didn't want to sleep with him anymore. I started sleeping in the back bedroom and he soon left and this time I didn't stop him.

I got a job downtown, a respectable one editing a newsletter for the Music Center Foundation, a collection of filthy-rich donors who helped keep the Mark Taper Forum, Dorothy Chandler Pavilion, and the Ahmanson Theater afloat. I bought a used Chevy Vega and found a place in a cheesy fifties apartment building on Beachwood Canyon, far from Mitch and West Hollywood (but only blocks from the gas station on Franklin and Argyle where Ronnie and Richie had landed) to start my life over yet again.

Unlike David Leach, who never spoke a word of protest when I pulled away from him, Mitch pleaded with me not to. I did anyway. What followed was the year in which I climbed off Brian and into therapy. Also the year it became undeniable that the prostate cancer with which my father had been diagnosed the year before would kill him.

I would like to say that my father died peacefully and beautifully, like Count Rostov in War and Peace, his deathbed surrounded by family whose forgiveness he begged for having left them penniless, forgiveness they tearfully, gladly gave him. Or that he died suddenly in his sleep or in his car or anywhere and anything but the agonizing and protracted three years it took him to die after the initial diagnosis of cancer that had already spread outside the walls of the prostate gland and was making its way slowly and inexorably into his bones.

It was as if life were punishing him—and us—for the happiness he'd brought to the world, the way we'd all basked in the quality of his attention, laughed with him to the point of tears, enjoyed the cocktails he made, the jokes he told. I felt lucky to have a father who lit up whenever I walked into the room—or had until that day I'd flown from California to see him and bounded upstairs to find him sitting at the edge of his bed, a panicked skeleton on the phone who, instead of lighting up at the sight of me, scowled and waved me off with a bony arm, desperate to hear what his doctor was saying. As if anything the doctor could say would have made a difference.

The time before when I'd been back to see him, I was with my mother and we were taking him home from the hospital well into his illness and after he'd survived a heart attack. I was pushing his wheelchair and when the elevator doors opened, a young man there waiting gasped in fright at the sight of him, my once-beautiful, handsome father, and I hated that kid. But now I was seeing what he'd seen: death personified, a wild-eyed, soon-to-be corpse.

The day of the elevator incident, my mother and I had driven my father home, and by prearrangement, his friends Frank and Raymond were waiting at the back door of the house on Wayland Avenue. They helped my father out of the car, into the house, and up the few stairs to the living room (we'd sold the grand piano), past the couch where he'd sat for the past

three months, wearing away the chintz fabric, any tiny move-
ment bringing what he called a "niggling" pain in his upper
back, watching my mother go about her chores, up and down
the stairs.

"She never stops," he'd told me. "She never sits still." It
sounded like a complaint.

Now he stood between Frank and Raymond at the foot of the
stairs, needing to be taken up to bed. I watched as his friends,
one older, one younger, both still hale and strong, made a seat between them by clasping each other's wrists, the way you learn to
carry someone when you're a child and are astounded when you
find you can. They made a seat between them and my mother and
I helped my father to sit and the two men carried their friend upstairs, never to come down again.

My brother's small bedroom had long ago been made into a
kind of den/TV room and it was there that my mother served
my father breakfast, lunch, and dinner, always just so, with a full
place setting and cloth napkin the way he liked it. And then,
when he couldn't make it into the den for meals, she served him
in bed along with the many pills she administered in spoonsful of
ice cream. And there came a day when my brother drove down
from New Hampshire to see him and my father had pleaded,
"Please, help me out," his meaning clear, but my brother, who'd
taken the Hippocratic oath, could only say, "I love you, Pop."

There had been a crisis before this trip home, one night at
the hospital. In the morning they were to perform an orchiectomy, which meant the surgical removal of his testicles, in hopes
it would slow the cancer down, and either from the fear of losing
his balls or fear period, he'd had a heart attack. I told my boss
at the Music Center I had to go back to Providence and she said
she couldn't spare me. I went around her to her boss and he said

of course you should go and I went, a good thing, because I was summoned to a phone at the hospital by a doctor who needed to talk to someone besides my mother, who'd been unwilling to hear what he'd had to say.

I told him my-brother-the-doctor was coming, but I couldn't say exactly when he'd get there because there was a snowstorm and he was on the road, but the doctor said, "Look, someone has to sign a do-not-resuscitate right now because if we have to do CPR, the bones in his chest have been so compromised by cancer that they will crumble under the pressure, do you understand?" What I understood was the expression *I felt as if a ton of bricks had fallen on me*, hit as I was by the full force of realizing that my father was actually going to die.

He had been dying for me in increments for a long time, as when my mother called to tell me he had fainted in the bathroom when he'd gotten up in the night to pee and she'd heard a crash and found him wedged between the toilet and the wall. It was at the exam that followed that the cancer was found.

Even before that, there had been a moment of foreshadowing when I'd answered my parents' front door to find a colleague of my father who worked for Gibson Cards. The man looked shabby—suit shiny, dandruff on the lapels—and I remember thinking that this was what it looked like when a salesman got too old for a job that depended on customers being cheered when he stopped in to take an order.

"How are you today, Ira?" customers would say to my dapper father when he showed up.

"Much better now that I've seen you," he'd say.

I'd read *Death of a Salesman* and now I was living it. I hoped my father would get off the road before he started to look like the Gibson salesman.

And then there was a day when we were taking a brisk walk together down Blackstone Boulevard, my father and I.

"I'm having a sort of, I guess you'd call it, moral dilemma," he said. "I'd like to know what you think."

"Sure, Dad, what?" I said, though he'd never said anything even vaguely like this to me before.

"You know Herb Sackett is a customer of mine," he said. "He's a friend but he's also a buyer. I sell him a lot of greeting cards for his stores."

"Sure," I said, "I know."

"Well, his business has expanded," my father said. "His father left him one store, but he's got thirty-two now and, really, it would be nothing to him, but if he increased my order by, say, just five thousand dollars, it would really make a big difference to me."

I knew what he was asking me but I didn't know what to say. I felt a seismic shift, not just in our relationship but in my relationship to the world.

"So, what do you think?" he finally said as we walked. "Should I ask him?"

"Sure," I said. "Why not?"

I knew why not, of course, but the damage was already done. He'd broken my heart when he asked the question. It didn't make me love him any less, just differently. And I figured that Herb Sackett would probably take it the same way.

And then he died for real. I flew through the night after my brother called to say this really looked like it. I didn't make it in time. My brother told me how, that night, when my mother had tried to administer the spoonful of ice cream containing that hour's pill, he'd pleaded, "Please don't make me."

Those were his last words. Shortly after, he looked at my brother, pointed to his heart, and then he was gone. He died at quarter to twelve on July 12, 1984, fifteen minutes before my mother's sixty-seventh birthday. "No, it can't be!" she wailed, in complete denial even then. At dawn, my brother called Sugarman's, the funeral parlor on Hope Street that dealt with all the East Side Jewish dead. They sent a van and my mother hid in the basement while they carried my father out.

My brother drove me to the funeral parlor to say good-bye. They'd already worked on my father and placed him in a temporary casket (we'd pick out his permanent one, a plain pine box, later that day), the lid of which was closed. Someone opened it so I could see him, and it was my father, all right, a white shroud placed over what had become his tiny body. Gone now, though, was the mask of pain he'd worn the last times I'd seen him and, in its place, peaceful repose.

"He's really handsome, isn't he?" I said and the funeral worker agreed. I asked if I could touch him and was told I could. The flesh of his cheek felt like cold wax. I could see his spirit was gone and he was in no way there. I said a silent good-bye as they closed the casket, and my brother put his arm around me as we went outside to the car, and we were less than a minute away—he'd taken the left down Doyle Avenue hill—when I let out a single wail, a primal scream, I even then realized, overcome by a terrible feeling of loss I right then remembered feeling for the first time when I was four and my parents were going away to Cape Cod for the weekend with friends and I'd wailed like a banshee at the idea of being without them. There in the car with my brother, I stifled the scream and that was that—except for the sea of sadness and depression and mourning in which I would drown in the coming months.

* * *

The year of my father's death, my life as I had known it stopped. When I'd returned from the penultimate trip to see my father, I'd been fired from my job at the Music Center. For one thing, I'd drunk too much champagne at a donors' gala recently. "She has a foul mouth," the president of Exxon told my boss when he called to complain about me the next day, "and it gets worse the more she drinks." She'd forgiven that infraction, but my going over her head to her boss to get leave to see my father was too much. She called me into her office. "The time has come," she said, "for us to part company."

I was hurt. I was angry. I was insulted. Until the realization hit me: I'd been fired, so for the first time in my life, I could collect unemployment, six whole months of not having to work, six months in which I would do pretty much nothing but eat, sleep, and walk around the neighborhood.

It was on one of these walks that I saw someone pruning the bougainvillea in front of a small Spanish apartment house I'd admired and asked if there were any vacancies. It turned out there were only two apartments—the owners inhabited the entire top floor—but one of the apartments was for rent. I moved in.

It was a sunny place with blond-wood floors, a fireplace, and views out the back onto Beachwood Canyon with its beautiful homes and gardens. It was near the Hollywood sign and Lake Hollywood, a man-made reservoir, an oasis in the city that you could then walk all the way around. One day and for the first time in my life—this was just after I'd returned home from my father's funeral—I found a twenty-dollar bill and some loose change in a gutter, money that I knew was a gift from my dad, a sign that he was with me and would always be.

Still, I sank deeper and deeper into depression. I gained weight, but I have no recollection of eating anything except popcorn and the mango I'd devour after I walked around the lake. I began to watch the small TV my parents had bought me a few years before—the first one I'd ever owned. I'd had absolutely no interest in TV since leaving home for college, but now I watched anything and everything, including, one New Year's Eve, all twelve hours of *Shoah*, a French documentary composed of interviews with Holocaust survivors and visits to extermination camps.

My six months were coming to an end. I would have to find work. At nearly forty, I felt too old to waitress. I could be a salesgirl, I thought, at a downtown department store. I was mulling this over one afternoon while I was watching TV, an old black-and-white movie about a newspaper reporter who was a drunk and who sank all the way into the gutter. A fellow newspaperman found him there and helped him get sober and his old job back. In the movie's last scene, the fellow newsman was stopping by the deserted newsroom to pick something up and saw the reformed drunk reporter at his desk, editing copy.

"Jim," he said. "What are you doing here so late? It's almost midnight. Go home."

"I am home," Jim said. And with that, I burst into tears. It was time to look for writing work again.

Chapter Fifteen

The Bitch Is Back!

Dying when he did, my father missed everything. He missed all those times on the red carpet at the Emmys, the limos, the private jets, the first-class plane tickets when there were no private jets. He missed seeing me on TV accepting my and Mitch's own private writing Emmy with the whole world watching. He missed seeing my credit on the many shows I wrote and produced and then that Mitch and I wrote and produced, and he missed seeing the show we created ourselves, still running after all these years.

He would have loved my flying him out to LA for the Emmys as I did my niece and her husband, loved his lavish suite at the Peninsula for which HBO footed the bill, loved donning the tuxedo from his salad days at the downtown Providence Biltmore that would have fit him still to walk the red carpet, watch the witty, glitzy show from the best seats, and then afterward attend the exclusive parties, would have loved all the special treatment, the handlers who would whisk him through crowds to the head of the line.

He would have loved the TV people too, the other writers and producers. Oh, and the actors! James Gandolfini, Edie Falco, Michael Imperioli, Dominic Chianese...and Lorraine Bracco, are you kidding me? And that's just *The Sopranos*. He would have loved all of them as I did through the years. And they would have loved him.

He missed seeing me rich. He missed seeing me married. He missed seeing me happy.

Instead, he was buried on a ninety-five-degree July day in an all-but-treeless Jewish cemetery crowded with gravestones in Warwick just off the exit to the Theodore Francis Green Airport (no relation, of course—our family name had been Gerstle or some such Litvak thing before my grandfather changed it). At the gravesite, someone read a prayer, then in the distance someone played taps; a gun salute was fired; an American flag was lowered and expertly folded into a neat triangle that a man in a U.S. Army uniform brought forward and handed to my mother, seated at the graveside. Then my brother gave what was meant to be a humorous little speech that fell flat.

"You're no Ira Green," Jane Sackett told him afterward, "and you shouldn't try to be."

In the limo on the way home from the cemetery, my mother gave me the folded-up flag "to hug when you miss your father," she said. Then why wouldn't she want to keep it and hug it? Later she gave me his Tiffany key ring, "because it was something he touched every day," she said. I knew she didn't want the flag and she had her own key chain, but I did want them and do. The flag is downstairs in the office next to Mitch's father's folded-up Marine World War II veteran's flag. The key chain is in my pocketbook on the hall table.

Back at the house on Wayland Avenue on the one afternoon of

sitting shivah my mother would allow—she found the prescribed week of it "ridiculous"—my father's friend Raymond cornered me as I was coming out of the downstairs lavette and ushered me back into the tiny powder room, where he pressed on me a check for seven-thousand-some dollars, saying it was money he owed my father—a lie, of course—and that my mother should use it to pay for the funeral. He and everyone else knew my father had left no money but that his life insurance would pay off the mortgages to the house and his continuing monthly Social Security checks would provide enough for my mother to live on.

I went back to LA and lived out the rest of my California State–sponsored six months of mourning and ease until the afternoon I burst into tears watching the old movie about a newspaper reporter on TV in my pretty apartment overlooking Beachwood Canyon and realized it was time for me to look for real work— just as I had done when I telephoned Alan Rinzler at *Rolling Stone* so many years before. I put in a call to Harold Hayes.

Harold Hayes had been the editor of *Esquire* in the '60s and '70s, was there somewhere on my one visit to its offices when I'd only had eyes for *Rolling Stone*. I'd come to appreciate since that he'd practically invented New Journalism, publishing Norman Mailer, Gore Vidal, Jean Genet, and the like, and now he was right here in LA, helming *California* magazine. I'd heard he was hard to please and, setting out to please him, I did what I'd never done before: wrote a piece on spec as a kind of calling card.

My essay, called "Gandhi Goes to a Party," about a press event I'd gotten wind of, led off like this:

> *"Anybody with the money to hire a P.R. firm and throw a party thinks they can get editorial space in your paper," said a reporter. True, perhaps, but it had to be a party with some kind*

of draw, which this one certainly had: Join Yogesh Kothari Gandhi (great-grandnephew of the mahatma) the invitation said, and someone named John-Roger for an evening at Chasen's. And who—especially a member of the chronically hungry press—would turn down an invitation to Chasen's? Who wouldn't want to see Gandhi—any Gandhi—at the same party as Zsa Zsa, who was also expected?

And so it went for a thousand-some words as I skewered John-Roger, a New Age huckster raising money for his "upliftment" (sic) institute; his acolytes, including then famous-for-being-famous jet-setting Arianna Stassinopoulos and TV actress Leigh Taylor-Young ("Had John-Roger taught her to hyphenate her name?" I wryly wrote), observing also that Zsa Zsa didn't show but Jerry Brown did, archly refusing a newspaper photographer's request to pose with Gandhi and John-Roger, and I even took a shot at my schnorring fellow journalists: "The salmon's not bad," said one scribe, "but stay away from the enchiladas."

The bitch was back!

I sent the piece to one of the editors at *California* and the word came that it would be published as a "Westword" essay on the closing page of the magazine, a coveted spot. After that, I got a few little freelance assignments there, but I had never spoken to, much less met, Harold Hayes, so it was startling to me, fat and depressed on the couch in my sunny little apartment, my eyes still wet from the movie on TV, when I telephoned and his secretary immediately put him on the line.

I explained who I was and that I wanted a job at the magazine, any job.

"Well, sure," he said in his booming Southern accent. "I know who you are! C'mon in!"

* * *

I loved Harold Hayes—loved, worshipped, feared. Feared, because he was a tough, sharp-witted, no-bullshit kind of guy who ran *California* editorial as he had *Esquire's*, as a fierce competition among editors (all male, surprise, surprise) for ideas, space, dominance. I existed pretty much apart from the competition, though, putting together a monthly column Harold had created for me to suit my ironic bent, a California-ized version of the Dubious Achievement Awards he'd instituted at *Esquire*.

In time, I was trusted with other stuff too, enlisting budding playwright Robin Baitz, who would go on to be nominated for two Pulitzers but was then just nineteen years old, to write a back-page "Westword," commissioning another "Westword" from a cartoonist whose syndicated strip *Life in Hell*, running in the *LA Weekly*, I'd admired: Matt Groening, in his pre-*Simpsons*, pre-five-hundred-million-dollar-net-worth days. Matt came to the office and I liked him as much as I'd liked his work. His father had been a literary man in Portland and from him Matt knew who Harold Hayes was and spoke of him and to him with deference and respect—unlike a lot of writers and editors in LA who thought of Harold as an antiquated has-been.

He was no has-been. He was very much a still-is, and if writers and editors didn't like him, it was usually because his standards made him hard on them. Or maybe I just thought that because (1) he liked my writing, and (2) I almost always agreed with his opinion. For instance, the time the editorial group attended a private, pre-release screening of David Lynch's *Blue Velvet* at the Dino De Laurentiis offices in Beverly Hills, and Mr. De Laurentiis himself popped in to pay his respects to Harold Hayes. The senior editors at *California* wanted to put *Blue Velvet* on next month's cover. Harold didn't. He hated the movie and so did I. The beginning of the thing was, like, a metaphor, Lynch showing a beautiful suburban lawn, then zooming down and into what lay beneath the grassy surface—darkness and creepy bugs and whatnot. Get it? If you didn't, the movie then proceeded to show one human example after another of the bad stuff suggested by the metaphor—murder, drug and sexual abuse, and so on. After ninety minutes of this, it ended pretty much where it began. A little birdy appeared, only now you were onto him. Plus worn out from having to watch the whole thing.

That's what I had to say about it. Harold's argument was considerably more erudite, invoking ancient Greek standards of stasis as regards to art, its being the opposite of what art should be. But the editors held their ground; they thought the movie was a masterpiece. And as it turned out, they were right, at least according to the hip-oisie who embraced the movie, which was to become a huge cult favorite.

Maybe Harold *was* behind the times. The magazine's publisher, the crass little Gordon Gekko wannabe Alan Bennett, certainly thought so, or certainly thought that when, after two years, Harold's remake of *California*, though it had initially spiked circulation, wasn't seeing any further rise. Harold was fired; the publisher had decided he himself could do a better job of editing. Which meant I was now working for the little cretin.

Meantime, though, my life outside the magazine was stabilizing. Through a friend from Berkeley, I was introduced to a wild-haired young woman who had just been lured south to become the editor of the *LA Times* restaurant section. She gave me a chance to try out as her second-string restaurant reviewer and sent me to Lawry's, a much-beloved LA institution on La Cienega Boulevard.

The place was an easy target, a corporate roast-beef theme

park, complete with a gift shop full of Lawry's mugs and aprons and, of course, bottles of Lawry's special seasoning, dinner itself an overproduced rigmarole including a spinning salad—iceberg lettuce in a glass bowl set in ice that a hypercheerful waitress spun with one hand while pouring viscous pale orange liquid from a bottle held on high of, you guessed it, Lawry's Salad Dressing— and, finally, what I called the Steaming Theater of Meat. It resembled a silver casket on wheels as it lumbered toward you up the aisle, obscuring everything else when it arrived at your banquette, the solemn Hispanic in chef's whites, the medallion around his neck reading MEAT CARVER, flipping open the lid and tripping a light inside that illuminated more roast beef than you have ever seen, or wanted to see, tableside, two entire rib sections of steer propped vertically and sweating. On my short stay in London, I'd taken myself to Simpson's in the Strand, seen the dignified waiter lift a silver dome from a single roast of beef and carve my thin slice. I sensed what I learned was true, that Lawry's founder had heard about it and re-created what he'd seen in his imagination, the Hollywood-extravaganza version.

After the piece was published came a hue and cry, furious letters to the editor. Who was this annoying smart-ass? He or she should be ashamed of him- or herself. Fired.

Instead, I was hired and in the next few years I wrote fifty-some second-string restaurant reviews, my night job while I worked at *California*. It was great fun; I wrote and wrote, some of the best and funniest writing I'd done, and I could take everyone I knew out for dinner on expense account. But even all that paled in comparison to what happened as a result of those reviews: they reminded John Falsey, my friend from Iowa, of my existence, prompting him to call me at the magazine one day and ask if I'd be interested in writing a script for his new television show.

* * *

That first script was the beginning of a twenty-five-year career as a TV writer in which I rose from staff writer to story editor to co-producer and on up to executive producer on *The Sopranos* and finally co-creator with Mitch of my own show, *Blue Bloods*, now in its eighth year and in syndication around the world.

I bought a glass-walled, midcentury house in the Hollywood Hills above Sunset Strip with a killer view of the LA Basin and, on clear days, the distant Pacific all the way down to Catalina Island. I acquired an agent, a money manager, and my first new car, a Kalahari Beige Metallic four-door BMW, and also a jet-black half–German shepherd, half-Lab dog that Mitch named Al.

Mitch had come back into my life, if not to live in my house, then to be often in my bed, and I in his. We had started writing and producing TV as a team and began to live together again only when we moved to New York City to do a new HBO show just starting up, *The Sopranos.* We worked on that show for its first five and a half seasons and would have stayed to the end of the sixth season except that the show's creator, David Chase, fired me, ostensibly for "not understanding the show." He said Mitch could stay if wanted, which he didn't.

"The time has come for us to part company" was what David said in my office that final day, parroting exactly what I'd once recounted in *The Sopranos'* story room (where I was, for all but four months of my time there, the only girl at the table with David, Mitch, Terry Winter, Frank Renzulli at the beginning, and Matt Weiner at the end), telling them apropos of some story we were working on what my LA Music Center boss had said when she fired me years before. I remember at the time seeing David register the phrase as he watched me with what had become by then his customary hate-rays, for while we'd begun as friends when I'd worked for him my second year in TV, sometime during the run of *The Sopranos*, he started to regard me with a distaste previously reserved for his mother.

I'd never had my heart broken, not really, but it did when he came into our office at a time when he knew Mitch would be away on the set and fired me; it broke my heart, and I reacted like I imagine a spurned lover would react. I didn't want him to see my face, and I turned my back on him and stayed that way until he left.

I haven't talked to him since, though it was inevitable that I'd see him, as I did at James Gandolfini's funeral a few years later, from which we'd been barred somehow—could it have been David's doing; could he really have been so petty?—me and Mitch, from sitting in the front section with the actors and other writer/producers with whom we'd worked from 1998 to 2005, and we were also not on the list for the gathering afterward in a restaurant only a few blocks from our house.

I'm told he'd been at James Gandolfini's father's wake just after my dismissal, as I was, but if I saw him there, it didn't register in my brain, something my brother posited could have been the result of a self-protective psychological mechanism. I did actually see him once, and I saw him see me, on a Writers Guild picket line, and I like to think that he saw me turn my back on him once more.

Oddly, the first time I laid eyes on him was during another WGA strike in '88 in LA. We weren't supposed to take meetings during the strike (that's what they call it in Hollywood, "taking meetings"—or do they say that in other businesses as well?), but we did. We met at an Italian restaurant on Ventura Boulevard in Studio City near the studio where David had a development deal. He had a show that he was staffing that he'd co-created with Larry

Konner, a Hollywood writer now known as the father of Jenni Konner, co-runner of HBO's *Girls*.

My agent had sent me a few DVDs of shows that were interested in hiring me, but David Chase's *Almost Grown* was the one I liked. It starred Tim Daly and Eve Gordon, a divorced couple who still seemed to love each other and flashed back to moments in their past that were cued by practical music—meaning that it came over car radios or some such and not sound tracks. It was charming and funny and had heart.

I was already seated when I saw a sour-faced man come in and be directed back to the table. David remained unsmiling and dour as we made our way through introductions—he liked my writing, I loved his show—but within a half an hour we were laughing to the point of tears, sharing horror stories about our mothers and how they drove us crazy.

I was hired and given a nice office in a bungalow on the Universal lot, right across from Robert Redford's private bungalow. I saw Robert Redford one day slipping through his door. I had never seen such a magnificent head of hair on a man, except maybe on Jack Kennedy so many years before.

We didn't have computers in those days; we typed on Selectric electric typewriters with white delete ribbons and carbon paper for copies. I couldn't proceed with a page, though, unless the typing was clean, so I'd end up typing the same page a dozen times, maybe more, until I had a perfect page. I wrote three episodes of the fourteen-episode order, finishing the last one even though the show had been canceled because I liked writing it so much.

By that time, David and I had become friends. He was a different boss than John Falsey and his writing partner Josh Brand had been the previous year, my first year in the business. Josh had made clear that life and work were to be separate.

"I have a family," he'd announced. "I have friends."

But David Chase was different. He came into my office one day early on, dramatically threw himself on the black leather couch like a fainting Victorian lady, the back of his hand resting on his forehead, and declared, "I'm so depressed."

My heart melted and stayed that way for years.

David had a reputation in the industry. He argued with what he called the Universal suits, the ones who worked in the lot's Black Tower where the business offices were housed. "Fucking pigmies," he'd call them when he came back from a meeting. "*Network standards?*" I heard him yell, presumably into the telephone, through an office wall when we later worked in adjoining rooms at Lantana in Santa Monica, the writing offices of *Northern Exposure*. "You're nothing but censors, that's what you are! How do you live with yourselves? How to you sleep at night?"

I thought he was wonderful. I never imagined one day he'd feel the same way about me as he did about the suits. I saw his temper trained on me only once that *Almost Grown* year. We were headed to lunch or a meeting somewhere and we were in the parking garage on the way to his car and I asked him what his wife did.

He turned and snapped at me. "She raises our child," he said. It was almost a snarl.

He was devoted to his wife, whom he had loved since high school, and their daughter. He seemed so basically unhappy, though, that I was sure I could make him happier. One day, after the show had been canceled and I was writing something else, I invited him to take a walk around Lake Hollywood with me. I had vague notions of seducing him somehow. But about halfway around the lake, he began to piss and moan about his aching back and I realized that this man was a full-time job. He was better off with his high-school sweetheart.

If he had any of that kind of feeling for me, I saw it just once. We'd all been drinking champagne to celebrate something or other in the loft that held *The Sopranos* offices at Silvercup Studios in Queens, a big, dramatic space, one side of which was a wall of windows looking out onto the East River and the Queensboro Bridge, beautiful in the daytime, even more so lit splendidly at night. We toasted and drank and then filed outside to wait for Teamster vans to drive us home.

We were out on the sidewalk, just Mitch, David, and the line producer, Ilene Landress. David, a little high on bubbly, walked into me, cockeyed. I don't know how else to describe it. I was just standing there and he walked into me, into my body, and then seemed to come to himself and backed off. It was just a moment. Maybe half a moment. But it happened. Mitch saw it too, so I wasn't imagining things.

We had had times, especially that first year on *Almost Grown*, when we talked and talked. I shared my bungalow with another writer, but it was just David and me one day, sitting on the couch in the bungalow's common room. He was going on about his mother, who had just been out from New Jersey for a visit, the outrageous stuff she said, how she belittled him, how small and angry and at the same time guilty she made him feel.

He was early–Woody Allen–movie funny, so droll and neurotic. I told him *that's* what he should write about, about his mother, their relationship, because here he was, this powerful man, to me, anyway, my boss, taking on studio suits and the network, and yet his mother could reduce him to, in his own words, a gibbering little gerbil.

He'd told me once, in the years before he began to hate me, that he remembered that conversation and that it had planted a seed, though in interviews with him I read later, he said it was his wife who had told him to write about his mother—and I'm sure she had.

There was much more involved, of course, in the genesis of *The Sopranos*. David had been nearing the end of a development deal with the Brillstein-Grey Company and nothing he'd written had made it, though he'd let me read his scripts, one a wonderful half-hour single-camera comedy about a superhero called Ultimo who was depressed and angry at the stupidity of mankind and who was always being sued for the collateral damage he'd caused to property and persons in the course of saving the world. Ultimo was David himself, of course, in tights and a cape and it was, like him, hilarious.

Lloyd Braun, who was a principle at B-G, told David one day that he knew he had a great TV show in him. Was there anything else gathering dust in his drawer? David thought about the pile of unmade movie scripts at home. He told Lloyd he had a treatment for an offbeat Mob movie he hadn't been able to sell. He said he'd see if there was something there for a TV show.

❖

Chapter Sixteen

Television 101

The new TV show that John Falsey had called me to try out for in 1986 was *A Year in the Life,* which he'd created with Joshua Brand, a former New York playwright he'd met working on *The White Shadow* and partnered with to create the Emmy-winning medical drama *St. Elsewhere. A Year in the Life* had begun as a miniseries starring Richard Kiley (*Man of La Mancha*), Eva Marie Saint (who starred opposite Marlon Brando in *On the Waterfront*), and talented newcomers Sarah Jessica Parker and Adam Arkin (son of Alan), among other actors, and it beat out the classy miniseries *Winds of War,* a World War II saga starring Robert Mitchum and Ali McGraw, for the Emmy in its category that year—that's how good it was.

NBC subsequently ordered a twenty-two-episode series that was to be, like *Hill Street Blues* and a few other shows that preceded it, a new kind of TV, what came to be known as quality TV, this one a subtle and realistic drama about what happens when the wife and mother of an upper-middle-class Seattle family dies in a car wreck. Well, good-bye, Eva Marie Saint, but there was still plenty to be excited about as I drove my sputtering Chevy Vega over the 101 to the Lankershim exit, then to the gatehouse at Universal Studios, where I'd been told the guard would have my name.

He checked my ID against a list, gave me a map, pointed out where to park, then lifted the gate, and in I went, onto the studio lot, vast and hushed paved acres that seemed as magical in the LA glare as it did later in *La La Land*—soundstages in giant hangars, electric carts whizzing around importantly.

Josh and John were housed in a swank suite in a swank, low-slung, landscaped office building in a shady part of the lot near the guard gate. Their pretty blond secretary showed me into Josh's office, where John introduced me to Josh, an avuncular young man, a first-generation Russian-American Queens Jew to Falsey's Darien, Connecticut, pretty-boy WASP (actually Catholic but passing for WASP), who said he'd really liked the restaurant review John had shown him, the lede of which said that the first thing you noticed about Prezzo on Ventura Boulevard in Sherman Oaks was that you couldn't find it.

"That's exactly what happened to me!" he said, as if it were the most remarkable thing in the world.

But the room turned serious and that was pretty much it for chitchat as they got down to the business of laying out the episode that I was going to write for which they'd already worked out the stories—an A story (twelve scenes, or "beats"), a B story (eight beats), and a C (four)—and melded them together into a four-act format, six scenes to an act.

John stood half in, half out of the sliding door to their sunny balcony, dragging on a cigarette and blowing the smoke out into the studio lot, and he and Josh ran through every scene, acting things out, throwing out dialogue, laughing, and relishing the whole thing while I frantically wrote everything down like a secretary taking dictation. It began to seem as if the work was being done for me. How hard could this be?

I'd been watching TV one day and seen a show in which one character calls to another, "Emergency! Emergency! Get the truck!" For the first time, it had occurred to me that someone had actually written those lines and I'd thought, *I could do that, I could write that. "Emergency! Emergency! Get the truck!"*

I had two weeks to write the script and I did. I sent it in and waited and fretted until word came a couple of days later—it stunk. John said, however, that I'd have another chance, that he knew from my short stories at Iowa that I could do this, that I should come in and they'd give me notes.

What they told me changed everything. What I'd written had no subtext, they said, it was all, as they called it, "on the nose." What they wanted was the tone I'd find in Updike's short stories; I should read "Here Come the Maples," among others, and take my cue from those. They'd take over the A story, they said, and I would rewrite the other two. I left with my tail between my legs.

I bought a collection of Updike's short stories at Book Soup on Sunset, read them, and spent the next weekend in my office at *California*, focusing as I had rarely focused before. I was desperate to succeed. I did what I had done in college when I aped Hemingway to write my first short story: I wrote the scenes as I felt Updike, an astute observer of suburban subtext, would have done.

In the B story I wrote, a young couple is looking for a nanny for their new baby. No one is good enough, for good reasons. Finally, a candidate appears who's educated, experienced—perfect.

The young father is delighted, but the new mother says the young woman seemed hostile. "Hostile?" the exasperated husband (Adam Arkin) says. "Did she *say* anything hostile? Did she *do* anything hostile?" The wife sticks to her guns but the husband realizes that she is having trouble relinquishing the care of their baby to someone else. His understanding and compassion loosens her resistance, and in the last scene we see the lovely nanny in place with their baby.

Okay, it wasn't Ibsen, but it wasn't "Emergency! Emergency! Get the truck!" either. It was subtext. And the word *hostile* itself was funny, reflecting psychobabblic jargon current to the times and funny, too, repeated so often. My education in TV had begun.

I messengered the rewritten half-script to Josh and John on Monday morning (no e-mail then) and the call came in a few hours: They loved it! I was hired! They needed me right away! When could I start?

On that same phone call, John asked me what I made at the magazine, and I told him, about forty thousand a year. I'd be making three times that, he said, and in only twenty weeks. That's got to feel pretty good, he said, and it did. But not as good as when *California* publisher/editor Alan Bennett came by my cubicle to congratulate me—begrudgingly, I thought—and asked what I'd be making. I told him and added, knowing it would gall him, that that the ironic thing was, I wasn't doing it for the money at all.

Which actually proved to be true. I loved this work so much I would have done it for free, though of course I never mentioned as much during negotiations for a new contract.

There would be a ten-week trial period on the show, after which John and Josh would decide whether to keep me on. I was directed to the building across from theirs, a squat, sixties-era motel-type structure that housed my office, which turned out to be a dark, dank room with shag carpet, a crappy old desk, and a ratty couch. I thought I had died and gone to heaven. An office with a couch? Actual walls and a door that shut? What more could a person want?

I left my few things there—purse, Updike book, half-script— and went down the dark inner hallway to introduce myself, as I'd been told to do, to the only other writer on the show. And there she was, Barbara Hall, a small blond woman in priestly clothes— black cardigan with a white chemise at the V-neck—sitting ramrod straight, her hands clasped before her on her own bare desk, a stern expression on her face.

My immediate response was fear. She looked severe, forbidding, reminding me of no one more than the mean-ass mother in the film of Steinbeck's *East of Eden*, whom we also come upon at her desk. But when I said hi, Barbara snapped to as if coming out of a trance and welcomed me in with a radiant smile.

We'd have lunch together every day after that, Barbara and I, and not in the commissary, with its cafeteria line, institutional tables, and trays, but in the real restaurant next door where Lew Wasserman and Sidney Sheinberg took their lunch, where Harrison Ford or Michael Douglas could be sitting in the next booth. That was Barbara's style.

I learned she was a Southern girl, born, raised, and schooled in Virginia, who had come out to LA after college to join her older sister, Karen, a writer on the sitcom *Newhart*. Whip-smart and drop-dead funny, Barbara was fifteen years my junior, but, as supervising producer, she was my boss. An actual female, a tough little number, seemingly fearless—though she admitted that it was partly fear I'd seen that first day, her first job on an hour drama (as opposed to a half-hour, three-camera comedy), and with the exalted title of supervising producer at that. I was no longer the only girl.

John and Josh called us the girls and we called them the boys. The boys worked out all the stories and we girls wrote a good many of them, rewriting freelance scripts when needed. We were expected on the set when our episodes were being filmed to keep watch over the tone in which our words were spoken, and we were allowed to sit in on the dailies in that pre-digital age when shows were filmed, edited, and spliced together manually with reel-to-reel equipment. Each day, the previous day's filming would be screened in an actual theater on the lot with Josh and John, us girls, the editor for that episode, and the line producer (also female) attending.

The first script I (half) wrote was also episode one of the series, directed by a prestigious Brit who did quality work for the BBC and PBS. We filed in and sat down to watch the first day's dailies, which were horrible. The scenes fell flat, and things that were supposed to be funny weren't. There was a terrible silence. John and Josh conferred, then left the screening room. I felt my career was over before it had even begun.

But I was wrong. The boys fired the Brit and talked their director friend and former colleague Thomas Carter into coming aboard. My stuff was suddenly good, smart, funny. They explained that British sensibility didn't seem to work with this material—the rhythm was wrong and Brits tended to throw jokes away. It became a guiding principle of mine in the years of hiring directors that followed: No Brits!

I wish I'd listened to myself years later when *the* Brit, Stephen Frears, showed interest in directing a pilot Mitch and I had written, a charming-if-I-do-say-so-myself hour called *Skip Tracer* about a low-level detective in Mar Vista, California. It was a solid script, got no notes from either the studio or the network—a rarity.

Having been nominated for an Oscar for *The Queen*, Frears was going to be in town anyway for the Academy Awards. He loved the script (though not so much the actor CBS had on contract and insisted we use), and who was going to say no to hiring an artist like Stephen Frears? Not, apparently, us.

The pilot was a disaster. We were at a wedding in Topanga Canyon the day it was tested in Las Vegas (testing is a brutal process in which Americans are lured away from the slots in Vegas or off the streets of Midtown Manhattan to watch and judge new TV shows, first with manual dials that record interest or lack thereof, then in discussion groups afterward), and we got a call from CBS that there would be no conference call about the test as previously scheduled. We never heard from them about the show again.

My second year, Barbara got a job on *Moonlighting*, starring Bruce Willis and Cybill Shepherd, and I went to David Chase's *Almost Grown* as an executive story editor with a beautiful office in a leafy part of the lot that was also on the tram route of the Universal Studios tour. I could hear the guides on their mics lowering their voices to hushed tones as they rode by. "We want to be quiet here because inside those bungalows are screenwriters busy at work and we don't want to disturb them."

David had his offices in the swank building where the boys had been, but his was a corner office downstairs overlooking the guard gate (where he and another producer were to witness just outside the office window the shooting and killing of a guard by a maniac stalking Mel Gibson). David didn't run his show the way Josh and John had theirs, where they worked out all the stories and the writer got teleplay-by credit only. Here, the writers were expected to be part of the story process, and it was here that I first experienced the congeniality of the story room, David telling Hollywood stories so hilarious your stomach ached from laughter, writer Andy Schneider one day somehow jumping from a complete standstill to land squarely atop David's desk—I forget in illustration of what.

It was glorious fun and I loved the characters and the actors and even the stuff I wrote and rewrote, loved blasting music in my bungalow—the Cowboy Junkies and the beautiful Irish folk songs of Mary Black on a CD David had given me as a present. But the fun was short-lived because only ten episodes of the thirteen ordered aired before the show was canceled in February due to low ratings opposite *The NBC Monday Night Movie* and *Monday Night Football*.

My education in television was only beginning. I was hired on a David Milch show for ABC, *Capital News*, about a DC newspaper, and experienced a new kind of show-runner, the archetype of the addictive personality for whom scripts were a last-minute emergency, unlike David and the boys, orderly sorts who were home every night by seven for dinner with their families.

Milch had a reputation as a wild man, a reformed heroin junkie turned gambling addict who pissed in the potted palm in his office and later pissed away his entire TV fortune at the track. Those who worked for him were as chattel. I'd shut the door to my office; he'd open it. I—and everyone else—would write scripts and he'd use them to rewrite, not writing per se but pacing with a rolled-up script in hand, improvising dialogue while his secretary dutifully typed every precious word. He'd still be rewriting on the set.

Network execs thought he was a genius, then and later, this despite *Capital News* being canceled after airing only three episodes, the first of other Milch shows to be canceled.

Immediately after *Capital News*, although I'd been in the business less than three years, CBS execs in their wisdom considered me ready to create my own show and paired me with Doug Cramer, a seasoned producer who had an idea for a show and who, with Aaron Spelling and other (to me) old-timers, was responsible for bringing such (to me) creaky shows as *Dynasty* and *The Love Boat* to what was then called the small screen. What did I have to do with shows like that?

My agent was Elliott Webb, another industry archetype memorialized in the *Doonesbury* cartoon as Sid Kibbitz (he was Gary Trudeau's agent too), "widely acknowledged as the first agent to use the car fax," according to press materials for a film version of the cartoon strip (though Barbara Hall's sister Karen, both of them his clients then, called him Agent Orange because of the peculiar hue of his hair). I knew pairing up with Cramer was a bad idea, but I let Elliott fast-talk me into it, another example (my first of many in TV) of the chicken-shittedness of not listening to that little voice inside me.

My experience so far had shown me that in TV, the writer was the boss—the boys, Chase, Milch—but here, in our offices far out in the broiling vastness of the San Fernando Valley near Six Flags Magic Mountain, I was anything but. I ran the writers' room, some distance from the production office and stages, where Doug Cramer ran everything else. My worst fears were soon realized, starting with the fate of Don Novello (who played the hip Father Guido Sarducci on *Saturday Night Live*) whom we'd cast as the lead and whose hair, I was horrified to discover on the first day of shooting, Cramer had had snipped off so that he now looked like someone else entirely, a discount-shoe sales-man at an Akron mall, maybe. When the network hated him in dailies, Cramer happily replaced him with Dom Irrera, a (to me) square and cheesy comedian.

All six episodes aired that summer with ratings that didn't en-courage a fall renewal. That was the bad, if expected, news. But the good news, what turned out to be very, very good news, was that another summer show had made it: *Northern Exposure*, cre-ated by the team of Falsey and Brand. I was hired on and it was where I spent the next five years.

Northern Exposure was a fish-out-of-water tale about a doctor from Brooklyn who'd gone to medical school on Alaska's dime with the promise that he'd work off the debt by practicing med-icine there. He'd been thinking Anchorage, but he was sent to a little town called Cicely in the middle of absolutely nowhere. As soon as I saw the moose stumbling into the town and down Main Street in the opening credits and heard the calypso-y music that played over, I fell in love with it.

I had a new used car by then, a wonderful little white two-door BMW 318i with the world's tightest turn ratio, and I didn't at all mind the commute from my new house in the hills of West Hollywood to the Lantana complex in Santa Monica where the writing and postproduction was done (the show was filmed near Seattle), forty-five minutes at rush hour but fourteen minutes at three o'clock in the morning, a drive I once made to pick up a script for what reason I can't quite remember.

At first it was just me and Henry Bromell and one or two freelancers, but for the second season, the boys changed their way of working. Now you were expected to meet with Josh and pitch him story ideas (John was busy launching another show, eventually taking Henry with him), and if and when the ideas were approved, you were to meet with fellow writers in the conference room downstairs to work out the beats of the A, B, and C stories, then marry them together into a script outline.

A couple weeks in, Josh asked my opinion about some writers they were thinking of hiring, Andy Schneider, whom I knew from *Almost Grown*, and his wife and writing partner, Diane Frolov, a former ballet dancer. I was familiar with their work—CBS had brought them onto my show with Cramer when its ratings began to flag—and told him what was true: they were good writers and very good with story, but they should watch out for a certain pat quality in their work.

The team was hired and things seemed to be going smoothly when one day I was called into the producers' suite and told that in generating stories and beating them out, I was not performing at a supervising-producer level (which, now that I had a created-by credit on my own show, had become my title). It was a horrible moment. I was told that I could leave the show or accept the lesser title of co-producer. I elected to stay, though a lesser title meant a reduction in pay of three thousand dollars an episode.

And I was glad I'd stayed on because the demotion had, for me, unexpected and momentous consequences. It was at this time that Mitch called me up—he had seen the show that summer and knew I was working there now and wanted to know about TV writing. We agreed to meet and I told him about the trouble I was having coming up with ideas. Maybe he could help me.

He was still working at the PR company in Century City and later recounted how he'd gone out into the plaza outside at lunch hour, sat at the edge of a tree planter, and focused with all his might, just as I'd done rewriting my first TV script years before.

He came up with two really good ideas, and I took them to Josh as my own, his and one I had come up with. Josh loved all three. I saw, or imagined that I saw, the hair on his arm beneath his shirt-sleeve stir with excited interest.

At least I had started, with Mitch's unheralded help, to redeem myself at work, and Mitch now began writing scripts with me. He proved to be great at dialogue. He was a natural. And it's so much better to work with someone than go it alone—the other person can be up when you're down, fluid when you're blocked.

It wasn't until years and years later, after I'd been fired from *The Sopranos*, after Andy and Diane had come on that show for the final season, rendering me and Mitch less necessary there in David's eyes, that I learned the truth about what had happened at *Northern Exposure* so many years before: Not long after they'd been hired, they complained about me to the producers, said they were carrying a disproportionate share of the work, that they should be bumped up from supervising to co-executive produc-ers because they wouldn't stay on with the same title as me. The producers, who now had two shows on the air and yet another in the works, didn't want to set a precedent for everybody and his brother to demand higher titles, with concomitant greater pay, and they had solved the problem by simply bumping me down.

That could be the end of a chapter on an education in television and its vicissitudes, but there is more to the *Northern Exposure* saga, at least, and Andy and Diane's part in it, because of what happened when David Chase came back into the picture.

We had done three great years of the show; it won all of us two Peabodys, two Golden Globes, and nominations for thirty-two Emmys, of which we won seven (one of them mine, shared, for Best Show, Drama). But most of it came to a screeching halt when Josh and John decided they would leave the show to pursue other projects and let other people take over. Andy and Diane were the logical candidates, but both the studio and network felt shaky about them because they had yet to executive-produce a show and *Northern Exposure* was prime property. Andy and Diane suggested that David Chase come on to help.

David was free now, having worked on one of Josh and John's other shows, *I'll Fly Away*, which, after a two-year run, hadn't been renewed. David had told me he hated *Northern Exposure*, that it pandered to its audience, "practically came out of the TV set to lick your face to make you like it," but when the studio and network called, with Andy and Diane's happy endorsement, he answered. It was to be his first million-dollar-plus yearly payday.

What Andy and Diane hadn't realized was that David's condition for being hired was that he be the boss—only one captain of a ship, et cetera. They were devastated. "We invited him into our tent," Andy said, "and he stole our camel." Still, they accepted the situation, and we all did some good work and won a few awards and had some fun—though the show's star, Rob Morrow, quit after a conflict with David, and without his character, the show devolved into something else not nearly as good, limping on with considerably less joy, at least for me and Mitch, for its remaining two years.

❖

Chapter Seventeen

Changing Television Forever

I finally confessed to Josh that I had given him Mitch's ideas as my own and that the two of us were writing together now, and Josh and John brought Mitch onto *Northern Exposure* as story editor. Now we were officially a team, an ampersand between our names, and we were sold as a team after that, sharing title and credit.

As a couple, though, we were wary. Mitch had had two relationships in the intervening years that I knew of, one with a fiery Italian and another with a pretty blonde I actually met at a party at Tom Boyle's new house in the Valley's Woodland Hills.

I wasn't jealous; I was glad for him. I wasn't having much luck myself. I had had a couple of really stupid relationships, one with a balding and emotionally withholding single father and the other with a day player on *Capital News* who had acted the role of a sadistic killer and who, while not an actual killer, was a few cans short of a six-pack, psychologically speaking.

I had been depressed in my beautiful glass house in the West

Hollywood Hills to the point that I couldn't stop crying and had suicidal thoughts, baby ones, like if I was going to do it, how would I? My therapist made an appointment for me with a psychiatrist and I drove to an address in Pasadena that I realized, once I'd parked, was a mental hospital. Somewhere in the middle of my interview with the admitting doctor, I began to feel a lot better—all better, in fact. I made a beeline for the door and drove home, never to return.

I did, however, take advantage of a prescription the man wrote for me for Prozac, which in time lifted my depression. I felt like my psyche had taken an elevator from a subbasement to the ground floor. *This is how normal people must feel*, I remember thinking.

Mitch wasn't doing all that much better. He had broken up with the pretty blonde—an issue with her difficult daughter from a previous relationship—and moved to a little house in Pacific Palisades where he chain-smoked, drank, ate large Jacopo's Pizzas by the delivery-boxful, and gained more than a hundred pounds.

Was it attrition that brought us back to each other? Exhaustion? Depression? We were battle-weary for sure. It had begun to occur to me that Mitch loved me. I remembered that it was Mitch who had driven miles through LA traffic to Beachwood Canyon to pay a condolence call in the months after my father died. And I remembered how David Leach, who had known and purportedly loved my father all those years ago in Providence, had been in LA, staying less than a mile away at Andrea's rock-star-manager brother's snazzy mansion/cocaine den in Hancock Park, and hadn't bothered to rouse himself to visit. I began to wonder about the exact nature of love and to ponder the wisdom of recognizing and accepting it when it showed itself.

We kept separate residences. Mitch found a house closer in and started shedding weight. We socialized, vacationed, sometimes slept together. But mostly we worked together, rewriting the Show-time movie about abortion, signing on to television shows—*American Gothic* and *Party of Five*. We also worked, briefly, with David Chase in an outbuilding of his house in Santa Monica Canyon on an idea for a show called *Beverly Hills Adjacent* about a ruined young lawyer starting up practice again in a Beverly Drive strip mall south of Pico. It was during that time that David's de-velopment deal with Brillstein-Grey was coming to an end, and, at Lloyd Braun's prompting, he had written a script that was being shopped around about a conflicted New Jersey Mob boss.

Mitch and I read various permutations of *The Sopranos* script, all terrific, one with no swearwords or nudity for the networks, another with both for cable. Fox and NBC declined. CBS too—Les Moonves didn't mind that the guy was a murderer, but did he have to take Prozac? In the end, Brad Grey convinced David they should circle back to an interested party, HBO.

At the time, HBO broadcast boxing on Saturday nights and had ventured slightly into original content with quirky shows like *Dream On* and the wonderfully sly *It's Garry Shandling's Show*, a send-up of late-night talk shows and TV egos. That year they were to air a fresh new half-hour called *Sex and the City*, but it wouldn't prove to have much of an audience—not yet, anyway. But com-pared to network TV, HBO was nowhere, an elephant graveyard, shuffling off to Buffalo, bye-bye big time.

Still, in David's discussions with HBO, their creative execu-tives were giving him all the right signals—he should film in New Jersey, spend what was needed, cast non-network types. (Imagine, for instance, if a network-star player like Anthony LaPaglia had been Tony Soprano instead of Gandolfini.) David signed on and by midsummer had directed, edited, and mixed the pilot. Late one night after Mitch and I had gone to bed, the phone rang and it was David, asking whether, were the show to be picked up to series, we'd want to write for it; we'd have to move to New York. It took us about a nanosecond to say yes.

But nothing happened. Not a word from HBO, zip. They had until the end of the year before the actors' contracts would expire. Meantime, David so loved the pilot he'd made that he arranged his own screening at Sony's studios, invited friends and colleagues, and had a catered Italian buffet set out in the lobby afterward. The show was wonderful—beautifully shot and acted. And, like the scripts, sharp and funny. But still, nothing from HBO.

David advised us to move on and we took a job at the popular Fox hour *Party of Five*. We tried, we really did, but we didn't have much feeling for the show, and the show-runners didn't have much feeling for us. It was not a happy few months. The day before we were all to head off on Christmas vacation, Mitch and I were in the bosses' office getting notes on a script when our assistant (no longer referred to as a secretary) poked her head in the door.

"I'm sorry to interrupt," she said, "but there's a Tommy Soprano on the phone for you." (Tommy was Soprano's original name, but when it didn't clear legal—meaning there was an actual Thomas Soprano in New Jersey—his name was changed to Tony.)

"You know somebody like that?" one of our bosses said, figuring just from the name it was some kind of gangster. We nodded and smiled, glancing at each other with the silent communication of twins, both realizing that this was David's way of telling us *The Sopranos* was going to series. We were saved!

"Tell Tommy we'll call back," we said, and our notes session resumed.

Party of Five let us go with no trouble—we had been a bad match there, so good riddance. We were heading, after all, into the then Nowheresville of cable TV. We were paid per episode, so that meant we'd be making about half the money we had on *Party of Five*, since that series, like most network shows, had an order of twenty-two, while *Sopranos* had only twelve. Our agent thought we were nuts, but we didn't care. We loved *The Sopranos* and it was—and remained, for a very long time—a labor of love. Especially in that first year.

While we were waiting for the editing bays in Oliver Stone's suite of offices down the street to be vacated, David, Mitch, and I met for long lunches at an Italian restaurant on the Third Street Promenade in Santa Monica, where David filled us in on his idea for the dramatic arc for the season involving Tony's conflict with his mother. Beyond that, he had four stories in mind—each show, while it served the overall arc, should be strong enough to stand on its own, he said, "like a little movie." But after those four, he said he had nada, that for all he knew, the whole thing could come crashing back to Earth like the Mir space station.

We ate pasta puttanesca, drank Chianti, laughed, and talked about Tony and Big Pussy and Uncle Junior and about both David and my familiarity with the Mob in our own hometowns. He filled us in about the writers he was hiring, Frank Renzulli in particular, a special case who, like the character Spider in *Goodfellas*, had served as a gofer for the boss of the Boston Mob at his Maverick Square social club/headquarters in East Boston. Frank was the real deal and a terrific writer too, but, David warned, he was also a compulsive talker, a mass of nerves and tics, and David didn't know how Frank would work in the collaborative setting of a story room.

Soon, the offices were ours and we met as a staff around a conference table—David, Mitch, Frank, Jason Cahill, James Manos Jr., Mark Saraceni, and me (once again the only female). And boy, did Frank talk. And David let him talk. And talk. For hours that day, until finally he'd talked himself out. And boy, he was worth it, providing so much of what someone later called "the authentic Italian marinara."

For instance, it was Frank who came up with one of the best ideas, an Emmy-winning idea, for that first season. We'd broken stories and created outlines for the first two episodes after the pilot when David came into work one morning and declared he was feeling claustrophobic and needed to get out of town—not David himself, but Tony. He'd had this idea that Tony should take his daughter, Meadow, on a college tour, already a wonderfully antithetic scenario for a hardened Mob boss, but he didn't know what to do with it. Something more than the delicious irony of a gangster driving around visiting ivy-covered campuses had to happen.

We all pondered for a stymied few minutes, until Frank piped up: Tony should come across a man he recognized as a Mob rat who was now in witness protection somewhere in remote New England. The idea was perfect: he had his daughter with him but still had to find time to kill the bastard. The back of the story for the fourth episode, "College," had been broken. David went immediately to the whiteboard, grabbed a Magic Marker, and wrote out the beats, scenes that just seemed to lay themselves out in a way that was almost automatic. Once David saw a story, he was a master.

In the morning, Mitch and I came back with beats for the B story, in which Tony's wife, Carmela, bedridden with the flu while Tony's off with Meadow, has an almost-dalliance with her priest and also learns from him that Tony's therapist is a woman.

The writers' assistant typed up the beats for both stories and then I cut those pages into strips, a strip for each beat, laid them on the table, and then, as if solving a puzzle, moved them around and married them to create a cohesive outline for the episode. (Unlike network TV, there was no four-act format with act breaks that were mini-cliffhangers to ensure viewers stayed through commercials. Here, it was one continuous fifty minutes or so with more of a movielike, three-act, no-break structure.)

Taking scissors to beat pages, rearranging them, and Scotch-taping them down was one of the things I loved most. Was it a craftsy/girly way of doing it? Maybe. After all, I'd learned it from a former ballet dancer. Whatever it was, I was good at it and it was deeply satisfying, much in the way that counting the words of all my *Rolling Stone* pieces had been.

James Manos, whom we called Macho Man behind his back, was to write the episode, though David ultimately shared writing credit because he rewrote so much of it. It seemed fitting when, more than a year later, at the Emmy Awards, Manos was outside smoking a cigarette when it was announced that he and David had won the Emmy for writing, and, since no one was allowed back into the auditorium while the show was on air, it was left to David alone to take the stage and accept the statue.

Finally, it was June 1998 and time to go to New York to start filming. Frank had stayed behind in LA with his wife and four children, but David and Mitch and I found sublets and moved east for the four-plus months it would take to shoot the series. Our writing offices were housed in a vast space in Silvercup, a converted bread factory in Queens across the East River from Manhattan. Downstairs and down the block were our stages and sets: the interior of the Soprano kitchen and dining room, an exact replica of those in the house in suburban New Jersey where David had shot the pilot, and also the Soprano Mob family social club and Artie Bucco's new restaurant (Tony having blown up his old one in the pilot).

The production spent half its time filming there and the other half on location in New Jersey. The trucks were loaded—wardrobe, electrical, makeup, props, the actors' three-bangers and two-bangers and Winnebagos—and Teamsters drove them over the Queensboro Bridge into Manhattan, through Manhattan, into the Lincoln or Holland Tunnel or over the George Washington Bridge, then onto the labyrinthine New Jersey highway systems to locations north, west, and south.

The day would last twelve or fourteen or fifteen hours and then it was time to load the trucks and go back again—highways, tunnels, bridges, and streets to Silvercup. The actors and other above-the-line personnel like David, Mitch, and me would make the trip in vans that would pick us up somewhere in Manhattan and drop of us back off late at night, sometimes well into the next day if shooting had started late enough, say at noon, the day before. We didn't shoot closer to home in New York because David rightly felt it would look inauthentic.

That summer, we filmed in the heat of New Jersey's marshy, mosquito-ridden suburbs, in a Trenton cemetery, and at the Bada Bing, the name on our signage for an actual strip club on Highway 17. Frank had originally called it the Final Lap, which, because it was the name of a strip club in Minnesota, didn't clear. In New York, when David learned it hadn't cleared, he called Frank in LA, and then and there Frank came up with a new name: the Bada Bing.

Before each episode, we had a table-read, all the actors reading their lines in the new script. "Look at us," Lorraine Bracco exclaimed in her lusty, growly voice at the first one. "Look at all these Italians!" And except for Nancy Marchand, Mitch, me, and Ilene Landress, the line producer, they all were, the rest of them, first-, second-, third-generation Italian.

Unlike network shows, which air while you're still writing and shooting, all our shows would be in the can by the time we went on the air in January, David working by phone with editors in LA, color-timing and mixing at Lantana once we'd finished in New York. Which meant that now we were working in a bubble—breaking stories, writing, casting, at tone meetings going over every line and scene with that episode's director to make sure we were all on the same page—with no idea how the show would be received. All of us—writers, producers, cast, and crew—were working for the sheer creative joy of it. That's what it felt like that first season.

Also unlike network shows, where getting script notes from executives at studios and networks has been likened to being pecked to death by ducks, there were no notes from HBO. Well, there was a note once, when Chris Albrecht, then head of programming creative, suggested David add a scene in "College" to further justify Tony's choking the witness-protection guy to death with his bare hands, since his having been a rat might not be seen as enough reason to kill him and could alienate Tony forever from his audience. The scene was added. But that was it for notes. And, also unlike the networks, there was no questioning of costs. HBO never said no.

Late one afternoon, when filming was done and the show was wrapping, Mitch and I were sitting around with David in his office.

"So, what do you think?" David asked. "You think this thing's got a chance?"

"I think," I said, "that it will either change television forever or sink like a stone."

David rolled his eyes. "Robin..." he said, trailing off with a world-weary shake of his head.

* * *

Looking back, I can see that the show might very well have sunk like a stone if, say, the Columbine massacre—in which twelve students and a teacher were shot to death by a couple of ass-hole seniors at a high school in Jefferson County, Colorado—had taken place the week before the show started airing instead of three months after. The audience most likely would have had no stomach for the violence of *The Sopranos*; people would probably have been repelled, unable to find any of it funny in the least. In that way, television is a crapshoot, dependent on the zeitgeist.

But there was no such pall over the premiere of *The Sopranos*. The screening was held on a cold January night in the basement theater of a record store on Times Square. After the show ended, Mitch and I went out to the lobby and watched as the audience filed out, and we could see from the expression on everyone's face that we had a hit. People were beaming. The energy was high. Even my highbrow friends were smiling ear to ear. We all headed into the night to the afterparty around the corner at John's Pizza.

The following year, we'd have our season premiere at the Ziegfeld Theater, the afterparty at a nearby Hilton. The next year we'd fill the Radio City Music Hall and the party afterward would take up all of Rockefeller Plaza, inside and out. After the very first episode aired, the show exploded. Scholars likened us to Balzac. HBO's ratings skyrocketed. We got nominated and won every award there was. And we did, just as I'd said we might, we ushered in a new golden age, changing television forever.

♣

Chapter Eighteen

Sellout Sunday

It was different the second year. For one thing, David became more tightly wound and more depressed at the same time. The full weight of *The Sopranos* rested on his narrow shoulders; it was great being the toast of the town, shit, the whole country, but now there were expectations and a lot of pressure on him to meet them. He was hard on himself, but he was just as hard on everybody else. If you were paying attention, you learned to be careful around him, as I had learned so many years before in the garage at Universal when I asked what his wife did and he turned on me.

That summer of the first season, when we were on lunch break on location in New Jersey, Tony Sirico, who played Paulie Walnuts on the show—he with the silver wings of hair—came and sat with me and Mitch. He told us about himself, how he'd been to "college," meaning prison (for extortion), how one of his brothers was a priest, the other a stockbroker, how he'd gotten into acting and it had saved him, and how lucky he felt to be on the show. He glanced over at David.

"Tell you one thing, though. I walked into the casting session and I seen him," Tony said, meaning David. "In the can, I seen a lot of tough guys and I seen a lot of 'em in my life, but the first time I seen David, lemme tell you, I took a step back."

Frank Renzulli was the sole writing holdover besides us from the first year. He still showed flashes of brilliance, though in time he began to phone it in, repeating dialogue and jokes, even writing on one draft that Mitch and I should do the Carmela scene, it'd come easier for us.

Still, Frank was enough in the show's good graces to plan a trip east with his family. The trouble started when David sent a Teamster van to pick them up at the airport and take them to their hotel, and Frank called David, apoplectic that it hadn't been a limo. Which pissed David off. Who did he think he was, the fucking *cavone* (Italian slang for an ill-mannered, lowlife Italian-American).

Things got worse when Frank paid a visit to the pork-store set in New Jersey, where we were filming an exterior scene (a storefront so realistic as a meat market that local cops stopped in for sandwiches when it first opened). The back room of it housed the practical set of the Mob family's onstage clubhouse, where they hung out, played cards and pool, counted money. Frank proceeded to boss the production assistants around, making demands: Where was his chair? Get him a Coke.

When word got back to David, he called Frank and gave him a bunch of shit. Frank gave him shit right back. David fumed around the office. Frank's TV writer friend Terry Winter, whom he'd helped get a job on *Sopranos* that year, called Frank and told him to back off.

"I explained to him that David was his boss," Terry told us. "I said, 'You want to keep your job, that's the ass you have to kiss.'"

At the office in Santa Monica where we first started, if Frank saw people sucking up to David, he razzed them, pursing his lips to make loud kissing sounds. No way was Frank going to kiss David's ass, which spelled the beginning of an eventual end to Frank's tenure.

When Frank finally did move on, however, hot from the success of *The Sopranos*, he landed a two-year, three-million-dollar deal with Reveille, a new production company. That kind of money was a revelation to me and Mitch, and when our current contract was up, and with HBO execs assuming a low take-it-or-leave-it stance in negotiations, as we would learn they always did, our agent went out with us and got an offer from NBC with Frank's kind of payday. We'd be going on a show called *Freaks and Geeks* with these young guys we'd never heard of, Apatow or something and Feig somebody.

We liked the show all right—it was sweet if not exactly groundbreaking—but our hearts were with *The Sopranos*. Elliott went after HBO to match NBC's money. HBO went to David. He told HBO to do it.

"But David has to come into your office and tell you in person he wants you to stay," Elliott said on the phone. "I'll let HBO know that it has to happen that way."

After a short while, David came in and asked us to stay. Looking back, I'm sure that grated on him. How could it not?

In the beginning at *Sopranos*, David had sought out my opinion—in the story room, at casting, and more. "He relies on you, it's obvious," Frank had told me. "He's always looking to see what you think."

"I'll make a geisha of you yet," David had joked more than once when I questioned him or disagreed.

As time went on, I began to sense that it was no joke, and by the third and fourth seasons, after 9/11 and even before, things were deteriorating in the story room to a point where David was assigning me and Mitch fewer scripts. I was being marginalized and he was looking more and more to Terry and then later to Matt Weiner when he came on in season five.

There had been overt stuff before that, such as on February 1, 2000, after a new contract had been settled. I know the date because we were celebrating Mitch's birthday at the posh then Biltmore, now Four Seasons, in Montecito, California, close to where Tom and Karen Boyle's Frank Lloyd Wright house sits.

We'd been shown to our hotel room, which was dark and dank, and I called the desk to ask if we could upgrade. The hotel was full but they found a vacancy and put us, at no extra charge, in the Ronald Reagan Presidential Suite, an absurdly huge and plush expanse on the second floor of the main building with a giant living room with a wet bar and a fireplace, a four-poster bed in the bedroom, plus a bath or two and a view over lush grounds to the Pacific.

We were in bed the next morning, the actual day of Mitch's birthday, when David called. You could hear in his tone he had smoke coming out of his ears. It wasn't the big money he was steaming about, it was Elliott's insistence to HBO that, since we were two people, we should receive two living allowances to what was most likely David's one, if he had a living allowance at all. He said our agent had made too good a deal before he hung up.

That beef, however, wasn't on the long-held list of grievances with which he confronted me in 2005 when he came into my office to fire me. Nor was his having to ask us in person to stay.

He'd never forgiven me, he said, for ruining the party at the Museum of Modern Art to celebrate the inclusion of *The Sopranos* in its film archive, five years before.

There had been the screening of an episode in the museum theater downstairs, then David and other panelists took the stage to talk about the show and answer questions from the audience.

It was a love-fest until a middle-aged man stood up and excoriated David for his stereotypically demeaning depiction of Italian-Americans as thugs, portrayals to which he and everyone else in the Italian-American Anti-Defamation League objected. That hadn't been the ruination of David's evening, however. What ruined everything for him that night, he said, was that at the cocktail party upstairs afterward, I interrupted a conversation he was having with one of the museum's conservators, and, after the man moved off, he said I'd disparaged Terry Winter. "You called him a *Flipper* writer," he said.

"I did?" I said. It was a long time ago. I didn't remember saying it. Maybe because of the gin and tonic—I remembered drinking that. "I'm sorry," I said, and I managed not to point out that Terry did write for *Flipper*, the 1990s remake of the 1960s show about a dolphin who solves crime, before coming to us.

Not on David's list that day was another incident I remembered—also alcohol-related—when, for the first time, I forgot to watch myself around David. The three of us were at a tony Upper East Side Italian restaurant. It was that first summer of *The Sopranos*, 1998, and David's wife hadn't yet come east and we often found ourselves somewhere at dinner together. We'd had some wine and I started in on David. I wanted him to reassure me that he'd hired me because he wanted me, not because Barbara Hall was tied up elsewhere.

Horrible and petty of me, I know, and add it to the list of

my faults, but I kept pressing until he blew, causing Isabella Rossellini, at the next table, to look at us askance. The following day at work, he said to me and Mitch, "If you're not happy here, leave now." Mitch said he didn't want to go. I told him how sorry I was. But the damage was done. I'd lost my cool with him and he became wary of me after that. And the warier he became, the more guarded I got.

That day when he fired me, he told me he'd been thinking about it for a long time, that the idea of firing me had kept him up at night, that he'd had many conversations with his wife about it. I told him I knew he'd been hating me lately. Larry Konner, who was briefly on the show, had even asked me how I could let him talk to me like that, meaning impatiently, derisively, contemptuously. I'd shrugged and told him it wasn't just me, David was that way with other women on the show—our casting director Georgianne Walken and Julie Ross, his assistant before Jason Mintner.

"This has nothing to do with your being a woman!" David yelled when I told him I'd said that, slapping the desk so hard I jumped. I sat back. Blinked. It occurred to me that David was afraid I'd sue.

At that point, Mitch came in, on lunch break from watching the set. He looked from me to David and back again.

"What's going on?" he said.

"David wants to fire me," I said. "He said you could stay."

Mitch took a seat next to me.

"The fact is, I haven't been happy with your work for a long time," David told Mitch.

"He says Terry and Matt get the show," I said, "and we don't."

David blew. "You have two of the funniest writers in the business sitting over there!" he said, meaning Terry and Matt's offices across the spacious former factory's floor. "Did you ever even think of going over and trying to learn something from them?"

Mitch and my eyes met. It was one of those twins' communications, as in, *Really?* It's not that we didn't think Terry and Matt were good writers, it was the insult of it all, with a good measure of *Then why did he ask us to stay and why did he have HBO pay us all this money when we renegotiated our contract every year or two? And if our work was the problem, why could Mitch stay on?*

David, an only child, saw this look between us. I could see him bristle, just as I knew he had when he'd learned we'd claimed two living allowances to his one all those years before.

Again, Mitch said he didn't want to go but would if I did. Mitch asked, though, for a chance to prove ourselves by writing another script, the one for which we'd all just broken the story and that we were in line to write. David reluctantly agreed. And added that I had to stop being such a negative presence around the office. I promised I would.

We went home and started writing, but midway through we realized that we were doomed, that no matter how good we might think our script was, David wouldn't, and it would serve as his excuse for getting rid of us. We kept at it, though, until we liked it enough to hand it in. The next day, while Mitch again was on the set, David came into my office, the script rolled tightly in his hand. He told me it didn't work at all, adding, "I'm afraid the time has come for us to part company."

I turned my back on him and he left. I called the set and Mitch came up. We'd already packed a box with our stuff. Mitch carried it through the office and we went home.

It was true that for a long time, I had been what David described as a "negative presence" in the office and in the story room.

As far back as the third season, when Mitch and I wrote the episode "Employee of the Month" that would, that fall, garner us our own Emmy for writing, I felt a schism. David's idea for the episode was that Dr. Melfi, Tony's therapist, would be raped and that Tony would exact revenge. I thought it would be more inter-esting if he never found out about the rape, so the show would be more about Melfi's moral struggle over whether to tell him or not, sure that if he knew, he'd probably kill the guy.

David said he thought it was a good idea. We wrote the script and it was shot scene for scene, except for Melfi's dream se-quence, which David, loving dream sequences, wrote in his own dream's image. But I could see when we screened it, he wasn't happy with the finished product—too dramatic? Turgid? Not funny enough? "Not my cup of tea" was all he said (a phrase I'd used when I'd read his unproduced movie scripts, a way to avoid saying I didn't think they were any good). He did tele-phone from New York to congratulate us after we won (it was the month after 9/11 and a lot of people didn't want to make the flight to LA for a celebration that had been postponed, and now that it was being held, nobody felt much like celebrating anymore).

But when we returned to New York, happily brandishing our Emmy at the office, all we got from him was a sour look from the loft space's communal couch and a reluctant nod.

But Mitch and I hung in and we did some really good work af-ter that—we all did. I fill with pride whenever I see a list of the twenty-three episodes on which Mitch and I have writing and/or story credit, pride in all seventy episodes, of the eighty-eight that were made, that we co-executive- and then executive-produced. I know my contribution the show, and each one brings back happy memories of the story room and casting, tone meetings and set, all of us creative and productive and, most of all, having the time of our lives.

But there remained an undeniable tension between me and David. As Mitch is fond of saying, "Nobody forgets where they bury the hatchet," and I felt a simmering resentment in him, as if he thought we were (or at least I was) too complacent in our jobs, behaved in too entitled a fashion when all we'd done was ride his coattails to our new wealth and comfort and success. Or maybe that was my projection. Or some of both.

I don't know what Frank-like hubris or misguided humor led me to bring back from a trip to Rome a souvenir for David that made a joke of everything: a little statue of Romulus and Remus suckling on a mama wolf. Maybe I figured that if what we knew David thought of us was owned, claimed, it would become a shared joke. Or maybe it was my way of saying go fuck yourself. Still, it was a gift from Mitch too, and Mitch doesn't have one passive-aggressive bone in his body. David seemed to see the humor in the figurine and put it on the window shelf next to his desk with other knickknacks and there it remained, where it may have served as a constant reminder of his gnawing disdain.

David, Mitch, and I shared writing credit for the finale of season four, though I'm sure David thought he wrote more than half of it himself. But I can say from years of experience, writing is the hard part; rewriting, not so much. It can come so easily, I had learned myself, that if you're not careful, you might start mistaking yourself for some kind of TV wizard.

In any case, I wasn't merely imagining that David resented our presence when we all took the stage to accept the writing Emmy for "Whitecaps." Mitch and I were standing behind him so he could be the one to receive the award, and he turned and held out the statue to me so he could retrieve the speech he'd written from the breast pocket of his tux, but then, as he saw me reach out to take the trophy, he must have thought better of it, for he snatched the Emmy away for, literally, all the world to see and ad-libbed his thank-you litany.

And then, in the fifth season, Matt Weiner arrived in the story room. He was fresh off a long stint on *Becker*, a network sitcom about a cranky physician, starring Ted Danson. The sitcom story room is a different animal than a drama's in that in sitcom, there's a constant and rapid-fire barrage of jokes and ideas from writers at the table, whereas in drama, in our story room, at least, there was a lot of silence and mulling; whole quiet minutes might go by. In fact, David might take to the couch, lying down and throwing his arm over his forehead as if in thought, though often, at some point, Terry, Mitch, and I would realize he'd fallen asleep.

I liked Matt but he didn't shut up; he rattled on, joked, brayed with laughter at his own jokes. Terry and David loved him. There was a lot of appreciative back-and-forth among the three, centering much of the time on *The Honeymooners* and Jackie Gleason—because who was Gandolfini's Tony Soprano but an Italian Ralph Kramden? To the moon, Alice! Or Homer Simpson? Doh! The writers' room was becoming a boys' club, a club Mitch by taste and temperament wasn't inclined to join. And me, girl or no, either.

In time, Matt settled down. Thought and focused exchange resumed. It was just the five of us with the occasional freelance writer coming in and going off with an outline. Then Terry went off to write. Mitch went to watch the set. And now there were three—Matt and David and me. Matt and David discovered in each other a love of cinema, particularly obscure French cinema. Their conversations were deep, arcane, and endless. Where was Frank and his kissy noises when I needed him?

In the fifth season the show became more Mob-centric—turf wars between New York and New Jersey, power plays, posturing, and wiseguy banter. As always, really good work was done, but the fabric of the original conceit of the conflicted Mob boss was wearing thin, in the room where the stories were woven, at least.

As the season was drawing to a close, David called an unprecedented Sunday meeting at the office—no Matt (it being a weekend, he was probably back in LA with his family), but me and Mitch and Terry Winter. David had also brought his wife, his trusted sounding board in all aspects of the show. David said he was exhausted. HBO was hounding him for eighteen more episodes but he didn't know if he had it in him. He wanted to know how we all felt. Could we go on? Terry Winter spoke up immediately—Absolutely! No question! Et cetera.

This would have been the moment for me and Mitch to bow out gracefully, to say that the office atmosphere (meaning David himself) had become increasingly toxic (Larry Konner's word for it) and intolerable to us, to confess that it had sent Mitch to the shrink for the first—and last—time in his life as well as contributed to giving me a mild case of shingles (though 9/11 may have played a part), and that we weren't really all that interested in the direction the show was taking.

Instead, we said of course we wanted to do a sixth season. And it's true that in spite of everything, we still loved the show and our part in it and felt the same responsibility to it as always. We were also thinking, of course, of our contract and the enormous amount of money we would forfeit if we said we didn't have it in us to go on, which would be tantamount to quitting. Because we didn't trust for a minute that David was really about to turn away what we'd heard were vast sums being offered him by HBO and end the show. So we said, Sure! You betcha! Et cetera. I think they call it selling out—on our part and possibly his too.

The Sunday meeting didn't end there. David said that if we went on he would need more help, that he wanted to bring on more writers. We went over some names, and then Mitch mentioned Andy and Diane. A show they ran had ended and they were looking for work. (It would be years before we learned how they had gone behind my back at *Northern Exposure*.)

"Great idea," David said, "they're good at story."

At the same time, it was as if a lightbulb appeared above David's head, a thought balloon next to it that said, *And then I can finally get rid of these two clowns*. Meaning me and, most likely, Mitch. Which, mid-sixth and last season, is what he did.

❖

Chapter Nineteen

My Little Life, Part 2

In October 2002, Mitch asked me to marry him. We were in Paris, at Taillevent, and we'd just finished lunch. He says that he got down on one knee beside our banquette. I have no such memory. I'd had a lot of wine and I remember only that I kept saying, "You're kidding," until he got exasperated and said, "Are you going to say yes or not?"

I don't know why I was surprised. We'd been living together for years, traveling together, working together. Even with all the tension at *Sopranos*, he'd stuck by me. Unlike my mother, who, when I told her I'd been fired, said, "Oh no! Why? What did you do?"

Not that Mitch wouldn't call me on my shit. He wondered why, for instance, when we were onstage taking questions on story process at a WGA symposium in Santa Monica way back when, I'd felt compelled to say that it was Renzulli's idea to have Tony see the rat on the college trip when I knew it would piss David off.

"Because it was true," I'd said weakly. Mitch just shook his head.

We had talked about getting married. It was after 9/11, and, in Manhattan anyway, there was a surge in marriage, that hideous calamity reminding us to hold closer what was dear. Mitch and I were in LA when the planes hit. We'd flown out from JFK the night before. The flight had been delayed for hours on the tarmac by heavy rain, the very storm whose passing had left the Manhattan sky so gorgeously blue the morning of 9/11, the city so sparkling clean.

At 5:45 that morning, Mitch and I were driving east to the Santa Anita racetrack on the Ventura Freeway when breaking news on the radio told us that a plane had hit a tower of the World Trade Center. The broadcaster didn't know much more than that and we imagined, as most people did at that point, that a small plane had gone off course.

We had come west for the Emmys early to research a script in which Tony Soprano bought a racehorse, and our stockbroker, who owned a few at Santa Anita, had offered to give us a tour. He showed us around the stables, the tack rooms, and the grooming stations, and we were watching the horses being exercised on the track when someone came out to tell us that a second plane had hit. There was a small TV in the office on which we watched repeating footage, the planes hitting the towers again and again, no one really able to fathom what was going on. Finally, someone's son who was in the military called his dad and said that everybody should get the hell home while they still could.

We were in LA for a week before we could fly back to New York. We'd left our two big rescue dogs at home and were lucky that our housekeeper, who was coming to stay with them that awful Tuesday morning, was able to get to our apartment, talking her way through police barriers set up to keep people away from downtown. From our returning plane's starboard window, we saw Lower Manhattan in the distance, the huge black crater, twisted steel where the World Trade Center had been, the two towers, the sight of which had so often welcomed us home in the wee hours after a long day's filming in New Jersey, gone.

We lived (and live) in Greenwich Village, about a mile away, but the stench reached us even there, an unholy smell of burning tires and something else less easily defined. It intensified when we went down to the site a few days later to pay our respects with a friend who had lost her best friend there, an odor that seemed to emanate from the thick, oily ash that covered everything. It was the smell of death.

I hadn't felt it was right to get married until everybody in the country, meaning my gay friends, could, but I went ahead and did it anyway. Mitch found someone on the internet licensed for the task who'd be available on a Sunday. Our only witness was a restaurateur whose place closed that day, and we were married in a room in a small office suite somewhere in the East Forties. There was a white parachute hung from the ceiling for atmosphere and a few lit votive candles around.

I said my vows and meant them—that was another thing I'd been waiting for, a time when I felt I was capable of making that kind of till-death-do-us-part promise. I'd heard or read or dreamed that love could be something that grew, but now I was living it. What had felt in 1976 like a crazy choice—the Lady and the Biker, as we were told the crew of one show we worked on referred to us—had morphed into something else entirely.

I enjoy telling people that I fell in love with Mitch again at the Richard Nixon Library and Birthplace in Yorba Linda, California, on the occasion of his forty-fifth birthday in 1997. Of the two of us, I'm the driver, and I told him I'd take him anywhere he wanted to go and that was the place he picked. We made the harrowing drive down the 405 from LA, bumper-to-bumper at sixty-five miles an hour, to Orange County, a scant forty miles away, but another planet. A Republican one.

We had lunch at a Chili's—salads as big as hubcaps and oily fajitas—and went to confront Nixon's legacy. Mitch had been a history major in college, an insatiable reader of newspapers, magazines, biographies, tomes about World War II. He'd been to the Herbert Hoover Library in Iowa, Truman's in Missouri, Harding's in Ohio, and now this.

Nixon's childhood home sat entire on the library grounds, a small, white two-story clapboard house with living room, kitchen, and parents' bedroom downstairs, upstairs a children's dorm. They were Quakers and the place looked it—no cushy couches for them, a wood bench facing a wood rocking chair before a fireplace. And on the white walls, nothing decorative, with one exception: a blue-and-white plate depicting the Great Wall that his aunt had brought home from a trip to China when Nixon was a child.

The sight of it led me to a recollection of Nixon's trip to the People's Republic of China in 1972. He'd been the first U.S. president to visit in twenty-five years and had been a proponent of warmer relations with China before that, and I'd written an article on it for *Rolling Stone* under the byline White House Staff. I was rocked when I saw that plate. Was that the reason behind his whole China thing? That one fanciful piece of art on the walls of his childhood home had spoken to his soul?

I began to think of him as human as we continued on to the main building, where we saw displays of gifts from foreign dignitaries, photos of Elvis shaking Nixon's hand, and an Elvis statue dressed in a replica of the clothes he'd worn for the visit. Finally, we came to a re-creation of the room so recently depicted in the Oliver Stone movie *Nixon*, where he'd crank up the air conditioner to freezing so even in warm weather he could sit by a fire and stew and curse on the phone and drink his bottomless glass of scotch.

No doubt it was because Stone's film had cast such a bad light on certain Nixonian items at the gift shop that, to be rid of them, those wares had been drastically reduced and set on a bargain table outside. For a dollar each, we bought two scotch glasses with *RMN* etched into the crystal and two pewter coasters similarly engraved, each surrounded with federal stars. Our scotch glasses have disappeared with time, but the coasters still sit on our bedside tables, for coffee in the morning and water at night.

I realized that day that with Mitch I would do things I wouldn't ordinarily do and go places I didn't even know I wanted to go. Since then, we have been to the libraries and birthplaces of Woodrow Wilson, Lyndon Johnson, Thomas Jefferson, George Washington, and James Monroe. We have also visited several Civil War battlegrounds, the Crater in Virginia the most vivid and horrible and interesting. And, of course, Gettysburg, where we spent the weekend after we'd been fired from *The Sopranos*, Mitch's thought being that it would be good for us to consider grief so much greater than our own.

And then there was the sex. Toe-curling, lubricious, ecstatic sex, the kind Germaine Greer had written about all those many years ago and that I'd wanted so much for myself, if inchoately, and now had—without being bound by the ankles and dragged through the woods, as I had been in Texas—and with the man I married, of all people.

I'd started talking about sex in therapy, more specifically about sex with Mitch, how we'd started in such heat when we'd met in 1976 but that, even then, there had always been some part of me that held back from the kind of cataclysm I imagined existed and that after a while, I'd become discouraged and began avoiding sex with him, though I'm sure the abortion and miscarriage played a part in my aversion. Now, so many years later, I'd started loving Mitch again—working with him, traveling; we were great companions—but I couldn't feel right about getting back together with him, not honorably, not unless I could feel right about sex with him.

My therapist asked if I'd ever had the type of sex I was after and I admitted I had—kind of, with the bald and emotionally withholding single father at times and unmistakably once with a cute guy from the art department at *California* who was in love with someone else but came by my apartment in Beachwood Canyon on some pretext one night anyway. Christine asked me to tell her about it and I did, and she pointed out that it was interesting that in both cases, we'd smoked a joint before we went to bed.

"People are wired differently," she said. "It may be something you need to know about yourself, that you might need this in order to free yourself."

I remembered what a friend had told me (this was when Mitch and I were living on West Knoll and I'd confided in her about my sex problem with Mitch). She'd told me to smoke pot; it's what she and her husband did and it made all the difference. (They're still married today, three grown kids and a hundred years later.)

I'd smoked plenty of grass with David Leach and it hadn't

done anything like any good, but I was a different person now in the mid-1990s, no longer the mute, frightened girl I'd been, staring out harmlessly from under my bangs. I'd found work that I loved; I'd become a woman of means. Wait—did I say *woman?* Was I? My mother had told me I wouldn't know what it was to be a woman unless I had children, and I was childless. And when I'd asked a friend why she was going through so much trouble to adopt, she had said, "Because I don't want to be one of those women without children."

Well, that's what I was and, at fifty years old, showed every sign of remaining: a woman without children. It was something that, at a time when bearing children was more a possibility, my therapist had wanted me to confront: Did I want children or not? I hadn't wanted to think or talk about it, but if I had, I might have figured out that, as with marriage, I wanted to feel self-reliant, more solidly myself, to achieve some sort of personhood before I dragged a child into it. And when I did achieve personhood, the time for motherhood had passed.

But sex? That was a subject I would address. I felt my life depended on it. I asked Mitch if he'd smoke some pot with me, and he was game, though he hadn't done it much since he was a kid. So we did, we smoked pot—and holy shit, the pot today!

It wasn't just the sex that was great, it was getting high together and being high before and after. And it would become a ritual for us, a time we'd set aside just for each other, a non-work, non-buddy time. We'd sit on the couch drinking good champagne and he'd fill a pipe and light it and I'd inhale and cough my lungs out. Then he'd smoke. He'd become more voluble, hilarious, in fact— I'd see the person he must have been getting high as a teenager, rapping with his cronies in Cedar Rapids, Iowa. He'd be smarter than ever. And even handsomer. We both grew younger by the minute.

When we decided we were high enough, we'd head for the bedroom. I'd feel something like a combination of fear of disappointment and happy anticipation as I lit candles—at a certain age, candles are key. He'd come in from another room and we'd see each other naked and I'd walk to him and we'd feel our undressed bodies against each other. In time, we'd go to the bed and I'd cry out as he entered me—it was such a rude shock and yet something I'd want desperately at that moment. And we'd fuck— a lustful, corporeal, carnal, and vociferous act.

His mouth would be at my ear. "Is this what you want? Is this what you want?" he'd say.

I'd be thrilled by the crude sexiness of it, out of my head with pleasure, actually, though sometimes I'd have a vague hallucination that I was in Montana or Wyoming, places I'd never been but where I imagined a person could be free to play the music loud and scream as loud as she wanted, and meantime we'd be fucking as if we were one thing until we'd both be crying out, until we were done and found ourselves landed on the bed on our backs, catching our breath, each of us with a shit-eating grin, or sometimes I'd feel emotional, both of us definitely feeling that we'd left it all on the field, as Mitch once put it. I'd feel beautiful then and strangely young, as young, in fact, and pleased with myself as the girl on the beach in the old photograph.

I wondered how such an animal, carnal act be called making love. And then answered myself: Because that's what you feel then, that you'd made, created love. And I'd congratulate myself for having had the good sense, or luck, to have found the right person to love and be loved by. And for finding what I'd been looking for my whole life.

Afterward I'd tie on a short gray satin robe I'd bought for such occasions and he'd slip into the cashmere set of loungers I'd gotten him for winter (James Perse cotton in summer), and, me still high, him taking a few more tokes, he'd put the music on—loud—Dylan or the Stones mostly. Sometimes we'd just sit and listen, Dylan's words striking us as especially profound, and sometimes we'd dance around the living room like kids and then it would just be me grooving while he went into the kitchen and fixed something us to eat. No food ever tasted as delicious as what he calls his fuck-night pasta (actually premium penne with basic homemade red sauce and hot and sweet sausage meat and good Parmigiano-Reggiano).

He'd have brought a good bottle of wine up from the cellar; the Iowa boy had discovered in himself a discerning palate with which, coupled with an ability to memorize that had once been trained on baseball stats, he'd become a collector of wine, I the beneficiary. One of our tasks in life now is to drink all of our excellent aged wine before we're dead.

We returned home to New York from Gettysburg to begin life without *The Sopranos*. Gandolfini reached out, wanting to know if we were all right, buying us lunch, offering us work opportunities; Lorraine Bracco called with sweet, reassuring words. We consoled ourselves for a while with a review in the (admittedly short-lived) *New York Sun* panning the new season, the reviewer saying he squirmed when he saw Chase's name as writer, that it was the team of Burgess and Green who knew how to bring *The Sopranos* to life.

I turned sixty the year we were fired—you'd think I'd have thought it was time for me to stop. We had two homes, money saved, I'd have my Writers Guild pension and Social Security too in a few years, and HBO had paid us the money that remained on our contract for the end of the sixth and final season. But I wasn't ready to stop—I had things I wanted to do and something I felt I had to prove—and Mitch, fifty-three now, didn't want to stop either.

Our agent secured a two-year development deal at CBS for us to write, and hopefully produce, two TV pilots. After the Stephen Frears/*Skip Tracer* pilot failed, we wrote *Greenwich Village PD*, a quirky hour about a precinct run by a transgender (male-to-female) captain, which might have been a few years ahead of its time, especially for network.

Not that it mattered. The Writers Guild called a strike and we were back to the picket line. When the strike ended (with little gain to writers), CBS force-majeured us, meaning they ended our development deal, meaning also that we were back on the street again and had to do then what we'd never done before—go out and pitch ideas to studios and networks—at the same time considering projects that came to us.

We pitched, and we traveled too. On a European trip, we stopped in Copenhagen to meet the writer and producer of a show we agreed to adapt for E One Entertainment. We pitched it around town, finally experiencing the supreme joy of selling it in the room, meaning that the creative executive (in this case, someone at Universal in the very same office building where I'd first met with Josh and John) said right then and there in the middle of the pitch that she loved it, wanted to make it, sold!

Sold, maybe, but never made. There were other deals, projects offered and rejected, consulting jobs on other shows, along with time spent in our glass house in the LA hills while our New York apartment was being remodeled. (I'd used professional designers there and in my LA house, just like my parents' rich friends' wives in Providence. But did it make me happy? Yes, it did. I experienced enormous pleasure and satisfaction whenever I came home to both places.) We were home in the apartment in Manhattan getting ready for dinner one night when the phone rang. It was our agent in LA with a favor to ask.

"This thing probably isn't for you," he said. "It's from an old-time producer, did *Charlie's Angels*, *Starsky and Hutch* with Aaron Spelling. But his sister works here at the agency and he has an idea for a show, so just listen to the pitch, okay?"

The old-timer called and halfway through his two-minute spiel we were looking at each other with our eyebrows raised: yeah, we could do this. And we did. We flew to LA to meet him and were seated in a booth at the Grill on the Alley, a power-lunch spot in Beverly Hills, when Leonard Goldberg came in—tall, ghost pale, white-haired, and, for such a square-looking gent, incongruously clothed in a little black leather racer-style jacket and slim black jeans.

Heads turned, and as we ate, a procession of men in suits stopped by our table to pay their respects and shake his pale hand. Who was this guy? With any sense, we would have Googled him before the meeting, for he turned out to be a genuine Hollywood éminence grise, a film and TV producer, former president of 20th Century Fox, now on the board of CBS, which was how Les Moonves, who ran the network, came to ask him if he had any ideas for a show.

At lunch, he gave us a two-page, single-spaced typed description of the show and its characters: a widower chief of police in a big East Coast city to be determined later; his father (a former chief), who lived with him; and his three kids, a hotheaded detective, a newly minted beat cop, and a DA daughter. There would be a crime to solve each week along with family stories and the set piece of a Sunday family dinner at the police chief's house.

We placed the show in New York, where we lived, and met with Leonard a few times more to flesh out our pitch and then took it to CBS. I was to do the talking, but strangely it was Leonard who seemed nervous as we waited for the executives to call us in. I had actually discovered a talent in myself for pitching—I proved to be, after all, my salesman father's daughter, especially when I felt sure of a project and enthusiastic about it, which I now was.

The pitch went well. We wrote the pilot script with Leonard's, Paramount's, and CBS's notes. One thing that never changed, though, not one word, was the nine-page family dinner, a very long scene for TV and the most fun for us to write.

The show was *Blue Bloods* and, if not a critical darling, it was always first for viewers in the ratings, doubling CBS numbers in that Friday-night time slot, which had until then been moribund at five million. Our pilot script attracted Tom Selleck back to series television and he is greatly responsible for the show's success, though he is also greatly responsible for Mitch and my demise as executive producers after the first year. From the minute he walked into the conference room at CAA to meet us, all looming six foot four inches of him, it was no longer our show, but his. Leonard knew it and it was fine with him, but it wasn't what I'd had in mind and I couldn't live with it.

❖

Chapter Twenty

RIP

My mother was born on an unlucky Friday the thirteenth in 1917, a month premature. Because her mother had already had a stillbirth and a preemie who'd died, she put this new puny child aside to die too until a neighbor lady came into the kitchen, saw the wailing infant, put her finger in the baby's mouth, and, when the child began to suck voraciously, declared, "This baby is hungry!" And, the story went, my mother hadn't missed a meal since.

I wrote a little play of this scene that was performed by my mother's great-grandsons on the occasion of her ninetieth birthday in a party tent set up in my brother's backyard in New Hampshire. I'd brought her friends Gloria, Dottie, and Ruth up from Providence in a rented stretch limo for the occasion (Ronnie's mother, Pearl, was now locked up in an Alzheimer's ward), and my mother's two middle-aged nieces, one with a husband, came to the celebration too. My brother, Ron, was there, of course, and so was his wife, Sue; their grown children, Becky and Jordy; Jordy's wife, Mandy; and my mother's five great-grandsons. We'd hung the tent walls with blowups of photographs from my mother's long life.

You'd think from all the hoopla that this was a mother whose children loved her, wouldn't you? But we didn't. Not completely. Maybe not at all. Or maybe just a little, because we loved her enough not to tell her that we didn't love her. Or would it have been more an act of love to have leveled with her instead of perpetuating this charade and its concomitant resentment?

My mother was living in New Hampshire by then. She'd managed life in the house on Wayland Avenue the twenty years since my father died, each day spent mostly on the phone with her friends (one day a week for an hour with me) until it was time to fix herself lunch and, later, dinner. She'd tell me how lonely she was, how she'd taken her toasted cheese sandwich to eat by the dining-room window because she'd seen a squirrel munching an acorn under the tree outside to keep her company.

I was living in Los Angeles then, so it was left to my brother and his wife to look after her, to drive the three-plus hours down when she had a health scare or needed care, needs that arose, in time, with greater frequency. And the house, with its old boiler and disintegrating window frames, was becoming harder to maintain, so even she recognized, if reluctantly, that her position there would soon be untenable. I gave her a narrative that eased her transition out, a story she could tell herself and her friends: she had raised a family in that happy little house and now it was time to give another young family a chance.

On a visit east, I took her for a tour of Laurelmead, a posh "active senior living" community on twenty-three manicured acres on Blackstone Boulevard in Providence, where I wanted to buy her an apartment. The place looked great—river views, a lovely dining room, cleaning services, a gym, transportation to and from doctor visits—and many of her East Side Providence Jewish friends were moving there.

Not her. She didn't have the right clothes for Laurelmead, one sometime bridge partner had been nasty enough to tell her, and it was true that my mother's non-beauty-parlor hair, faded jeans, and denim shirt really wouldn't cut it there. When I offered to buy her clothes, she scoffed at the idea, and I understood—she'd already fought the East Side Jewish status wars; she didn't want to spend the rest of her life worrying about being popular in the dining room and at bridge.

She elected instead to move to Hanover, New Hampshire, to be near my-brother-the-doctor and Sue, first in a nice apartment they found for her to rent, then in a condo Mitch and I bought for her with the attached garage she required, and then, at age ninety-one, when even the condo became untenable for her, at Wheelock Terrace (these names, right?), an assisted-living facility that, with its white clapboard and green shutters, resembled a New England inn. "Death's waiting room," she wryly called it. She hated it there—the food, the people, the fact of a locked Alzheimer's ward on the ground floor.

She did allow that she liked her little suite for which I'd done a diagram so the furniture we'd had moved from Providence, to the apartment, to the condo, and now here could fit. It looked like Wayland Avenue in miniature—her treasured antique English breakfront, the tall, handsome bar where my father had mixed so many cocktails, the small Early American kitchen table and chairs where she'd eaten her breakfast and ate it now, and the chintz love seat and matching couch, the very couch on one end of which my father had endured his final months downstairs. She admitted it pleased her when the staff brought by prospective "inmates," as she called them, to see how nice the apartments could be.

Still, and though she never said it outright, we all sensed she wanted to move in with my brother and Sue. It would mean the end to the loneliness she'd suffered all these years and especially here in New Hampshire, where she'd waited at the rented apartment, then the condo, then at assisted living for what she felt were my brother's all-too-infrequent visits.

"I'm hungry for you," she'd say when she finally couldn't keep herself from calling him.

Back when she still lived in Providence, she was diagnosed with colon cancer at eighty-two and stayed at my brother and Sue's house for a monthlong course of preop chemo and radiation at the hospital where my brother practiced and taught medicine. The day after *The Sopranos* premiere, I rented a sturdy SUV, drove up, and stayed there too, ferrying her through snow and ice to and from her hours of treatment. As weeks wore on, Sue spent most evenings upstairs, leaving my brother and me stuck with our mother.

What crimes had my mother committed that she was so avoided? Why did we feel so compelled to hold her at arm's length? Was it her insatiable need of us? That we'd always feel her waiting, longing? That whatever we did, it would never be enough? Is that what my father had meant when, from his hospital bed after his heart attack had spared him an orchiectomy, he'd said to her, "I never loved you enough"?

She told me that when she'd asked him what he meant by that, he said he didn't know, and the question remained unanswered. Was it like that song of regret Willie Nelson sings, a man who realizes he could have been more generous with his love? Or was it what we all seemed to feel about my mother, that for self-preservation, it was necessary to hold ourselves back to keep from disappearing into what seemed a black hole of need?

Not long before what would turn out to be her end, I'd spend time lazing around with my mother in the bedroom of her small apartment in assisted living.

"I wasn't very nice to Nana," she said in a ruminative mood one afternoon, Nana being my father's mother. "Maybe I should have been nicer." I suspected she was thinking about my brother's wife, how my mother's treatment of her own mother-in-law might be karma coming back to bite her in the ass, a suspicion confirmed when, in what seemed like a fishing expedition, she later said, "Sue must love me very much to want me to move up here near her..."

We were lounging on the double bed in which she and my father had slept, nestled like spoons, for forty-three years, in which the whole family had cuddled and watched late-night TV, the bed in which my father had died and in which she would soon die too.

I was lying with my head propped up on pillows at the foot of the bed facing her when she said that, about Sue loving her very much. There was a silence. Here was my chance to tell her the truth—she'd always said she wanted the truth, that she herself was honest to a fault. "I don't play games" was one of her favorite sayings.

Oh yeah? Well, here would be match, point, and game if I said, *Actually, she doesn't love you very much at all. They wanted you up here because Sue didn't like her husband driving through snow and sleet for three and a half hours every time you had a hangnail, and he didn't like it either—that's why you're here.*

Instead, I smiled and said, "Yeah, she really must."

* * *

Mitch and I were in Toronto filming the interior scenes for the pilot of *Blue Bloods* on stages there, and when we returned from dinner to our rooms at the original Four Seasons Hotel (since torn down), the phone rang. It was a friend of David Leach's— the same friend in whose garage room I'd lived—calling to tell me that David had died that day, a heart attack, age sixty-five. As shocking as it was, as death always is, an unopenable door slammed shut in your face, it was hardly a surprise. David, with all his excesses, had been a poster child for heart disease.

The year was 2010, but it was seven years before I found myself in the Bay Area and could pay a visit to my old boyfriend's widow. I had called and asked if David had kept any photographs of the time we were together, and when I got to the house in the Berkeley Hills, she had waiting for me an artsy shopping bag containing two eight-by-ten orange cardboard Agfa-Gevaert Brovira photography-paper boxes that, when I got back to my hotel room, proved to be filled with prints, contact sheets, negatives, and a folder with pages of color slides in plastic sleeves, all of them marked with subject and date in David Leach's familiar scrawl.

His handwriting and the orange cardboard boxes brought him acutely back to me along with the autumn, winter, and spring nights we spent holed up in his Hyde Park apartment in 1968, both of us stoned on pot, me on the bed that doubled as a couch listening to music, studying liner notes on the album covers, while ten feet away, David spent hours and hours in a darkroom in the closet that had been the then-fledgling photographer Danny Lyon's darkroom before David moved in, the same photographer who had since become famous in the art world and spent a night with me on Tamalpais Road.

I could almost smell the chemical stench from trays of developer, fixer, and stop bath, see David standing over them with tongs as I watched with him the miraculous emergence of images in the bath in the dim red light of the darkroom when I went in to say good night. I had to go to bed and get up early for my job at the University of Chicago, where I answered the phone for George Shultz—yes, Reagan's future secretary of state, then dean of Chicago's graduate school of business, though he was always off somewhere and if I met him, I don't remember it.

In my hotel room years later, looking through the contents of the orange boxes, I could see the evidence of all those hours and hours of tinkering—sometimes a dozen prints of the same thing, the differences undetectable, to me at least. And these were only the prints he'd kept.

But there I was in the photographs, young and also naked in his camera's eye much of the time. Spread before me on the hotel bed was a visual record of who I've said I was in those pre–*Rolling Stone* years, me staring up from under my bangs or with my head tilted to the side, wearing expressions I'm sure were meant to be coquettish. I may have been naked, but the photos themselves reveal nothing of the person I was beyond an (admittedly) beautiful object. Possibly because at that point, there was nothing, or little, to reveal.

I am pictured here. I am pictured there. I am nowhere.

And David? What did it mean that there were so many photographs, all these and also in the boxes and boxes collecting mildew in the basement of the house in the Berkeley Hills? Had photography been more than something he was merely "into"? Had he been an artist after all? But if he hadn't claimed or owned or professed such a vocation or ambition, was he? It might have made him feel better about himself if he'd let himself think that's what he was or wanted to be. But did it matter, now that he was dead?

When we were much younger and still lived in Providence, David's father, Jonah, telephoned me one morning.

"I want to talk to you," he said in his thick Russian accent. "I'll be in the parking lot behind the slaughterhouse, ten o'clock."

Jonah Leach had immigrated to the United States in the beginning of the twentieth century. He'd gone to Chicago, where he peddled boxes of strawberries on downtown street corners, and he could still tell you what they cost him and what he sold them for. Soon, he found work in the stockyards. There were photos of him on horseback among the cattle. In time, he owned a cattle slaughterhouse in Providence, which he eventually deeded over to David's twenty-five-years-older porcine half brother Maurice, who sold it and bought one that slaughtered pigs.

When I drove in, Jonah was already waiting in his Caddy and waved me into the passenger seat. I knew I shouldn't be here. I knew David wouldn't like it, that I was betraying him somehow. But I was curious. And flattered. It made me feel important to be summoned to the parking lot of a pig slaughterhouse by a seventy-some-year-old Russian-immigrant millionaire.

Looking out the windshield, I could see a long line of fattened pink pigs being prodded up ramps to a third-floor kill room, from whence gravity would do the rest as they were processed, pieces of them making their way down to be packaged and sold.

"Tell me," Jonah said once I'd settled, "what's the matter with David? What's the matter with my son?"

What could I say? That I suspected David was ruined and that Jonah himself had ruined him, that he was too critical of him, too competitive with him, but that he'd also spoiled him, given him too much money, cars, freedom?

"There's nothing wrong with David," I said. "He's fine." And that was the end of it.

As I continued looking through the photos that night in my hotel room, I came across the few of David himself, ones I might even have taken, though I had no memory of having done so. He looked so sweet and vulnerable. And attractive. And I remembered that I loved him all over again.

I had at home another photo from those days that delivered a similar message, a snapshot my brother and Sue had sent me when I told them David had died, one taken at their old house in Vermont in 1970. In it, David and I sit across from each other at a chessboard. He's smoking his pipe. Both of us are smiling. You can see in the snapshot more of who I was in those days: a goofy, happy, possibly stoned young girl. And if you didn't know what a sexual fake I was then, a girl very much in love.

My mother died the Tuesday before Thanksgiving 2011, at ninety-four. Though her brain had remained sharp, her body had been in slow decline. She'd shrunk from a model's height of five nine to five three, her spine fracturing and collapsing into itself over time, her frame gradually bending so that near the end as she walked, her gaze was directed to the floor. Her heart function had slowed to the point that doctors were at a loss to explain how that exhausted organ kept her going. Those last few years, I tried to do my part, to spell my brother in service of her. Mitch and I had sold the LA house by then and lived full-time in New York and we'd drive up often, renting homes nearby for long stays when we had time off, all so we could visit her, take her out to dinner, take her shopping for shoes, clothes, makeup, shampoo, and toilet paper, and drive her for a day at my brother and Sue's new place, a Charles Platt estate of twenty-seven acres south of Hanover, New Hampshire.

I tried to be patient and kind—until the day I wasn't, two weeks before her death, when my anger and resentment surfaced. We were on the phone, talking about Thanksgiving. I'd volunteered myself and Mitch to come up and be with her so my brother and Sue would be free to drive to Virginia and spend the holiday with their recently divorced daughter and her two boys.

My mother had nixed Thanksgiving dinner at Wheelock Terrace, even the catered one I proposed in the lovely private dining room there, wanting instead to go to the new hotel in town, since the relatively charming Hanover Inn was closed for remodeling.

"It will be so much fun!" she said.

"Fun?" I said. "What are you even doing, Mom?" Thinking only of my importuned self as entertainment committee, picturing a grim meal, the three of us in the stark, sterile restaurant of the new hotel, me fearing another bathroom emergency or reeking mishap such as one that past July that I'd handed off to my brother. Apparently, my mother wasn't the only one who didn't "*do* shit."

"It will be fun for *me!*" she snarled. "I've got to get out of here!"

I realized at once I had poisoned everything, ruined any possibility of enjoyment, not to mention blown my whole volunteer/martyr bit. But the cat was out of the bag.

"I'm sorry, Mom," I said.

"That's all right," she said in a calm, even tone. "I understand."

I apologized some more; I begged; I cajoled. But the damage was done. I had fulfilled my grandmother's curse: she had a mean daughter just like her.

Two weeks later, on a Monday, when for the first time my mother didn't appear in the dining room at Wheelock Terrace for lunch or dinner, her one friend there, a cigarette-smoking (outside, in all weather), Harvard-educated landscape architect twenty years her junior with incurable lung cancer that had spread to her brain and with whom my mother played Scrabble in the facility's living room for hours every day of her stay there, came upstairs, also for the first time, to my mother's rooms.

In the weeks and even months before that phone call, my brother told me after she died, her health had been deteriorating, her energy flagging, and she was spending most of her time on the bed, no longer even wanting to read or watch TV—in fact, she had asked him to remove all books from her bedroom—hauling herself up and onto the walker gizmo she used only to make her way oh so slowly to the elevator to go down to meals. She was living, as her doctors said, on pure will.

Whether or not it was my cruel outburst that finally sapped her of her last bit of it, this final Monday she told her friend, who was sitting at her bedside, that she simply couldn't gather herself to go downstairs.

My mother said, "This is it for me," the friend told me later.

"Robin's coming tomorrow," the friend said to her. "Don't you want to wait?"

I asked the friend what my mother had said to that.

The friend made a dismissive gesture with her hand, as if batting the idea away, a gesture I recognized as my mother's. The friend immediately realized what that said and tried to walk it back, telling me, "She said she didn't know."

My mother died the next morning. My brother and Sue didn't go to Virginia. Instead, Becky came up with the boys and we all had Thanksgiving dinner, along with Jordy and his wife and their boys, in the restaurant of the soulless and stark new hotel in town. And it was—it was a lot of fun.

There remained, of course, the matter of what to do with her now that she was dead. There had been a conversation on one of those days I'd just hung out with her, an afternoon when we were lazing around on her bed. She'd put down the magazine she was reading and said, out of the blue, "I don't want to go to Lincoln."

It took me a moment to realize she was talking about Lincoln Park Cemetery in Warwick, Rhode Island, where my father was buried.

"Wait, what?" I said. "You don't want to be buried next to Daddy?" She knew there was already a plot that had been bought for her long ago right next to him.

"It's the other ones," she said. "I don't want to be there with them." She meant her mother-in-law and poor, sad Uncle Lenny. She had nothing against my father's father that I knew of.

"Are you sure?" I said. Was she really that crazy?

"I want to be cremated," she said, and she went back to reading her *New Yorker*.

At some point later, another day lying around, I asked what she wanted done with her ashes. She said she didn't care. I said we would have to do something with them.

"I don't know," she said, "what do you think?"

"Maybe at Canochet?" I said, meaning the beach she loved so much.

"Okay," she said, "that's a good idea. Or maybe somewhere outside at Ronnie's house."

In the early 1980s, as a journalist in LA, I attended a press event at the Playboy Mansion, a must-see and mythical place for a girl like me whose life had been affected by Hugh Hefner's *Playboy* magazine philosophy, David Leach, with his hedonism, his pipe, and his attitudes toward sex and marriage, having been an early adherent.

Described as Gothic-Tudor Revival, the twenty-two-room, twenty-thousand-square-foot monster of a house was set on more than five acres of groomed prime real estate in Trousdale Estates, though we reporters were allowed only in the downstairs public rooms—the bunnies and Hef lived upstairs—and outside in something called the grotto, where the sex orgies supposedly took place.

I suppose Hef was somewhere around in his silk paisley pajamas and bathrobe, but it was the Playboy girls who caught my interest. They were such singular creatures, whip-thin as nervous little Italian greyhounds, but with these preternaturally big round breasts stuck on, looking like nothing else on earth except each other.

I started up a conversation with a friendly bunny, introducing myself as a journalist, asking some question or other about whatever this event was for before asking her about herself. Yes, she lived there. Hef? He was really, really nice. She was smiley, engaging, and sweet, but I saw something else in her eyes, a kind of vulnerability, a mute appeal that said, *Don't say anything mean about me, okay? Be nice to me. I'm helpless.*

And I understood at that moment what it must be like to be a man attracted to women like these and how appealing it must be to take one home and put her on your bed like a pretty stuffed animal, a woman who was helpless, who'd be grateful, who'd want nothing more than to be protected and taken care of, petted, and clothed.

And later I wondered if this was what my father had been

trying to tell me when I'd complained about what I saw as my mother's indolence and uselessness and he'd said that I had to remember that she was completely dependent on him. And that there were two messages in that. One, that her helplessness made him feel like a man. The other . . . to make sure for my own good that I myself turned out to be something other than that.

Which is what, in my life and time, I have tried to be.

❖

Chapter Twenty-One

RIP RSX

In the years after the 2007 RSX—the *Rolling Stone* ex-employee reunion in San Francisco—there were more, albeit smaller, reunions right here in New York City. They seemed to occur randomly—a couple of luncheons at the Blue Ribbon Bakery at Bedford and Downing Streets in Greenwich Village; two potluck suppers at the town house on Grove, also in the Village, where Christine Doudna and her husband raised their two kids; and, more recently, a cocktail party for Ben Fong-Torres and his wife, Dianne, in town from San Francisco, at the book-lined apartment in a Bing and Bing building overlooking Abington Square where Sarah Lazin, her hair now a halo of white frizz, has lived since the magazine's move to New York.

Annie never comes—she didn't come to the first—and neither does Jann. But David Felton does, and Paul Scanlon, Laurel Gonsalves, Harriet Fier (or she did; she recently died, after a long battle with cancer), Christine, and Sarah, as well as others who came after me—Barbara Downey Landau, Roger Black (who headed the art department for years after I left), and, on occasion, writers Don Katz and Greil Marcus, who was at the magazine from the beginning and who happened to be in New York the night of one get-together.

Something pulled us there to one another, maybe to relive for a little while the time in our lives when we were having the time of our lives, when *Rolling Stone* was young and we were too. As Hunter Thompson wrote so eloquently on the magazine's pages, it was

> *the kind of peak that never comes again. San Francisco in the middle sixties was a very special place and time to be a part of. Maybe it meant something. Maybe not, in the long run...but no explanation, no mix of words or music or memories can touch that sense of knowing that you were there and alive in that corner of time and the world. Whatever it meant...*

We'd all come to the Bay Area and ridden that 1960s countercultural tide as long as we wanted to, or could, right into the 1970s. How lucky we all were to be there when it was happening and do our parts, whatever they were, in putting out a magazine that was more than a magazine—it was a state of mind, something all at once raucous and insightful and smart and funny.

So what if the counterculture became part of the culture? So, eventually, did all of us.

As head of *Rolling Stone*'s new book division, Sarah Lazin made her way into the publishing business and now heads her own eponymous literary agency. Harriet Fier worked as an editor at the *Washington Post* before founding a film business with the man she married and raising their children in Westchester.

Christine Doudna went on to write and edit, married a tall, handsome partner at Salomon Brothers, and the two of them enjoyed a house on Martha's Vineyard as well as the one on Grove. They had also eventually partnered with Marianne Partridge to publish the *Santa Barbara Independent*, with Marianne as editor, she herself having married a rancher with a huge Spanish land grant near Santa Inez. And me, married and living my bourgeois life in a town-house duplex on Washington Place, passing my winters in the warmth of St. John in the U.S. Virgin Islands.

The year 2017 marked the fiftieth anniversary of the founding of *Rolling Stone*. A fifty-year anthology of writing was put out (I was disappointed to see that my work wasn't represented, though it had been in the twenty-fifth-anniversary anthology). It was a year in which Jann closed his *Us* and *Men's Journal* magazines (having sold *Outside* long before), a year in which he finally sold off his controlling interest in *Rolling Stone* magazine.

The year also saw the publication of *Sticky Fingers: The Life and Times of Jann Wenner and* Rolling Stone *Magazine*, described by Knopf as "a delicious romp through the heyday of rock and roll and a revealing portrait of the man at the helm."

Ben had gotten hold of a pre-pub bound galley, and at a cocktail-hour gathering for Ben and Dianne, it made its way through the party and fast became dog-eared as we all took turns ego-surfing through the pages to find ourselves. Later, after the book had come out and we'd had a chance to read it, there was a flurry of disappointed e-mails, Facebook posts, and blog postings, one ex-*Stoner* cc'ing some of us his outraged letter to the author, book reviewer, and publisher, none of whom bothered to respond.

The actual life and times of Jann Wenner and *Rolling Stone were* in fact delicious and a romp in many ways, but maybe you had to be there. Because the book just didn't get the times or Jann. Which left those of us who had been there feeling betrayed, especially those of us who'd spoken to the writer and saw how he'd twisted our words. Had I learned nothing? Me, of all people, who should have known that a writer was always selling somebody out, had put such blind trust in a reporter on the phone. I'm still left to wonder, though, what I could possibly have said to prompt him to write that, when covering Joe Conforte's whorehouse in Sparks, Nevada, Annie Leibovitz and I had worn bikinis, which we most certainly did not.

The morning after the party at RSX in 2007, we all gathered at a movie theater in San Francisco's Mission District to see a short video and clips from a BBC documentary about the old days and afterward to take the mic and share any stories or thoughts. There were many antic tales of Hunter. Antic deadline stories. And antic-for-the-sake-of-being-antic tales, like photo editor Karen Malarkey's story of her and Annie's three-bridges game, which involved their doing a bump at Annie's apartment on Union Street, then flipping a coin to see who'd get the better route—the Golden Gate to the Richmond Bridge to the Bay Bridge home. The loser of the toss was consigned to the reverse route. Then they'd set out, Annie in her Teardrop Porsche, Karen in her '55 VW Bug with the rebuilt engine, and tear around the bridges, the first to get back to Annie's rewarded with the next few lines of coke.

Jann's name came up a few times that morning in jokes about those he'd fired and then immediately rehired, like Felton, Fier, Doudna. The accountant at the time said she wished she had a

dollar for every final paycheck she cut for David Felton. Someone else thanked Jann in absentia for not coming because "he
would have tried to take over," and then went serious, calling on
us to remember that it was Jann after all who had brought us
together. Michael Lydon, who'd been one of the first editors in
1967, said that Jann really pulled it off, he was the guy with the
vision and needed other people to get his vision across and that
was why we were all here.

I'd forgotten about the Saturday-morning gathering until, at a
kind of mini-reunion—a dinner party at Christine's a few years
ago with just Mitch and me and Christine and her husband and
Don Katz and his wife—Don reminded me of it. I didn't know
Don back then. He had come to *Rolling Stone* just after my time,
in 1975, at age twenty-three, filing stories on politics from the
London office. Then, in the summer of '76, he covered the Democratic Convention, where he also wrote and rewrote speeches,
including Ron Kovic's speech, and it was Don who wheeled the
Vietnam vet onto the convention floor, a scene that ended the
Tom Cruise movie based on Ron Kovic's life.

After *Rolling Stone*, Don had gone on to write well-regarded
nonfiction books and in the '90s had founded Audible, since sold
to Amazon, though he remained CEO.

"You know, what you said that morning really stayed with me,"
Don said at dinner.

I had no memory of the event, let alone what I'd said.

"You said you felt so lucky to be at *Rolling Stone* then," he told
us, "that the music was so great, that it was so good to be young
then. That you felt sorry for people who were young today that
they didn't get to do it.

"And that's exactly the way I felt too," he said. "How we all
felt."

Laurel Gonsalves, an organizer of RSX with Sarah and Roger Black, supplied me with a CD audio of the event, and there was my voice, right after Felton told a story of his time living with Barbara Downey, when she was out one night at an office women's consciousness-raising group at Marianne Partridge's apartment, how Annie had come to their own apartment with Mick Jagger, and how, when they left, he'd called Barbara to tell her and could hear all the consciousness-raised women squealing and shrieking like teenagers in the background at the news that Jagger himself, in the flesh, had been at Barbara's house.

When I took the mic, I introduced myself, explained that I had been a contributing editor to *Rolling Stone*, that I wrote cover stories. I told about David and Annie and my wearing those stupid disguises to Hunter's speech in Chicago and about David's taking me to the printer to see my first cover roll off the presses. And then I did, I said what Don said I said, that I felt so lucky to work there when I did. But I had also gone on to say that though it had been this huge high point in my life, such a big deal, and that I had had so much fun, they had been hard years in some respects…

I realize now that's why I traveled all the way across the country to go to RSX: to claim my place in that life and time and to fill in the blanks in a part of my past that was largely a blank. To see that Alan Rinzler had survived and flourished. To see Felton, married to a woman who didn't seem to show up at these events and once again find myself seeking the safety of his company at the party, asking to sit next to him at lunches in New York, and, finally, seeing the look in his eyes when Barbara Downey showed up late to the last lunch, how he couldn't keep them off her.

I had always felt invisible at *Rolling Stone*, eclipsed by brighter lights (to all but maybe Felton or Rinzler), so it was a revelation when Don said what he said at dinner—to be told flat-out I'd

been seen and heard—just as it had been to learn that Christine
and Sarah had noticed, even admired me way back then, and it is
such a gift that we have now become lifelong friends.

There was another such gift at one night's post-reunion reunion in New York when Greil Marcus came up and introduced
himself to me—Greil Marcus, the holy grail at *Rolling Stone*, the
music and cultural critic who had been there since the beginning and gone on to author 1975's *Mystery Train*, which placed
rock and roll in the context of American cultural archetypes from
Moby-Dick to *The Great Gatsby* to *Stagger Lee* and was listed as
one of *Time*'s 101 best nonfiction books since 1923.

"Robin Green," he said, shaking my hand. "I've always wanted
to meet you!"

You have? I thought but didn't say.

It took me a while to summon the nerve to ask him why. But
when I did, he told me it was my work, that it had stood out, that
I took on ambiguous and difficult stories and approached them
with a sense of both modesty and amazement. I could have died
of happiness right there, but he went on. My stories were so different, he said, from the panic mode of Hunter Thompson and
all of his tough-guy imitators. The reader got the idea there were
both real people in the stories and a real person behind them...

Me. That girl in the photograph at the beach I couldn't remember having been—who, I can see now, was a strong girl in some
respects, a girl just beginning to come into her own as a person in
the world.

I finally also got to know Paul Scanlon, who'd been managing
editor when I was there, when I was Felton's writer and he and
David occupied different, and opposing, camps, Paul's supposedly workaday and David's farther out. Paul had gone on to other
magazines but eventually come back to *Rolling Stone* and even

now had a cubicle in its offices on Sixth Avenue near Radio City Music Hall.

We'd meet at the White Horse Tavern here in the Village for a drink or two, talk about the old days, his memory sharp and clear, his perceptions funny and deep. He took me on a tour of the offices once, leading me through hallway after hallway hung with every *Rolling Stone* cover that ever was, a literal trip down memory lane.

I managed to screw up my courage with him too one day and ask him what he had thought of me then. I told him that I always had the feeling he and the other editors didn't like me.

"No," Paul said, "it wasn't that we didn't like you. We didn't know you."

I was glad for him finally to know me a little now. It seems important now for me to make myself known. And to that end, I have herewith written 89,329 words. I know how many because my computer counted every one.

Acknowledgments

[TK]

About the Author

TK

I came across a photo of a girl I knew was me, but I had no memory of ever being her. *(Stanley Summer)*

When my father was away at war, my brother toddled around, gripping this photo and eventually wearing away the corner. *(Robin Green)*

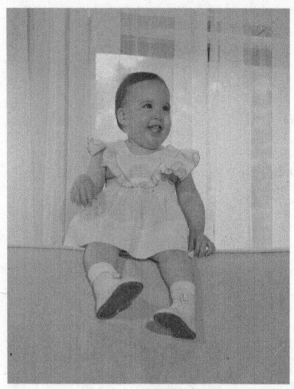

My mother's sad attempt to prettify and feminize me at age one. *(Robin Green)*

Mom, big brother, and me. She's holding him up to make him look taller. *(Robin Green)*

As editor of Brown University's literary magazine, I was the only girl. *(Robin Green)*

I showed up in Providence in a dress that looked like somebody's college bedspread.
(David Leach)

One ear up, one ear down, Reuben the Dog was up for anything. *(David Leach)*

We chicks peered at the world of men from under our bangs and posed with our heads tilted coquettishly. We weren't threatening anything—yet. *(Robin Green)*

Me with Reuben under the loft on Fox Court. David's Persian chair is at the right. *(Robin Green)*

Annie in 1975. *(Marc Pokemper)*

At my twenty-seventh birthday party, Hunter's sidekick Oscar Acosta put a small hill of coke on the kitchen table. Annie gave me a $20 gift certificate for Lyle Tuttle's tattoo parlor. *(Robin Green)*

A birthday card for me:. To "Little Bird," signed "Brown Buffalo [what Hunter called Oscar], and Doggie Diner [Annie]." The diner was where all the take-out food at the office came from. I don't know why Annie called herself that. Maybe she thought she looked like their doggie logo. *(Robin Green)*

Marianne (standing) saw the brain power she had in (left to right) Sarah, Barbara, Christine, and Harriet. *(Max Hellweg)*

At a time when Annie and Jerry Garcia were circling each other, she and I drove up to Stinson Beach, ostensibly to get his autograph on her photo for the January '71 cover as a birthday present for me. He wasn't home, so she left the print—with this result. *(Robin Green)*

With David in 1970, a goofy, happy, possibly stoned girl—a girl (if you didn't know what a sexual fake I was) very much in love. *(Robin Green)*

The hardest part about leaving David was leaving Reuben. *(David Leach)*

My first cover of *Rolling Stone*. Herb Trimpe drew The Hulk. *(Robin Green)*

Cassidy wanted a cover, so we gave it to him. *(Robin Green)*

At work on the roof-
top on Tamalpais
Road. *(Robin Green)*

In my backyard in
Berkeley. Off the mast-
head, miserable, and
homely. And what's with
the dress? *(Robin Green)*

"Iowa's most dissolute couple," Jack Leggett called Mitch and me. The sexual heat between us was there for all to see. *(Robin Green)*

We drove from Iowa City to L.A. in a $200 Impala that we bought from Mitch's little brother. *(Robin Green)*

I showed Ronnie this photo of Mitch. She said he looked conceited. *(Robin Green)*

Mitch and me, back together again but wary. *(Robin Green)*

At the 2003 Emmys with *Soprano*'s creator David Chase. *Cent'anni!* *(Getty Images)*